Letters from Fairhaven 1890

**The Life, Love & Legacy
of W.R. Gray, Pioneer Physician**

My Darling Anna

by

Brian L. Griffin
&
Neelie Nelson

Knox Cellars Publishing Company

My Darling Anna
Letters from Fairhaven 1890
The Life, Love & Legacy of W.R. Gray, Pioneer Physician

Copyright© 2009 by Brian L. Griffin & Neelie Nelson

First Edition 2009
Knox Cellars Publishing Company, Bellingham, Washington USA

Knox Cellars Publishing Company
1801 Taylor Avenue
Bellingham, WA 98225
info@mydarlinganna.com

ISBN #978-0-9635841-5-1

Library of Congress Cataloging-in-Publication Data pending
Griffin, Brian L. & Nelson, Neelie
History / Mount Pleasant, Iowa / Bellingham, Washington

Design/Composition/Cover: Kathleen R. Weisel (weiselcreative.com)

Printed in the United States of America

Front cover photograph of Anna Kurtz courtesy of Iowa Wesleyan College Archives.
Photos and images not attributed to others are from the authors' collections.
All *Fairhaven Herald* and *Weekly World* newspaper articles are from: Newspaper Collection, Center for Pacific Northwest Studies (CPNWS), Western Washington University, Bellingham, WA 98225-9123.

Dedications

Brian Griffin dedicates his share of this book to Marya, his wife, who like Anna, was engaged to marry, kissed goodbye and left at the train depot as her fiancée headed West for an undetermined period. Unlike Will Gray, Brian was sent off to Korea for eighteen months by the U.S. Army; however, like Will Gray, he wrote his fiancée letter after letter describing the experience and attesting to his love and longing for his sweetheart. Like Anna, Marya eventually married the guy and they have spent the rest of their lives together.

Neelie Nelson dedicates her share of this book to her wonderful husband, Steve, who displayed great patience during the creation of this work and endured with loving good nature, the disruption that Will and Anna created in his life. In the words of Will Gray, Neelie declares that Steve is indeed the "light of my soul."

Oil painting of Fairhaven, painted in 1889 on a window shade. The artist is unknown. Painting includes buildings in the planning stage. The design of the Fairhaven Hotel was subsequently changed. This painting hangs on the ground floor of the Whatcom Museum's History Building (Old City Hall).

Introduction

MY DARLING ANNA relates the story of a man, a woman and a time in history. It speaks to the life and love of an educated, sensitive and idealistic young doctor seeking to find his place in the world just as the nineteenth century was about to roll into the twentieth. This book is also about a place, Fairhaven, in the wild newly settled Pacific Northwest. It illustrates how the raw new town was to be influenced by the cultural contributions of its new immigrants from the long-settled areas of the eastern parts of the nation. It particularly speaks to the contributions of Mount Pleasant, Iowa, from which Will Gray came to Fairhaven, as did a remarkably large group of his acquaintances.

The personal letters of Will Gray to his fiancée, Anna, reveal the hardships, loneliness and excitement of living in the rollicking boom town of Fairhaven, as well as the melancholy of the lovers' separation and the nostalgia for their childhood and youth in the peaceful old Iowa town of Mount Pleasant.

My Darling Anna celebrates the cultural legacy carried by Dr. Gray from Iowa to his new community. Mount Pleasant is a commanding presence in the book because of its formative influence on Dr. Gray and Anna, and through them on their daughter Margaret. The Gray legacy to the cultural level of Fairhaven and Bellingham came through his interest and participation in the theatrical arts and his many years as a member and president of the community's Board of Education.

This is a book about Will and Anna Gray, their contributions and their era; and yet the authors felt it would not be proper to ignore the huge role that their daughter, Margaret Gray, played in enlarging and passing on their legacy. "Miss Gray" became an almost legendary figure in her own right. For that reason we have published a special edition which relates Margaret Elizabeth Gray's personal story.

The special tribute includes a particular treat for those who remember Miss Gray. We have uncovered two 1971 interviews of Margaret Gray, one done by the late historian Galen Biery, and the second by retired radio personality Haines Fay. An even rarer find was a 1946 recording that includes two duets sung by Eloise Tweit and Norris Brannstrom, the teenage leads of the 1945 and 1946 Bellingham High School operettas. The interviews and duets have been recorded on a 60-minute CD which is included with the special edition.

We hope you will enjoy My Darling Anna and join us in our tribute to the Grays and their cultural legacy.

Brian Griffin & Neelie Nelson

Contents

✤ ✤ ✤

✤ ✤ ✤

Well this will be a book
if I don't stop soon.
So with great love
I will say "goodbye sweetheart."
Yours devotedly,
Will

W.R. Gray, May 25, 1890

Prologue

HISTORIANS ARE A STRANGE AND INQUISITIVE BREED. They get immense pleasure from poking around in boxes of musty old documents and collections of photographs. They are hoping to find some revelation of the past that will be meaningful to them and will add to their collection of facts from bygone days. They also seem to enjoy sharing their finds with others of the "ancien" persuasion and can endlessly converse about the meaning and relative importance of their finds. Any little tidbit of information can add to their understanding of an era, a place or a person and so those bits are searched for in private and public archives with great vigor and enthusiasm.

Brian with drawer from Anna's desk.

Two such victims of the "archive disease" are the authors Griffin and Nelson. Their collaboration on this book is a result of their individual interest in the history of Fairhaven, in Bellingham, Washington, where they both reside.

Brian Griffin had in 2007 written a local history *Boulevard Park & Taylor Avenue Dock on the Old Bellingham Waterfront*. His research for that book illuminated the fact that the complete history of Fairhaven had never been written and it was to that task that he was devoting a great deal of research.

Neelie Nelson, a relative newcomer to Bellingham, had become fascinated by the history of her new home and has been researching Fairhaven's historic buildings in order to update and expand the City's website describing these turn-of-the-century structures that define the Fairhaven Historic District.

Neelie with Will's letters.

The impressive collection of the Northwest Regional Branch of the Washington State Regional Archives and the additional collection of Western Washington University's Center for Pacific Northwest Studies (CPNWS) are housed in the Goltz-Murray Building on the WWU campus. Both Griffin and Nelson have spent many hours grazing through their collections, sometimes searching for a relevant fact; sometimes just satisfying their curiosity about Fairhaven in general.

One day in the Archives, Nelson came upon a large collection of hand-written letters dating from 1890, the height of the Fairhaven Boom. The letters had been written by a young pioneer doctor to his fiancée in the Midwest. She knew Griffin would be interested. Upon reading them Griffin, a Bellingham native, immediately recognized the names of the young lovers. Touched by the quality of the letters and a personal connection to the family, he proposed to Nelson that they publish the letters collaboratively.

With the generous permission of the Northwest Regional Archives, the two authors digitally photographed each letter and Nelson began the arduous task of transcribing them.

The letters are important historic documents and at the same time a heart warming and poignant love story. They offer a deeply personal glimpse into the lives of a young couple while also providing a unique view into early life and times in Fairhaven and the developing Pacific Northwest. Will Gray's letters touch on subjects that lead into never imagined realms. The Endnotes are used to elaborate on those facts.

Their research uncovered many unexpected, and to the authors, thrilling discoveries. Among the most exciting was the finding of Anna's desk, identified in an 1892 photograph of her bedroom in Mount Pleasant and discovered 117 years later in Bellingham. The story of this discovery is told in the appendix section dubbed Side Stories, in which the authors have assumed the privilege of expanding various subjects in greater detail than would fit in the narrative of the book.

The provenance of the Gray letters is not complete. Somehow their donor and the circumstances of the donation to the Northwest Regional Archives were not recorded. The authors believe that the letters were purchased at the Margaret Gray estate sale by a stamp collector interested only in the stamps and envelopes. Fairhaven historian Gordon Tweit corroborates that theory. He was given two of the original envelopes by a stamp collector to add to his history museum collection. Our community and the authors are indebted to the donor for recognizing the unique value of the letters and for donating them to the Archives.

The Western Adventure

A SMALL KNOT OF PASSENGERS and well wishers gathered on the dimly lit platform of the Mount Pleasant Depot, waiting for the midnight train for Burlington. The train was late; it was 12:30 before the locomotive could be heard puffing along the Chicago Burlington & Quincy track through town. As it approached the North Main Street crossing the engineer hung on the whistle cord and a long, perhaps needlessly long, moan burst from the steam whistle, piercing the soft spring night and no doubt disturbing the sleep of countless weary residents of the little college town. Just past the crossing the fireman began the rhythmic tolling of the great bronze bell as the locomotive slowed approaching the Depot. It finally stopped with a burst of steam and a loud hiss from its huge drivers, its three ornate passenger cars centered neatly before the depot platform. The handful of waiting passengers was illuminated by the yellowish glow of the gas lamps.

Among those few on the platform were a tall, spare young man and a diminutive young woman, obviously very much in love and visibly in the grip of strong and sorrowful emotions. He was William Radford Gray, recently graduated from the medical school at State University of Iowa (now University of Iowa). She was Anna Allen Kurtz, a school teacher employed in Mount Pleasant and a graduate of Iowa Wesleyan University (later renamed Iowa Wesleyan College). Their mournful demeanors and their heartfelt embrace were occasioned by Will's departure for the West in search of a place in that far away land to establish himself in a practice of medicine and to earn enough money to consummate the marriage they had pledged to each other twenty-one months earlier.

It was mid-May in that year of 1890, a time for new beginnings and of opportunity for the young and enterprising in a West just recently opened by the transcontinental railways. Will and Anna hoped for a rapid establishment of Will's practice so they could soon be together again.

With the waiting train before them, the tearful couple fell into each other's arms for one last lingering embrace, then Will, writing case in hand, mounted the passenger car steps and with sinking heart took his seat to begin his great adventure.

Postcard of Union Depot, Burlington, Iowa.

He was to write to Anna almost every day until he saw her again fifteen months later. The letters began in Burlington, Iowa, less than two hours after his departure.

Courtesy Mount Pleasant, Iowa, Public Library.
Partial 1869 Birdseye of Mount Pleasant town square.

Mount Pleasant

MOUNT PLEASANT IN 1870 was a quiet Iowa college town that boasted a population of about 4,000 souls. It had long been a cultural haven which its citizens liked to call the "Athens of Iowa." Because it was the site of Iowa Wesleyan University, the county seat, and a large state mental hospital, Mount Pleasant had attracted a large number of doctors, educators and other professionals. It was an unusually enlightened community for its day.

The town, set in the gently rolling plain of southeastern Iowa, had become prominent nationally for its forward thinking citizens who were leaders and active in the reform movements of the time. Mount Pleasant had long been a center of abolitionist thinking and had been a stop on the underground railway in the years prior to the Civil War. One of its leading citizens, James Harlan, had gone to Washington, D.C., to serve first in the U.S. Senate and later in Abraham Lincoln's and Andrew Jackson's administration.

It became a hotbed of women's suffrage in the years after the War. Iowa Wesleyan, founded in 1842, had accepted women into its student body from its early years, a policy which very few institutions of higher learning followed at the time. This forward thinking practice resulted in Lucy Killpatrick Byrkit becoming the first woman to achieve a college degree in the United States in 1859. Later, in 1885, Susan Mosely Grandison matriculated from Iowa Wesleyan, possibly becoming the first African American woman to graduate from a U.S. college or university. The first Iowa women's rights convention was held in Mount Pleasant in 1870.

Among several outstanding women who attended Iowa Wesleyan, Belle Babb Mansfield broke barriers in the legal profession as the first woman in the United

States admitted to the Bar. That same year seven women founded P.E.O. Sisterhood, which would become an international women's organization with a membership of close to 250,000, dedicated to the higher education of women in the United States and Canada. Its record of freeing women from their ancient bonds is evident in the achievements of many of its members.

Mount Pleasant in 1870 was a prospering small city with a rich cultural history. It was into this citadel of liberal and enlightened thought that William Radford Gray came with his father, Thomas, and mother, Elizabeth Long Gray.

Thomas Gray was a carriage maker and the 1870 census shows the family living next door to an owner of a carriage manufacturing company. It is likely that the Grays moved to the city for a job and also to be near Elizabeth Gray's parents, William and Mary Long.

Thomas Gray died prematurely when Will was only eleven. The bereaved widow and her young son moved in with her parents, the Longs. Soon they would be joined by another husband-less Long daughter, Alice Long Taylor, and her son, William Byford Taylor. Will Taylor was a year younger than his cousin Will Gray, and the two boys grew up together, becoming close friends.

William and Mary Long had been farmers who had emigrated from Manchester, England in 1845 with their two daughters. They had two more daughters, Rose and Jennie, born in the United States. By 1880, the Longs, now elderly, had moved to a large rented house on North Main Street between the railroad tracks and Iowa Wesleyan.

Around 1883, William Long returned to England to live out his final years. Mary stayed in Mount Pleasant with their daughters until her death in 1887.

Elizabeth Gray supported the family by taking in male college students as boarders. The house came to be called "Gray Club" and later became the headquarters for the local chapter of Phi Delta Theta fraternity. Elizabeth's sister, Alice Taylor, continued to live with her. Alice was active in Mount Pleasant's cultural and literary affairs and was instrumental in founding the Ladies Literary Association and the Mount Pleasant Free Public Library. In this atmosphere young Will Gray grew up, surrounded with literary and cultural influences that were to form him and would later allow him to leave his mark on another community half a continent away and on many generations after his life had run its course.

Will Gray's life had begun far to the north in Port Huron, Michigan, where he was born on March 15, 1862. His father, Thomas Gray, was born in English-speaking Canada. His father's early death placed great responsibility on young Will's shoulders; he left home to learn a trade and help his mother. He apprenticed as a printer. The 1880 census finds eighteen-year-old Will Gray living in his birthplace of Port Huron and listed as a printer. We know that Will worked printing jobs in Chicago and in St. Paul. By the very early 1880s he had decided to get a formal education. He returned to Mount Pleasant and entered Iowa Wesleyan. School records show him enrolled as a senior in 1885.

When the young Will Gray moved to Mount Pleasant, the city was the new home of an orphan child, Anna Kurtz. Anna was the only surviving child of James Kurtz, a Civil War veteran and a grocer in Iowa City. He had died the year after her birth. Her mother, Theresa Allen Kurtz, next married another grocer, S.L. Saunders. She soon gave birth to another daughter, who was christened May. In a tragic succession of events for little Anna, her mother died at age 29, leaving the seven-year-old Anna with her stepfather and her one-year-old half sister May. The stepfather Saunders married again. Anna was sent to live with blood relatives, the Hervey Cranes, in Mount Pleasant.

In an act of compassion, Anna was taken in by her aunt Ella May Allen, known as May, and husband Hervey Newell Crane in 1870, the first year of their marriage. The Cranes were members of a large and socially prominent Mount Pleasant family. May and Hervey would have four children of their own, but to their credit they treated Anna like their own child.

Anna lived in their large stone house on the corner at 401 E. Washington Street and grew to be an intelligent and pleasing girl. She entered Iowa Wesleyan in 1883, pursuing a course of music and elocution and seeking a teaching certificate. Anna and Will Gray met at Iowa Wesleyan. We don't know the circumstances of their acquaintance but their meeting and subsequent romance was surely not unusual for two socially active young people, members of the very small Iowa Wesleyan student body. Will was a member of Phi Delta Theta fraternity and Anna had been initiated into I.C. Sorosis, an early women's sorority.

The records of Iowa Wesleyan show Will Gray in an unclassified category in 1887, and in 1888 enrolled in the Conservatory of Music and also studying elocution. Those same records show that Anna had been enrolled in the Conservatory and graduated with a B.S. degree in 1887.

Will left Iowa Wesleyan before graduation, determined to become a homeopathic physician. In 1888 he enrolled in the Homeopathic Medical Department at the State University of Iowa in Iowa City (now University of Iowa), and graduated two years later at the top of the class.

Anna used her education to secure a teaching job in the Mount Pleasant schools. She taught at Willowbank School while also attending advanced college classes. She received a Master of Arts degree in 1890.

Anna and Will fell deeply in love. On August 21, 1888, a date that Will referred to frequently in his letters, he proposed marriage. Anna was 24, Will was 26. Anna accepted but their engagement was to be kept a secret for reasons that we do not fully understand. Possibly the secrecy was because of the fear that Will's mother would not approve. There was a dark cloud hanging over Anna's family history. Anna's father, a Civil War veteran, had died in the Iowa State Hospital for the Insane at Mount Pleasant. Another possibility was that Anna's teaching job could have been in jeopardy if the school authorities had learned that her marriage was imminent. In the 1890s, elementary school teachers were not allowed to be married.

The two lovers were destined to continue a long courtship, delayed by Will's financial condition and their desire for him to establish a secure medical practice before they could set up housekeeping.

Partial Fairhaven Birdseye, 1891.

Boom Town Fairhaven

THE FAIRHAVEN OF 1890 was simply a gol-danged, consarned madhouse. The frenzy began in 1888 when Nelson Bennett, a hard-driving railroad contractor from Tacoma, envisioned Bellingham Bay as the place where the transcontinental Great Northern Railroad would meet the sea. This important northern route being built by his old friend James J. Hill would link the burgeoning industrial heartland of the nation with the Pacific Ocean and the shortest sea route to the Orient. Hill was even then pushing his tracks across the plains and mountains and would soon be selecting a route through the Cascade Mountains to a port on salt water. The selected site was sure to enjoy a remarkable growth and become a city of fabulous wealth. Bennett was confident that Hill would choose Fairhaven, a sleepy little village with a well-protected deep water harbor.

In 1853, Daniel Jefferson "Dirty Dan" Harris had jumped ship from a whaling vessel provisioning in Victoria Harbor, procured a wooden skiff and rowed it to Bellingham Bay. He moved in with the original settler, John Thomas, who had just filed his donation land claim and was building a shack above the beach in what would become the Fairhaven waterfront. Thomas died that winter of tuberculosis but Dan stayed on, eventually buying the land claim from Thomas's heirs.

Harris built a dock and a hotel and tried to promote his little settlement by the bay. He developed a reputation for being an energetic character with little interest in personal hygiene. Harris platted his town in 1883, naming it Fairhaven, and what would become its main street, Harris Avenue. He hoped to sell lots and make some money.

Whatcom Museum.

First known photograph of Fairhaven taken in 1889. Arrow notes Fairhaven & Southern Railroad office near 10th Street and Mill Avenue. The large building at right is the Fairhaven Land Company office and warehouse at 7th Street and Harris Avenue.

It was pretty slow going until 1888 when he got a visit from Bennett and, a few days later Bennett's new partner and investor, C.X. Larrabee. The two speculators bought all of Harris's Fairhaven minus the few lots that Dan had already sold. They then quickly bought the neighboring town of Bellingham, which Erastus Bartlett and Edward Eldridge had platted, also in 1883. The original owners had sold a few lots but there were plenty left for the new Fairhaven promoters. In addition, the newcomers bought a half interest in the big saw mill that Eldridge and Bartlett had built to jump start the Bellingham economy. Neither the town site nor the mill had been very successful for the sellers.

The new players incorporated themselves as "The Fairhaven Land Company" and quickly filed a re-plat combining Bellingham with Fairhaven. Their now enlarged town reached from Julia Avenue in the south to the very northern end of what is now Boulevard Park.

The Fairhaven Land Company owners were all wealthy and successful businessmen. Bennett had made a fortune as a railroad contractor building track and tunnels across the land. Larrabee had discovered the copper in Butte, Montana, sold his stake for a fortune and then made more money investing in real estate in Portland, Oregon. Their lieutenants were all tested, competent and well-to-do in their own right: Edgar Lea Cowgill, E.M. Wilson, Alexander McKenzie and J.J. Donovan. Together they were a terrific public relations team. The new "Boom Town" of Fairhaven was advertised all across the nation and even in Europe. Their promotions praised Fairhaven's beauty and location, its mild climate, the richness of its timber and mining resources, and its unlimited future. It was called the "Focal City" and the "Imperial City."

In addition to their superior sales skills, the leaders of the Fairhaven Land Company had the foresight and resources to invest in the infrastructure that a great new

Fairhaven City Directory, 1890. R.L. Polk & Co., Washington State Archives: Northwest Region.

city needed. Their personal commitment of huge cash resources was evidence that they truly believed in Fairhaven's future.

Soon an iconic hotel began to rise at the top of Harris Avenue; its tower could be seen by approaching ships and from all over the fledgling town. It stood as evidence of the power of Fairhaven's developers and the certainty of its prosperity. They organized a water company and laid pipe from nearby Lake Padden. A coal-operated electric company and then a gas company making gas from coal followed. The Fairhaven Land Company even built a railroad to their newly purchased coal mine in Skagit County to the south.

Their financial commitment, the physical evidence of growth, the obviously immense potential for prosperity, were the railroad to come, and their consummate selling job worked. Immigrants came from all over, people of all sorts, wanting to be in on this great opportunity and stake their claim early in this "gold mine" on the waters of Bellingham Bay. By 1889 the "boom" was on. The Fairhaven Land Company would sell a lot in the morning for $1,000 and by afternoon it might have changed hands twice, the last sale for $2,500. The next day it would sell again and someone would begin building a house, or a store, or a hotel on the lot. Every steamer brought another shipload of "boomers," packed elbow to elbow; men with no money and men with money to invest. There were families looking for a fresh start, gamblers, prostitutes, con men, tradesmen and merchants, professional people, card sharps – everyone seeing a chance to "strike it rich."

Fairhaven was indeed a "boom town" even though the promoters insisted that they were not "booming" Fairhaven. "Booming" was the practice of building up a great and false enthusiasm, getting rich on the resulting speculation and then letting the boom collapse. According to the Fairhaven Land Company, Fairhaven's success was to be certain. The December 29, 1890, *First Holiday Edition* of the *Fairhaven Herald* announced with joy and pride that the population of Fairhaven had been 150 on September 1, 1889, and just over a year later, 8,000. "Now that is progress," it trumpeted. An advertisement in the *Fairhaven Herald* newspaper boasted, "Recollect that the Western Terminus of the Great Northern Railway is Absolutely Fixed at Fairhaven." "Boom fever" was running hot and heavy.

The pattern of migration to Fairhaven was not much different from that of immigrants coming to American shores from the countries of Europe. One adventurous soul would respond to the call of a new land and make the move. He would quickly report back to friends and family with glowing reports of the beauty and opportunities of this new country. Soon, more and more of his fellows would be emboldened to come.

So it was with a large number of people who came to Fairhaven from Mount Pleasant, Iowa. Somehow the sophisticated folks from "The Athens of Iowa" had heard of Fairhaven and were intrigued. Perhaps the economy of Mount Pleasant had begun to stagnate by this time. Perhaps it was simply the excitement of this new land that appealed to the young people of staid and cultured Mount Pleasant. Whatever the cause, one after another, they migrated to Bellingham Bay. Even an established second-generation dry goods business, Templin & Woods, closed their Mount Pleasant store, held a big moving sale and re-located to Fairhaven.

Fairhaven in 1890 was the place to be for the young, the adventurous and the far-seeing.

Harris Avenue in the 1890s, looking east from Deadman's Point.

Cast of Characters
May 1890

William Radford Gray: Will, age 28. Attended Iowa Wesleyan 1885-1888, but did not graduate. Editor of the *Iowa Wesleyan*, member of Phi Delta Theta. Recently graduated from the Homeopathic Medical Department at the State University of Iowa at the top of his class.

Anna Allen Kurtz: Anna, age 26. Graduated Iowa Wesleyan University in 1887. Member I.C. Sorosis (now Pi Beta Phi). Enrolled in the IWU Normal Training to receive her full teaching credential. Teacher at Willowbank School in Mount Pleasant. Engaged to William R. Gray for almost two years.

In Order of Their Appearance in the Letters

OVER 100 NAMES ARE MENTIONED in Will Gray's letters. Many are classmates of Will and Anna's in Mount Pleasant, Iowa. The following people will be highlighted in **BOLD** the first time they are mentioned in the letters.

Will Taylor: Cousin William Byford Taylor, age 27, President of the Taylor and Myers Pharmacy Company, a homeopathic pharmacy manufacturing company in St. Paul, Minnesota. Married in 1884 to Golda Murdoch, the couple has three children. Will Taylor and Will Gray are extremely close, as they grew up living in the same house for many years when they were children. (Letter 2)

Harry Grahn: Cousin Harry, age 28, native of Pennsylvania, currently residing in Minneapolis, Minnesota, working as a clerk in a bank. Harry's mother, Mary Catherine Kurtz, is the aunt of Anna Kurtz. (Letter 2)

Aunt Rosie: Rose Long, native of Richmond, age 46, one of three sisters of Elizabeth Gray, Rose is married to Jacob Richmond, a real estate and insurance agent. Resident of Minnewaukan, North Dakota. (Letter 3)

Ed Richmond: Cousin Ed, age 22, son of Rose Long and Jacob Richmond. Currently living in Minnewaukan, North Dakota, with his parents. He is hoping to move to Fairhaven in the near future. (Letter 6)

May Weir: Maria May Weir, age 23, graduate of Iowa Wesleyan. Member P.E.O. Currently teaching at Willowbank Public School and engaged to be married to Carl Williams. Her father, Clay Henry Weir, owns 500 acres of one of the finest and most well cultivated farms in the county. (Letter 7)

Ed Robinson: (not to be confused with Cousin Ed Richmond) H. Edgar Robinson, age 30. Son of Mount Pleasant physician D.W. Robinson. Recently dropped out of Medical School to pursue his fortune out West. Listed in the 1890 Directory of Fairhaven as "Real Estate Speculator." (Letter 11)

Clint Howard: Clinton Woodbury Howard, age 25, native of Ohio, graduated University of Michigan's law school in 1887. Former associate at the Mount Pleasant law firm of Woolson & Babb before his move to Fairhaven in November of 1889. He is planning to move his law firm Evans, Sherman & Howard into the Mason Block when it is completed later this year. (Letter 11)

I.C. Templin: Isaac Clinton Templin, age 48, native of Indiana, graduated Iowa Wesleyan in 1862. Married with five children. Although he is co-owner of Templin & Woods in Mount Pleasant, he has moved on to real estate in Fairhaven. In 1889 he founded the real estate firm Henderson & Templin. He has successfully encouraged many Mount Pleasant friends to move west and buy property from him. (Letter 13)

Det Bird: Leslie L. Bird, age 28, son of wealthy and prominent citizen of Mount Pleasant, physician Wellington Bird, and brother of P.E.O. founder, Alice Bird Babb. Attended Iowa Wesleyan in 1885 as a sophomore. He is a good friend of Ed Robinson and is listed in the Fairhaven Directory of 1890 as "Real Estate Speculator." (Letter 13)

Ross Sullivan: William Ross Sullivan, age 35, Illinois native, lived in Mount Pleasant down the street from Anna Kurtz on East Washington Street. Recent arrival to Fairhaven on the advice of friend I.C. Templin. His family includes wife Anna, son William Ross (age 10), Zetta (age 9) and newborn daughter Edna. (Letter 13)

Jessie and "Jeff": Jessie, age 22, is the daughter of Carrie Crane Brenholtz, sister of Hervey Crane. Jessie's fiance is William R. Jeffrey, age 26, is currently studying Theology at Iowa Wesleyan. Member Phi Delta Theta. Resides at Gray Club. (Letter 15)

Mother: Elizabeth Long Gray, age 49. Native of Manchester, England. Widowed in 1873 at the age of 32. Proprietor of Gray Club, a boarding house for male students of Iowa Wesleyan and fraternity for Phi Delta Theta. Active member of the Methodist Episcopal Church. (Letter 15)

Anna Crane: Anna, age 23, is one of nine children of Baron Hutchison Crane. Currently attending Iowa Wesleyan College. Anna's father (now deceased) was a prominent hardware merchant in Mount Pleasant and brother of Hervey Crane. Anna has been engaged to Leigh Woolson since she was 19. (Letter 18)

Mr. Woods: John T. Woods, age 53, native of Indiana, lives in Mount Pleasant and is married to Sarah Killpatrick, sister of Mary Killpatrick Templin, wife of Hugh Templin. John is one of the partners at the Templin & Woods dry goods and is planning to close the Mount Pleasant store to join the Templins in Fairhaven. The Woods have five children: Edward, Lulu and Charlie, Alice and Ella. (Letter 23)

James H. Heacock: Dr. Heacock, age 48, native of Ohio, graduate of St. Louis Homeopathic Medical College 1872. Veteran of the Civil War. Farmer and Doctor until 1882, accepted position with Northern Pacific Railway Company. In 1885 he sold his 320-acre Ohio farm for $20,000 ($470,000 today). Married with six children. Moved to Washington state to work with his brother, Howard P. Heacock, owner of several patents for use in saw mills, and owner of the new Heacock's Mill in Fairhaven. (Letter 24)

Hugh and Mrs. Templin: Hugh Worster Templin, age 51, native of Indiana. Brother of I.C. Templin. Part owner of Templin & Woods dry good store in Mount Pleasant. Worked for the railroad in Mount Pleasant. Hugh left for Fairhaven in 1889. He and his wife Mary, have seven children. (Letter 34)

Aunt Jennie: Jennie Long McCulloch, age 42, sister of Elizabeth Gray, native of Wisconsin. Married to William McCulloch. Resides in Victoria, British Columbia, with two daughters, Nellie (age 14) and Jennie (age 11). (Letter 33)

Aunt Alice: Alice Long Taylor, age 48, sister of Elizabeth Gray, native of Manchester England, resident of the United States for 47 years. Widow of Dr. John Scott Taylor, surgeon in the Civil War. Charter member of the Ladies Literary Association and Trustee of the Mount Pleasant Free Public Library. Alice is known to thoroughly enjoy reviewing many of the books that she deemed inappropriate for public consumption. She lives well, but not extravagantly, with her sister at the Gray Club Boarding house. She has a secret that the town of Mount Pleasant is not aware of. (Letter 34)

Uncle Hervey and Aunt May: Hervey N. Crane, age 49, owner of a prominent jewelry and stationery store on the Town Square in Mount Pleasant. Married to Ella May Allen, known as May, age 39. May's niece, Anna Allen Kurtz, has lived with the Crane family on East Washington Street for almost 20 years, growing up with their children Frank (18), Mary (age 14) and Lewis (age 12) and Leigh (age 4). (Letter 38)

Leigh Woolson: James Leigh Woolson, age 24, entered Iowa Wesleyan in 1884. Member Beta Theta Pi. Currently attending Boston University Law School. Described by his college friends as "mischievous," Leigh is living up to his reputation while he is in Boston. (Letter 48)

Clara Cole: Clara, age 23, native of Iowa. Recent graduate Iowa Wesleyan. The Cole Family is one of the wealthiest families in Mount Pleasant. Clara is a very active member of P.E.O. She is engaged to Dr. Robert Carothers of Ohio. (Letter 48)

Mrs. Babb: Mrs. W.I. Babb, age 40, native of Iowa, is also known as Alice Bird Babb. Graduated Iowa Wesleyan University in 1869 with Honors. One of the founders of the P.E.O. Sisterhood. She is the sister of Det Bird. (Letter 107)

Courtesy P.E.O.

Folks back in Mount Pleasant
May Weir
Lulu Satterthwaite
Clara Cole
Leigh Woolson
William Jeffery
Mrs. Babb

Will mentions more than 80 other
people from Mount Pleasant.
Many were connected with
Iowa Wesleyan.

Will's Family
"Mother" Elizabeth Long Gray
"Aunt Alice" Long Taylor
Aunt Rose Long Richmond
Aunt Jennie McCulloch
Cousin Ed Richmond
Cousin Will Taylor

Anna's Family
Uncle Hervey Crane
Aunt May Crane
Cousin Anna Crane
Cousin Jessie Brenholtz
Cousin Lollie
Cousin Harry Grahn

Mount Pleasant
Folks in Fairhaven
Det Bird
Ed Robinson
I.C. Templin
Hugh Templin
Mary Killpatrick Templin
John T. Woods
Sarah Killpatrick Woods
Clint Howard
Ross Sullivan

According to Will there were
27 residents who had moved
from Mount Pleasant, Iowa, to
Fairhaven by 1891.

The Letters

Again I have just sent off a letter today,

but want to commence another tonight,

if only for the sake of having the opportunity of writing

"My Darling Anna."

W.R. Gray
1890

Will's first letter, May 19, 1890.

Letter 1

Union Depot
Burlington, Iowa
2:10 a.m., Monday, May 19

My Darling Sweetheart,

It is little more than an hour and a half since I left you, and I feel utterly desolate.

With the exception of two or three men walking about the depot it is entirely deserted. My train to St. Paul does not leave until 5:15 a.m. so I have about three hours to wait. Pretty prospect isn't it? Add to this the great sorrow that I have looked upon your face and held you in my arms for the last time in a year and a half at least and perhaps you can realize my state of mind. I know you can for I believe you think enough of me to be in much the same condition. But this is not exactly the way to start out – on a consolatory letter is it? I want you to not feel so very bad but think that this trip means the making our union possible the quicker. But do you know I never realized it before now that this struggle means a bigger struggle in the world for a while than I have ever had. It means new and greater responsibilities and I will need all my strength, and all your love to enable me to come through it with credit. Maybe you don't know what a powerful stimulus your love is. It's what gives me all hope and all pleasure in the work that is to be done. So you see each will have our work to do. I to go into actions, yours to give loving words and encouragement to sustain where things look darkest.

We can be mutually helpful if we are separated by a great distance. Taking this view, maybe we can lighten the burden of our separation. We can leave work for the future too, and that will be helpful. And I want you to look to the future hopefully and without any misgivings, Anna, whatever comes to you, you will always have my love, a love that will suffer all things for your sake. I will not write any more now as I think it will be well to try and get a little sleep. Be of good cheer dear, and remember that I am thinking of you and that my thoughts are all love.

Yours for good or ill,
Will

Letter 2

St. Paul, Minnesota
Tuesday, May 20, 1890

My Darling Sweetheart,

Here I am in St. Paul once more. The journey from Burlington was fairly comfortable. Had a chair car all the way and a good dinner at Albert Lea. I arrived here at 7:29 in the evening decidedly weary. I believe I told you in my letter from Burlington that I was going to try and get some sleep. You may have seen a picture of a tramp who has laid down on a seat in a park. It was one of those benches divided into separate seats by arms similar to the ordinary depot seats – when he got up he was twisted into various curves and angles where he had lain over each arm of the bench. Well that was pretty nearly the picture I presented when I arose and I hadn't done much sleeping either.

Minnesota Historical Society/CORBIS
1890. The boys at *The Minnesota Pioneer* newspaper, started in 1849.

*I am staying at **Will Taylor**'s house. There is no one there except Mr. Clark, Will's partner who sleeps there. Take my meals at the same restaurant where I used to board. I called around on the boys in the Pioneer this morning and had quite a cordial welcome. I shall not stay here to work under any circumstances, now inasmuch as the workmen of this city are going to undertake to put the nine-hour movement[1] into operation on the 2nd of June and it will be resisted by the employers so that there will likely be a strike or some trouble at least. As I do not want to be involved in this will go straight west.*

*There was a letter came for me from Ellensburg last Friday and Mr. Clark forwarded it at once to Mt. Pleasant so that if I had gone to the office on Sunday I should probably have received it. Now I will have to wait until it gets sent back … to say nothing of the suspense of having to wait. Am hoping that as the Ellensburg mail was answered so promptly that there is something favorable in it. Fortunately I can put in my time profitably. The annual meeting of the Minnesota State Homeopathic Society commences a three day session in Minneapolis today. Think I will attend tomorrow proceedings. Am making out my order of supplies in case my Ellensburg scheme falls through. Will call on **Harry Grahn** while in Minneapolis.*

I hope you have been getting through the time comfortably though if you have felt as miserable as I have you have had far from a hilarious time. I will be anxious to get your first letter. Will write tomorrow to tell you where to send the second one. I am bound to hear you from along the road some way. Will stop now and say goodbye for the present and always think of me as yours,

Lovingly, Will

Letter 3

St. Paul, Minnesota
Wednesday, May 21, 1890

My Darling Anna,

Well it gets pretty tedious here though today will be pretty well filled in my going to the State meeting for which I will start in a few minutes, so this will be but a note, to let you know that I am all right and tell you where to send a letter on the way.

I am all impatience to get to Minnewaukan for your first one. If I can get my mail from Mt. Pleasant so as to know how things stand from Ellensburg. I will start tomorrow afternoon, and will arrive in Minnewaukan Friday morning and then I hope to hear from your own dear self.

How dear, I begin, is more than you realize as I think of getting farther and farther away. I went to the general offices of the Manitoba railroad this morning and secured my passage to Butte, Montana. By the way, unless you hear, say nothing about the pass to anyone. I think that you had better write first to Helena, Montana. We will have about an hour there and that will give me a chance to get to the post office. A letter on the road will be a great solace. Write as soon as you get this so that the letter will have a good enough start to arrive there before I do.

*It will cost me thirty four dollars to get from Butte to Ellensburg. About what I thought it would take. It is going to cost a pretty nice little sum for board on the way. I may so far succeed in putting my pride in my pocket as to ask **Aunt Rosie** to put up a lunch(!!) for me. Think of it; dream of it! Then sleep if you can!! But what will a man not do when he is long on journey and short on cash. Yea, he may even descend to a lunch in a square pasteboard box. At least is must be a square box – No! Never will I carry a basket or a round box! Ha! Ha! I have sworn it! But please take notice this wild scheme is not yet consummated. It is but in embryo, so to speak and may never see the light of fulfillment.*

Tomorrow morning will end my suspense in regard to Ellensburg I hope. I wonder if you share in my suspense in regard to this matter. I believe you do for do you not love me, and is it not of great investment to us? It means much to us Anna. Maybe a years shortening of our separation and consequently the consummation of our happiness a year sooner. So why should we not both be in suspense.

I will write to you at once the contents of the letter when I get it. This will be rushing in three letters in as many days. But what of it? I believe they will be welcome and are a pleasure to me to write. See how conceited I am? I know they will be welcome – does that not sound as if it came from a man who is sure of the love of the one to whom he is writing? I guess I will stop now and get over to Minneapolis or I will have nothing to say tomorrow and will be late to the meeting besides.

I will say good bye now dear until tomorrow, but how different from our goodnights when I was home. It makes me feel lonely and desolate to think of it, but it will all end sometime, oh that sometime!

Good bye sweetheart, Devotedly, Will

Letter 4

St. Paul, Minnesota
Thursday, May 22, 1890

My Darling Anna,

Will start in half an hour for Minnewaukan. The letter came all right. This morning. It is such a letter as a cautious conservative man would write who did not want to raise too great expectations in his correspondent. He says that he wants to take in a young man but not just see his way now. But he also says that as I will be there in a few days he will wait and say his say when I arrive. He also says that he liked the tone of my letter very much. It is just such a letter as would lead me to suppose that when I get there he will make me an offer but that it will not be a very good one.

Well in my present circumstances any offer will be a good one, so I have him there. While I do not expect anything to come from it, I am hopeful.

Saw Harry in Minneapolis and told him all he wanted to know. Of course much of it was about you. And now I am off for Minnewaukan. So good bye once more.

Lovingly,
Will

Harper's Weekly.

The Northern Pacific train from St. Paul to the Northwest.

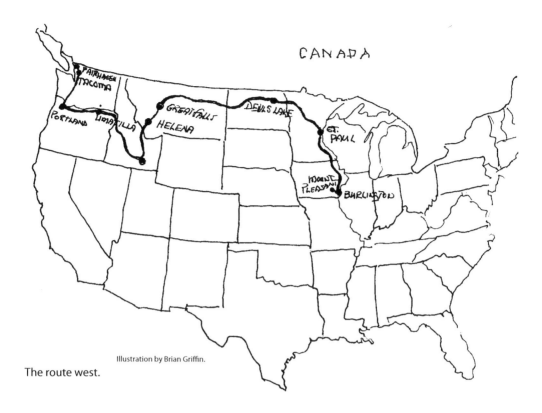

Illustration by Brian Griffin.

The route west.

Letter 5

Church's Ferry, Dakota
Friday, May 23, 1890

My Darling Sweetheart,

Truly I have been having a time along this stage of my journey. Church's Ferry is called Church's Ferry I suppose, because a man by the name of Church started it – and also because there is not a sign of a ferry any where near. And how do I happen to be here? Well, this is the nearest point to Minnewaukan which town is about sixteen miles from here.

I landed here today at noon and contrary to my expectations found no one to meet me. As a result I am stranded in this town (?) and will have to get a livery rig to take me over to Minnewaukan for which I will have to make the owner a present of three dollars or more.

In fact I have been having a time ever since I started. I lingered in St. Paul until I had to run to catch the train. Made it all right. Next the car that I was in was left at Grand Forks and when I moved I left my rubbers in the car. (Rubbers always were a confounded nuisance.) Next I had a scene with the conductor about allowing to lay over at this place.

He wasn't sure whether his instructions allowed him to permit it or not and it took us some time and a good deal of talk to make him see it my way. Then to cap the climax when I got off this train I left my overcoat which contained my instrument case in the car. Never thought of it until I saw the train pulling down the track about three hundred yards. Then had to telegraph to the next station to secure it and send it back by the next train which could be at four o'clock. So I am now waiting for my coat. And to make my misery complete there is a storm coming up which bids fair to keep me in this place until tomorrow at any rate, And such a place. Right on the prairie without a tree or shrub or fence within ten miles. A few little wooden shanties thrown down on the ground apparently in whatever positions they chose to alight. Unpainted and weather stained and the wind moaning and howling among them as if it had lost its last friend. And cold! Say as I came along on the train this morning I saw men driving along with great heavy fur coats on and they acted as if they were none too warm.

And to complete my misery, vegetation is barely started here. The grass is just starting and the few shrubs and trees that we passed by the way were just budding out so that it is not a very inviting prospect that greets one on every hand.

There was one pleasant little oasis in the wilderness of trouble that I have had. Now don't say that is just like a man but what I refer to was the supper I had on the dining car last night. To begin with it was one of the handsomest cars I have ever seen in that it was genuinely artistic. The wood work was entirely in carved oak with here and there a panel inlaid with hammered brass. Between each window, which were very large and excellent plate glass, were three columns handsomely carved in wood. The car was handsomely carpeted in Brussels[2] and instead of being seated with the usual car seat had ordinary movable dining room chairs so that the whole effect was that of a handsome dining room.

Now as to the bill of fare. I will just give you part of it. Tenderloin steak with mushrooms, broiled quail on toast, chicken salad, plain omelet with jelly, stewed potatoes with just a dash of onions in them to render the taste piquant, some buttered toast, a cup of black tea, strawberries, ice cream and cake. Perhaps it is unnecessary after that list to state that I was hungry and that I did full justice to all of it.

I mustn't forget one little thing that pleased my fancy very much and furnished me with not a little enjoyment. The round water bottle was in the end of the table opposite the window. In it was reflected the window and all that was in sight through it and there in miniature was the scene without and as the train moved swiftly along, something was imaged there and actually changed like a panorama. It was really exquisite to watch the ever changing scene, and nothing looked any prettier than the scene as it drifted by.

My old friend Grand Forks has changed considerably. The train passes through the heart of the city and I see many handsome buildings. At Devil's Lake City – I got out of the car to stretch my legs a little when behold about the first man I saw wore a great big Phi pin[3] in my plain sight. Mine was just as plain and as soon as he caught sight of it he held out his hand and said "How do you do brother, what chapter do you come from?" His name is Higler from Bloomington and he is a lawyer here – that is at Devil's Lake and his partner is likewise a Phi. I had quite a pleasant chat with him while the train stood there. He was anxious to have me stay on, and spend the day with him, but I couldn't do it of course, though I don't doubt he would have made it very pleasant for me.

Well, I guess I am rambling along pretty well this time. If I don't stop soon you will not have time to get this read before the next one comes along. And now, you may well imagine I am anxious to get in to Minnewaukan not only to see the Richmonds but to get your letter. I will just naturally burst with impatience if I don't get them before long. It is clearing up a little and if I didn't have to wait for that overcoat, I might get off this afternoon. By the way, there ought to be some good fishing in Devil's Lake so expect to hear something astonishing in my next letter.

Immediately on receipt of this write to Ellensburg, Washington so that I will get it while there while traveling this way. I have to keep you posted somewhat so that you will catch me at the different places. I am a little afraid that unless I should stay at Ellensburg that you won't catch me there as it is.

Just consider this letter as loaded with love from the first word to the last.

Good bye dear.
Yours devotedly,
Will

Letter 6

Minnewaukan, N. Dakota
Sunday, May 25, 1890

My Darling Anna,

Here I am ensconced at the town situated by the side of the lake that is named as belonging to his satanic majesty. To take up my adventures where I left off in my letter from Church's Ferry. When the afternoon train came in they had forgotten to put my overcoat aboard at the next station so I had to stay still longer. I had resigned myself to losing the overcoat, but about six o'clock brought a freight train with my outer covering on board. I then settled myself to stay all night in the place.

After supper I had secured a copy of Haggard's "Jess" and was just settling down to be in the time when I heard a buggy drive up front of the house a moment later a man stuck his head in the door and called out "Dr." (I'm getting my title of "doctor" now). "Mr. Richmond is outside and wants to see you." You can image that it sounded very pleasant. I went out and found Ed there. My card from St. Paul had been delayed and did not reach him until four o'clock that day. He immediately hitched up and was over there by fifteen minutes of seven. Pretty good traveling for sixteen miles. We had a very pleasant night ride. The moon was up; the horses stepped off quite lively. Ed and I had a good deal to talk about and so the time passed quickly, though it was not as pleasant as the ride I took the Saturday night before from Rome to Mt. Pleasant.

I do not see how the Richmonds stand it here. There is no society, the town is but a collection of wooden shanties while the farms around are mostly inhabited by Norwegians who live in regular houses, some of them built of sod. It looks like a vast wilderness of prairie around here. All day long the wind howls across the wide expanse making traveling around a rather undesirable proposition. One of the worst features about the place at least as far as the outlook for the future is concerned is that the waters around about here seem to be drying up. The shore line of Devil's Lake is several hundred feet from where it was when I was here four years ago. The dock where the steamers used to land are away up on dry land and the steamer itself can no longer ply in this part of the lake. I have found out why Church's Ferry has that name. When the town was first started there was a lake at that point – about seven miles in length and five in width. Across this was a ferry run by a man named Irvine Church, who, by the way I knew when I was in Laramie and at one side of the lake where the boat landed the little town sprung up. But in four years that lake has completely dried up and this year a crop is being planted where the bed of the lake formerly lay. This will perhaps give a little idea of what the drought must have been like in this county for the past two years.

I feel sorry for **Ed Richmond** being obligated to stagnate in a place like this. He is naturally very bright but gets but little opportunity to keep polished.

Yesterday I assisted at a surgical operation performed on an old Norwegian by one of worst looking old specimens of a doctor that I ever saw. He is one of the regular old timers that you sometimes hear about. After seeing him work I felt quite encouraged. If I couldn't handle a knife more skillfully than he did, I will, as old Polonius says, "Keep me a farm and carters."[4] Well do you know Anna I am beginning to realize how far it is out to Washington. It has been quite a long journey up here but it is just a beginning compared with what is to follow. Your letter was awaiting me when I arrived here. It came the same day. You can hardly imagine with what eagerness I received it. I don't believe I could have waited longer. Ed told me on the way over here that the letter was here and it seemed to me that the horses crept along like snails hitched to a mountain.

I wonder if I will get letters at Helena and Ellensburg. It looks now as if I am to do most of the writing for a while until I have a regular address. This being so long on a journey is no fun when one has to wait for letters and then not know whether they will reach him or not. It makes the letters very precious when they do come. You may be sure I am very glad that I wrote from Burlington if it was a consolation to you. I would just like to go on doing things all my life that would be a consolation and a source of happiness to you and would consider the life well spent if I could feel sure that I had accomplished that. It would be sufficient happiness for me to know that I in any way added any joy and pleasure and above all peace and contentment to your life. I shall go on doing what work I can in the world but I feel my ambition is all wrapped up in your well being. Whatever will most conduce to make your pathway through life a joyous one, that is the thing I want to do. If I should fail in this it will be through lack of judgment and the knowledge as to how to accomplish it and not from any lack of desire on my part.

As I write, Ed Richmond is stretched out on a sofa in the room with a cigar held in his mouth, smoking away and seeming to extract solid enjoyment from that weed. I think sometimes that I miss a good deal of comfort from not using the narcotic weed. Say Anna, suppose I commence smoking again? But no, when I come to think of it that would not add to your comfort in the future whatever it might do to mine, so I will ever leave the fragrant (?) cigar alone.

You think that your letter partook of the little things? Well it is the little things that go to make up life and so if you tell me all the little things that come with yours, I will be able to know about what it is, and that of course will be of great interest to me, so don't be concerned about the kind of letters that I will have to receive for the next year and a half (?).

While I was in St. Paul, I got (obtained, I should say) a piece of chamois skin to make a covering for my instrument case and Aunt Rosie has made it up, binding it with blue silk. It makes a very pretty covering. There are some pieces of the skin left, which I send you to make the needle case out of. I have cut them about the size that I want the case. Two halves of chamois skin will be about right for the inside of the case. The outside I leave entirely with you. You may fix it up to suit your taste, and then it will suit me. Don't feel badly because you did not get it made while I was home. I will not need it for some time, and besides, you know you want something to keep you busy that will serve in a small way to do it.

I hope you will get up to see mother quite often, she will be pretty lonely, especially after the boys are gone.

Well I think I will stop now and give you a chance to breathe. I will stop writing but will think about you. Do I not carry a blossom in my pocket of which Ophelia said, "There's pansies, that's for thoughts"? And how can I forget the night that blossom was given to me? That night, and the afternoon at Rome will be long remembered for were we not happy if we were to part so soon?

I have looked at that pansy several times. My note-book is not very tight so that as it dried it had a chance to shrink, so that is quite small now, but that makes no difference. It is the same flower and the same sweet girl gave it to me as if it were the largest blossom in the world.

Enclosed you will find some flowers that Aunt Rosie wanted me to put in and send to you "from Dakota." And as I send it, remember the heliotrope means the same thing the world over.

Well this will be a book if I don't stop soon. So with great love I will say "good-bye sweetheart."

Yours devotedly,
Will

HELIOTROPE

Illustration by Brian Griffin.
Heliotrope, in the language of flowers means "Eternal Love."

Letter 7

Helena, Montana
Thursday, May 29, 1890

My Darling Anna,

Here I am six thousand six hundred feet above the level of the sea in the Rocky Mountains. I have stopped here because I make better time on the Northern Pacific than by going down to Butte, which is south of here, so that a loop would be made by going there. But I will have to linger here until tomorrow afternoon. The way the Manitoba and the Northern Pacific roads manage their connections here is enough to exasperate a man. The N.P. train for the West leaves just twenty minutes before the Manitoba comes in and as neither road runs more than one train a day that necessitates a twenty-four hour's stay here – less than twenty minutes. Just before sitting down to write things I received your letter. You needn't make your letters short for fear I will not get them. I intend to manage, so that they will all reach me. There may be a little delay sometimes, but I will get every one of them. You will never know how delighted I was to get your letters. I couldn't tell you if I tried. Just think a little through and perhaps you can imagine. It was the second letter in nearly two weeks. Just think of it – only two letters in that time.

This journey seems harder and harder all the time. It is a long ways and it is only two-thirds through with yet, and all the time as the train speeds along I think it is taking me further and further away from all I love on earth.

If there is anything in one mind acting on another at a distance, you must surely have known – have felt – how often I have been yearning for you since I left Mt. Pleasant. Maybe it will be easier when I get to work – indeed I hope it will, because, I don't want to suffer all the time as I have from the moment that I last held you to my heart and kissed you goodbye. And now, alone in this strange town, it all comes over me stronger than ever. I want you tonight Anna, want you so badly. Don't you feel that as I do as I write this? I wonder if you feel the need of me as badly tonight. Do you know I believe you do, for I remember that today was **May Weir**'s wedding day, and you will miss her very much and you will couple this loss with mine. There is a lover's conceit for you but don't I know myself beloved and so what should be more natural than that I should suppose and believe that my beloved one would miss me.

I feel tonight that you are nearer to me than ever. Do you know, dear one, that I believe if I were with you tonight that there would be no silence when we are alone and have a chance to lay our hearts bare to each other's gaze. I think I could tell you all the feelings of my heart. I cannot put them on paper. They would be but words,

Courtesy Iowa Wesleyan College Archives.
May Weir.

without what I feel I could put in my voice and eyes, if I could just look into your sweet face while I was saying them. Yes, as far as I have gone I want this to be a love letter pure and simple. That's all I have any room for now. Tomorrow I will add what I have to tell about the journey.

Tonight I cannot put your image out of my mind's eye in order to admit even the grand view that passed before my eyes today. Just your image, sweet, lovely and loving. You cannot know how sweet it is in my eyes. You used to laugh at me when I used to want to see your hair flying about. You would not wonder though, if you knew how I love to see it so, I think because it was like no one else's. It was a part of your individuality. I have the lock you sent me once, with me, and I carry it all the time in the back of my watch. It is a great satisfaction to have that much of you with me. I feel as if I would like to go on and write nothing but love all night, but it might grow tiresome to you because I know that I don't put it as an ideal love would. But I am just a plain fellow that feels deeply without saying much very often. You will not think this a silly letter will you dear? It bears with it a man's strong and lasting devotion at any rate, and I don't think that can ever be silly to the one whom he loves. I believe I will say good night now. I had to sit up all night in a crowded car last night and will have to again tomorrow night and hence feel the necessity for plenty of sleep tonight. Tomorrow I will continue this letter and endeavor to tell a little about what I saw along the journey. And so good night my darling loved one. I shall dream of you tonight – as I have for the past week. Once more good night dear. Tho almost as hard to say good night, this time as it was when you were with me, and I could receive a loving good night – kiss. How long, oh how long before I can again. It must not be long before I can receive the caresses of a wife. Good night.

Friday morning *– Good morning dear – I have spent the morning in a mountain scramble and am now writing from notes taken on the highest peak near Helena. When I started it looked like a little climb but it took me over two hours to reach the top. I had to stop several times to get my breath and rest and once or twice thought of turning back, but I determined that as I had set out without any intentions of stopping short of the highest point, I would do what I intended. It was more of a climb that I bargained for and has about tired me out. But the top once gained it was well worth the effort. I have used the word magnificent before to express small things but with the scenery spread out – before me here I never will again. Below me looking like a small hill is an elevation, which when I started seemed to turn up into the heavens. I am sitting on a ledge of rocks and right before me is a sheer precipice of at least a hundred and fifty feet. Beyond and away down the mountains lying in a valley that is surrounded by mountains like a protecting wall is the red city of Helena, spread out in a birds eye view. On the left the valley stretches out as floor and, beyond that rise range after range of mountains, stretching out seemingly into infinity. To the right and behind me are peaks with their heads above the clouds and the snow lying on their summits. The mountains here are not above the perpetual snow line, but there was a snow storm up in the range last night while below in the valley it rained.*

From this point I can look around in every direction. The grandeur of the scene is a revelation to me. In some places where the sun breaks through the clouds the mountains look green and smiling. In other places where the shadow of the cloud rests they are dark and frowning. In some places the mountain sides are golden with a yellow flower like something that grows in Iowa. The prettiest thing that grows on the mountain side is a moss that clings to the rocks and bears a little blue flower, something like a forget-me-not only a little larger. I tried to press some to send to you but it was a failure. I put them in. Maybe you can get an idea of them as they are. They seemed to me the most beautiful and dainty thing I ever saw. Maybe they impressed me that way on account of their rugged surroundings. Helena is quite a town and has such beautiful buildings and dwellings but looks rather bare and bleak because there are no trees. The only trees to be seen are a kind of stunted pine that grows on the sides of the mountains.

The journey here was very tedious until Great Falls, Montana is reached. It is almost a dead bore of the barest looking prairie. At Great Falls we strike the Missouri River and then the course of the railroad lies for a long time on its banks, following the winding course of the river among the hills that commence to rise from that point on until the "Gateway of the Mountains" is reached. There the scenery becomes grand. The Missouri on one side and the mountains turning up in the most fantastic shapes on the other make a scene that one will not forget. Very soon, five tunnels are going between here and Great Falls. A new sight to me was to see after we passed the Montana line, over the doors of certain buildings, the world "licensed gambling room." Here in Helena that sign may be seen anywhere almost. I passed one block this morning where I think every place on each side of the street was either a gambling room, saloon or a place where revolvers are sold. I am going to go most of the way to Ellensburg by the Union Pacific. I have a scalper's ticket to Portland and will save about five dollars on it though it will take about four hours longer. Anyway, however that will save, anything is the way to go out of here.

I hope to get to Ellensburg soon so as to know my fate. Well, I guess this is as much as you can stand this time so I will stop now. I expect the next letter will be from Ellensburg and will tell about what my luck is. Goodbye my dear.

Yours lovingly,
Will

Letter 8

Umatilla, Oregon
Monday, June 2, 1890

My Darling Anna,

Here we are again, once more waiting for a train. Tell you what it is, if my success out here is to be attained through the same proportions of difficulties as has attended my journey out here, I am going to have a hard row to hoe. At Helena I wrote you that I would hear on Friday. Well, I didn't know. I thought I would hear Friday, but I didn't. When I went down to the depot to depart, I found that the transfer company had not transferred my baggage and so I had to stay over another day. Was I mad? Oh no! I wasn't mad. My hair hasn't got back to its original color yet. Then my beautiful cheap ticket didn't turn out to be so cheap after all. I will take a day longer which of course means added expense of living on the way. Then I got into this place about three o'clock this morning after two nights and a day on the cars and cannot get away until two o'clock this afternoon. Hotel bill to pay. Have to make two changes yet before I get to Ellensburg.

And what a magnificent lot of territory has been covered. Do you know that at one time I was within one hundred and twenty five miles of Ogden, Utah? That was at Pocatello, Idaho. I wrote to you from Helena, to mother from Pocatello, Idaho and to you now at Umatilla, Oregon. Quite an extent of country isn't it? The mountain scenery between Helena and Butte was the grandest and wildest I have seen on the way. About midway between the two cities the highest point is reached, known as the continental divide. On the east of this is the Atlantic slope and on the west is the Pacific. Since leaving the mountains, it has been one almost unvarying scene of sage brush. The most barren and dreary looking landscape I ever saw. It is no better here. And yet in the places where the land has been irrigated it looks beautiful and is said to be wonderfully fertile. I can well believe it from the few prices that I saw. At this place, which is just a little junctions point, the great Snake River runs by.[5] It is as wide as the Mississippi at Burlington and gets to be a great expanse by the time it enters the Columbia – not far from here.

Inasmuch as I didn't go to bed until three o-clock, I slept until noon, and so haven't much time to write. Speaking of noon, I have put my watch back two hours since I left Mt. Pleasant. At Minot, one hour to correspond to Mountain Time and here to be square with Pacific Time. I will stop now and the next you hear from me will tell what the final decision is at Ellensburg. I am getting very anxious.

Good bye dear,
Hastily and lovingly,
Will

Letter 9

Ellensburg, Washington
Wednesday, June 4th, 1890

My Darling Anna,

 At last my destination has been reached. I arrived here Monday night. I would have written yesterday, but I wanted to wait until I could write a letter definitely in regard to my prospects at this place. Well I don't know that things are any more definite now than they were. I have made the acquaintance of Dr. P. P. Gray[6] and found him a very pleasant gentleman of about fifty years of age. My getting in with him depends upon certain projects of the town of Ellensburg. Just at present the place is very dull owing to the great boom across the mountains along the Sound.[7] And a thousand people have left here within the last two months. So that real estate values are at a stand still and little is being done in that line. There are two schemes on foot now to make the town grow. One is for another railroad. The other and chief project is for the funding of the county for the purpose of building a ditch for irrigating purposes. This latter scheme will be settled in about four weeks. So that I cannot know definitely, very likely, short of that time or possibly a little longer. And yet I feel that it will come out all right. If I get in at all it will be a better thing than I had expected. Dr. Gray says that if property looks up so that he could dispose of what he has here at a good price, he would work a new man into his practice and then go away from here and leave the whole thing to him. I seem to have made

a pretty good impression on him. One thing that makes me rather hopeful is that the Dr. has evidently been talking about me before I arrived. Several places where he has introduced me he has done so as the young man that he has been in correspondence with. I have not had very much conversation with him about the matter as yet but he wants me to stay a few days here anyway, so that he can introduce me to the people of the town. He is a rather wary old fellow, I imagine, and every once in a while he drops in a question on medical subjects and then wanders off again.

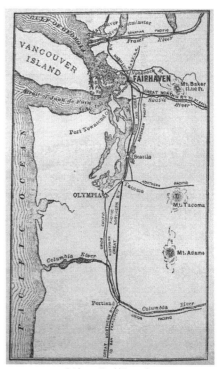

 I think he is trying to find out how much I know, so I have to be pretty cautious and careful in my conversation with him. He has one of the nicest residences in the town, though he has only been here for two years. During that time he has put about $15,000 on his books of which he collected all but $3,000. It is a stake worth playing for.

Fairhaven Herald, December 29, 1890. CPNWS.
Map of Puget Sound.

If the irrigation scheme goes through[8] *everything will be all right and the town will boom.*

The town is situated in a small valley and is the prettiest place I have seen since leaving St. Paul. It was almost wiped out by fire last year[9] *but the buildings have been rebuilt in brick and the business part of the town presents a more substantial appearance than any new town I ever saw. To the west are the Cascade Mountains and just northwest can be seen the snow covered summit of Mt. Stewart. On a perfectly clear day they say that the top of Mt. Tacoma can be seen from here. This is the first glimpse I have had of a genuine snow covered mountain. In the valley there is a great profusion of flowers. The wild roses are very thick and just in their glory. Since I will have to wait to know whether I can stay here or not, I suppose that in a few days I will have to go to Tacoma or Seattle and try to get work because of course I can't afford to stay here and do nothing on an expectation that may come to naught. However send my letters here until further notice because it is but a few hours travel to Tacoma or Seattle and I can have them forwarded so that they will reach me all right and just save the time it would take to get a letter from either of those places to Mt. Pleasant. Probably day after tomorrow. The Dr. and I together with two or three others will take a trip of twenty five or thirty miles into the mountains on a fishing excursion and then look out for some wonderful stories for I will do my best to tell an interesting one at least.*

I received your letter all right and am wondering when I will get another. I imagine that my scrawls by the way have arrived in rather an intermittent way on account of my being obliged to scratch off a few lines just as I had an opportunity along the way. Say, this morning I was up in the State Register office of the place and there was a huge map of the United States hung on the wall and then I had a full view of the distance between Mt. Pleasant and this place and it wasn't a very consoling thing to see. Excuse me a few minutes please and I will go and get my dinner.

There I feel better now. Am going to assist Dr. Gray this afternoon in making an examination in a suspected case of consumption brought on by the "grip."[10] *Another little test "you know."*

As so the first Sunday was rather difficult to get through, was it dear? Didn't I have a case of it in Helena? Well I think I did. Say don't count up the Sundays in two years Anna. It will only make it look harder. Two years is a mighty long time but there is no telling what may happen in that time. Maybe I can get both you and mother out here before that. I am sure that I hope so. Say, while I think of it, when you go to call on mother, don't stop at the front door, but knock (a good sound knock) on the door at the end of the hall. And then if you don't raise anyone, go to the next door. That's what everyone does who calls at that house, often they have been there often enough to "know the ropes." It is a long way from the front door to the kitchen in that house and the way I have given you is the only way to raise the folks. Mother will be glad to see you anytime and especially when the students are all gone and she will be alone.

Snipes Block, Ellensburg.

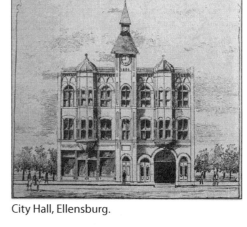

City Hall, Ellensburg.

Davidson Block, Ellensburg.

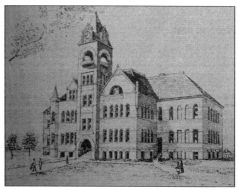

Ellensburg School.

Washington State Archives: Northwest Region.

The above sketches from the *Graphic, Washington Special Edition 1891*, are buildings which rose from the fire of July 4, 1889. Today, only the Davidson Block still exists.

I am trying to keep a stiff upper lip but I tell you this suspense in regard to prospects here is not very conducive to ease of mind. I think I would breathe easier if it were settled even adversely. I would know exactly what I have to do there and if it was to go to work at the trade for awhile I could stand it. Tell you what it is. I don't believe there is much to be gained by waiting on the action of another person. The best way is to go to work independent of anyone then one knows that every failure and disappointment is his own doing and any success is his own as well. So you laughed or no. That wasn't it, you were "amused" over my little troubles on the way, were you. That's all right for you. However, I'll take your advice and the next time I make that journey have someone along to look after me – you. How do you think you would like the responsibility? It would be a pretty big one – the responsibility I mean. And so "Baby" Warren was smitten was she? Wonderful are the ways of women. To a man up a tree it would look as if she were madder than a wet hen. I actually shivered and needed an extra overcoat whenever I met that frigid bow of hers on the street. I think Frank must have been indulging his imagination a little.

Something that will interest you a little about this town will be the fact that although it has over three thousand inhabitants, it has not a public school. It had one however until the fire of last year. A new $40,000 building is to be constructed at once to be ready by fall. The place is lit entirely by electric light. And one of the prettiest little things here to my notion is a stream that runs through the town that is just as clear as crystal and the water is as cold as ice. It is ice water in fact, for it comes from the frozen tap of the mountains.

Well, I must stop now and go out with the doctor. Hope that the next time I write – I will have some better news to tell. And don't get blue. Remember that we will end it as soon as we can and that may not be as long as we anticipate. So good bye dear. Love to "Aunt May" and "Cousin Mary."

Yours devotedly,
Will

HOMEOPATHY IS A HEALING SYSTEM developed in the 18th century by the German physician Samuel Hahnemann.

Monument to Samuel Hahnemann, Washington, D.C.

According to the National Center for Homeopathy, Hahnemann believed the substances that cause disease could, when administered in tiny amounts, provoke a healing response. Over decades, Hahnemann built a pharmacy of thousands of "remedies" derived from natural substances such as herbs, minerals and animal products. Homeopathy quickly built a great popular appeal. By the mid 1800s, thousands of homeopathic doctors, hospitals, pharmacies and medical schools appeared worldwide. Homeopathy faded from popularity in the United States beginning in the early 1900s as a result of successful efforts by conventional medicine to limit access to it, and later with the advent of antibiotics and other effective pharmaceuticals. Today, increased interest in alternative therapies has led to a revival.

ALLOPATHIC MEDICINE was a term also coined by Samuel Hahnemann and refers to the broad category of medical practice that is sometimes called Western medicine, or modern medicine. Homeopathy, from the Greek word *Homeo,* meaning similar, used substances that cause similar effects as the symptoms of a disease to treat patients. Allopathy, from the Greek word *Allo,* meant different. Allopathic medicine differed from the homeopathic approach as conventional medical treatments directly countered a patient's symptoms. In 1848 the allopathic doctors created the American Medical Association (AMA) as a response to the popularity of Homeopathic medicine.

ECLECTIC MEDICINE, popular in the latter half of the 19th century, made use of botanical remedies. As its name implies, "eclectic" referred to those physicians who adopted in practice whatever was found to be beneficial to their patients. Eclectic medicine is still practiced today, but mainly by medical herbalists rather than physicians.

Letter 10

Ellensburg, Washington
Sunday, June 7, 1890

My Darling Anna,

Your letter written on the 31st reached me the fifth of this month so according to that it takes five days for a letter to reach here. Think of it, five days if it has good luck.

Well I guess my chances here for the present at least are rather slight. The march across the mountains has made things very dull here and Dr. Gray's business, according to his books, has fallen off considerably. If the projects that I spoke about in the previous letter should materialize things will look differently, but in my present financial condition I can't afford to wait. Dr. Gray has rather advised me to start independently here, so that we can have the benefit of consultation, but I told him that if I start independently that I shall do so in one of the growing cities on the Sound. He has very kindly offered to give me an outfit of medicines sufficient to start with wherever I may go and also lend me some books. This will save me the cost of freight from St. Paul and what is more important, the three or four week's delay that is likely to ensue on all goods ordered from the latter place. This offer of the doctor is proof of confidence at least and shows that his reasons for not wanting me to go in with him at present are genuine.

I shall start for Tacoma tonight and see if I cannot get work in a printing office for a few weeks. That will enable me to get enough money to start up somewhere and also will give time for the Ellensburg projects to be consummated.

Don't know how I will succeed in getting employment as there is a great rush to the Sound. There were five printers on the train in which I came here, bound for Seattle. If every train brings in five printers the supply must be more than equal to the demand.

I expect also that under the new medical law here that I will have to take an examination in all branches before the state board. The allopaths last winter managed to put through a bill providing for a board of nine members all of the "regular" school to examine all applicants for license to practice medicine. It was passed by both branches of the legislature but the governor vetoed the bill on the grounds that it was class legislation with the intention of giving a larger class of citizens no choice as to whom they should employ. He said however that even if he had not vetoed it that he should have so construed the meaning of the word "regular" that if he had wanted to be could have appointed nine homeopaths and still come within the meaning of the term – that regular physician meant one who had graduated at a school regularly chartered under the laws of the land for the tracking of medicine without regard to doctrine. A new bill was passed in which the word "regular" is not found. And there the governor said it was his intention to so approve the members of the board that no one school would have a majority. As a result the board stands four allopaths, three homeopaths and two eclectics. But I believe that the law requires all applicants to be examined whether they have a diploma or not. All that hurts me about this is that the examination fee is ten dollars.

Well, so much for the medical question. Now a little more about the country. Of course as yet, I can only speak for this side of the mountain. The climate is much like that of Iowa that is as regards temperature. They tell me that it sometimes gets to be one hundred in the summer and twenty five below zero in the winter. But that there are few sultry days and the nights are always cool. The winter season is not as long as it is in Iowa, real cold weather lasting only three or four weeks. The springs are much earlier. You will believe that when I say that cherries here have commenced to ripen and grain has headed out. Owing to the lack of rain, the atmosphere is much dryer here so there is not as much catarrh or throat troubles.

Yesterday we went fishing – that is we went after fish but the fish were in a contrary mood and refusing, yes refused to be caught. But to me the scenery was well worth the trip. We went about ten miles up into a canōn in the mountains, where there is a rushing mountain torrent. It was too rushing. That was what was the matter. About a month later, when the water is down so that there will be quiet pools here and there the fishing will be good. Yesterday, though there was not a spot where the water wasn't tumbling down the canōn. It was reached by the roughest road – it was ever my good or bad fortune to ride over stumps, rocks, hills, underbrush, made it like Jordan, "a hard road to Trouble." On each side of the streams the rocky sides of the mountains rose in great cliffs for three or four hundred feet, great pine trees projecting out wherever the roots of one could find a lodgement. Down in the canōn the bottom was filled with the wildest growth of shrubbery and trees that you can imagine, making it a regular tangle, and through it, danced and leaped and tumbled the stream, the clearest and coldest water I ever saw. We were all fixed for trout. Regular sportsman's outfit – basket strung over the shoulder, slender, flexible, jointed rod, reel and fly hooks. Rubber boots coming up to the thighs for wading. But the fish wouldn't bite. But the scrambling, the wading, the scenery, the hum and the roar of the water were all glorious to a greenhorn without the fish. I don't like fish anyway. Had a little lesson in distance and perspective.

And so May Weir's wedding was a sad one was it? And you actually wept. Anna, I have a good mind to be jealous. Cry when May Weir is married, but not when I went away. I would believe I thought that tears were the measure of one's feelings at all times. But as I don't – I don't believe I will be this time. I will wait until I get glowing reports of the antics of the McAdam twins, Jim and Ed, and thus I will turn green, not exactly with jealousy but with envy. But that's right, have as much fun as you can. I am hoping that one of us can. There won't be too much fun for me until I know what I am going to do or at least whether I am going to get work. Talk about being jealous! Why Anna, I would be an unreasoning brute if I could possibly be jealous of one who would stick to such a poverty stricken wretch as I am. But there I am talking foolishly again. Why should I say anything about poverty. I'm all right. I feel though that it would be useless to think of fitting in there. I could never have such luck. Kind of fuming though how some fellows can fall into rosy beds so easily while some – speaking of rosy beds, I should have said that about half the underbrush up the canõn was wild rose bushes – the odor was delicious. I will get things told if you just give me time enough.

Oh! I'll have a chance to get my "ten dollar" horse out here I guess. There was a pretty good looking "cayuse" being sold on the street, the other day for eight dollars and a half. A "cayuse" I will state for your information is a native Indian horse. Hay sometimes costs $40 a ton however, so the beast wouldn't be so cheap after all. Well I guess I told about all I think of this time. My next letter will be written from Tacoma, the "City of Destiny." Write to me there though there is no telling where I will be by the time the letter will reach there. If I didn't have your love to think of and sustain me, I think I could without much difficulty, get down in the depths. But having that I won't. And see how selfish I have been, I have said nothing to make things a little bright for you when I know that you have not been very happy with May going away, but you know that you have my love and sympathy even if I can't always express them. I suppose that before this reaches you your school will be out. I am glad of it, though you may not be, because I think you need the rest. In fact I know you do.

Well, I must stop now, or you will surely need a rest before you get this read. So goodbye darling. Hope I will have some good news next time.

Lovingly,
Will

Letter 11

Tacoma, Washington
Monday, June 9, 1890

My Darling Anna,

One more step on the way and I must say these steps are getting to be decidedly tiresome. I arrived in Tacoma yesterday (Sunday) morning, three weeks after leaving Mt. Pleasant. Much of the journey over from Ellensburg was in the night so that we missed a great deal of the mountain scenery but as day breaks early there was much to see after daylight. It was the wildest, grandest and most beautiful that I have ever seen.

The peaks of the Cascades are higher than any that have been passed. On this side of the mountains too, the vegetation changes. It seems like passing into an entirely new country. Three hours travel changes the landscape from a dismal stretch of sagebrush in the prairie and pine trees on the mountains to a growth of ferns, tropical in their luxuriance, and the great fir and cedar trees. The fir trees are a sight to behold. Some of them rise up for fully two hundred feet if not more. The most curious sight to me and a very beautiful one, too, is the extreme slenderness of the trees in proportion to their height. A fir tree is little more than trunk anyway. The branches at the great height at which they come out seem like small mossy limbs stuck around the trunk. The tops are rounded instead of going up to a point like the pines. This whole Sound country is one great forest and milling is the great industry. Tacoma is a beautiful city, or will be when it is built in a little more. At present, owing to rapid growth it presents a very crude appearance. A great business block will rise up into the sky, and right alongside will be a little one story wooden building.

Booming was taking place up and down the Sound. The Tacoma Hotel was built by the Tacoma Land Company and is now Stadium High School.

The Graphic, Washington Special Edition 1891. Washington State Archives: Northwest Region.

I never saw so many wooden structures before. Lumber is so cheap here that every house is built of wood. But at least the people here prove what can be done with wood in the way of beautiful designs. There are some very elaborate buildings, all wood. The city is situated on a hillside so that the streets running east and west are quite steep. While those running north and south seem to be terraced, one street rising above the next. At the foot of the hill are the green waters of Puget Sound. There are miles of wharfage along the shore where ocean vessels come up to take on lumber. The air smells delightfully fresh with the salt water and the odor of fir, pine and cedar lumber mingled. The business streets are about one hundred feet wide and are laid with planks three or four inches thick. But the great sight here are the roses. The choicest tea roses that back East require the most tender nursing and then do well if they produce three or four blossoms during the season, just luxuriate here. Many of the residences here are up quite high from the ground and are terraced. Along each terrace are rows of roses. Just one mass of blooms of every possible variety from the purest white to the deepest crimson. I saw one branch yesterday which rose way up in the air and then hung over a perfect arch, fairly laden down with the richest crimson roses. There must have been a hundred flowers on that one stalk. Transportation can be had from the business center to almost any part of the city – by steam or electric motor.

The Graphic, Washington Special Edition 1891. Washington State Archives: Northwest Region.

Seattle: A view of the city from the harbor.

Seattle is thirty miles down the Sound ("down" means north of here) and steamers are plying between the points along the Sound all the time. There are about a dozen steamers daily each way.

Clint Howard *and Ed Robinson were here Saturday on their way home (to Mt. Pleasant I mean) so I just missed seeing them. I called on LuLu Woods and her husband yesterday. They made things quite pleasant for me. We went walking for a while along the water first and then took a drive around the city. Lu is looking about as she did when she left Mt. P and has developed into a great "boomer." I think she can give her husband points in the line of booming Tacoma. I guess boomers judging by appearances that they can boom Tacoma with good reason as they have done well. They have a beautiful house here in a nice quarter of the city and they have a splendid view both of the waters of the Sound and of Mt. Tacoma. The house is built in the wooden villa style and has ten rooms, with fire places (tile) in several of the rooms. Leroy Palmer is building a very fine residence next door to* them and they are going to have a large barn and stable in common. *Lu says she was down to Seattle a short time ago to see Ed Howard and his wife and that as soon as Mr. Palmer's house is finished, Ed and wife will be here for a week and are visiting Mt. Pleasant people. Well, that will do I guess for the town and of people at present.*

I received your letter today with the account of May's wedding. It was forwarded from Ellensburg. You may be sure I was delighted to get it especially as I had expected it before leaving Ellensburg. About the pressed flowers. I quite like your idea of keeping a collection. A very pretty one might be kept in a book made for that purpose. You make the collection and I will send the flowers. Will try and get them and press them in such a way that they will arrive in good condition for fastening in a book.

I don't know what I will do here yet. Am going to try and get work for while. Will have to pretty soon, as I can't travel much more. The railroads out here are perfect wolves. They charged me six cents a mile from Ellensburg to this place. Fortunately from here all the points I want to see can be reached by boat – and that is a cheap way to travel. Am going out to call on homeopathic doctors today and find out about the best medical examination. If I just had money enough to hold out for awhile I should like to stay right here. It is a growing town and will be a larger city. There are about 40,000 inhabitants now.

If I was acquainted with Leigh Hunt I would go to Seattle and see if I couldn't get on his paper, the Post Intelligencer.[11] But I don't, you know. Well I think I will sally out and see what I can see and learn what I can learn. Will tell you the results when I get back so au revoir dear.

Tuesday morning – *Well didn't get back yesterday until quite well on in the evening. Looked around the town for awhile. Then went up to call on Drs. Munson and Wisner, the two most prominent homeopathic physicians in the city. Found them both very pleasant gentlemen, but was especially impressed by Dr. Munson. He is a rather elderly gentleman of very courteous dignified carriage and is an unusually intelligent man. Perhaps the most interesting thing about him from my present point of view is that he is one of the homeopathic members of the state examining board. It makes me rather provoked to reflect that if I had arrived in this state a little over a month ago I would not have been obliged to pass an examination. All that would have been necessary was to get my diploma registered in the county in which I intended to practice. I got along pretty well with the doctor. Am going out to take lunch with him today. I understand he has one of the finest residences in the city.*

After I left the Doctor's office I met Mr. Hedrick and was invited out to dinner with him at six o'clock. Went out (saved a meal, you know). The conversation was almost exclusively real estate. We had town lots with the first course, and ended with town lots during the last. Perhaps if I had money to invest the subject would have more interest for me, but as I have not it becomes rather monotonous. Lu was the worst one of the lot. She apparently knows what every lot in town was worth six months ago, what they are calling for now, and what they will sell for six months hence. Say Anna, when you come out here promise me that you will not become a real estate fiend. I may be one myself by that time and one in the family would be enough.

Am going to look for work today. Cannot get my examination until the first Tuesday in July and will have to go over to Olympia to take it. Expect it will be a pretty stout one because it will be the first one under the new law and there has been such a fight between the two schools that all the old school members of the board will be on their muscle and will see that the homeopathic candidates get a thorough test. I will have to study some as will have to be examined in diseases of the eye and ear and diseases of the nervous system and as they are both special branches very much attention was not given them at Iowa City. Think I will stop now and visit the town some more. I suppose that if you waited until school was out before writing again I will not get a letter until the first of next week.

Good bye dear.
Lovingly,
Will

Illustration by Brian Griffin.

Letter 12

Tacoma, Washington
Thursday, June 12, 1890

Light of My Soul,

I wonder if you are becoming as tired as I am of not knowing where I will be found any two days in succession. I know I am getting heartily sick of it. Am going to start by boat for Fairhaven this afternoon at four o'clock so thought I would drop you a line or two before I go. Have been looking this place over quite thoroughly since I wrote last. It is a fine place, but think I will look for one a little smaller. The doctors here tell me that they think there is no homeopath at Fairhaven, so I am going to investigate. Direct letters to this place until further notice, as I will have to return here to get over to Olympia for my examination. Am beginning to feel a little shaky on that subject. Don't just fancy the idea of going before a lot of allopathic physicians for exams.

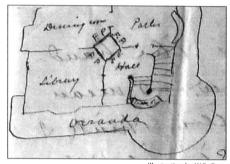
Illustration by W.R. Gray.

As I told you in my last, went to a lunch with Dr. Munson, one of the Board. His residence suited me a little better than any I ever saw, that is, the interior arrangement. The unique part of it – is that when the corners of four rooms come together there is a great chimney with a fireplace in each room, something after this fashion.

In the hallway where you see the circular arrangement, is a Turkish couch made to fit a stained glass window. It is placed on the landing that is three steps up from the hall. In the parlor is another couch, built into the window in the same way. The furnishings throughout are each on the Turkish order. There are no carpets, but a great profusion of rugs; the doorways which are all large with sliding doors are hung with heavy curtains suspended from heavy brass rods that are set-in between the casings. The fireplaces are all in tile work, each one of different design while the mantels over them, also each one of different design and material, are of carved wood reaching to the ceiling.

The hallway especially is the handsomest thing I ever saw. I mean by that it suited me better. Think I will have something like it – when I pass my "exam" and get a practice. Am hoping that things will look favorable at Fairhaven. If not I shall go over and see the towns in Gray's Harbor.

Was up to see more homeopaths yesterday. Found two of them from Iowa. One a graduate of the State University. They have only been here two years and now have beautiful residences, handsome offices and good practices. Well I will stop now and write from Fairhaven and tell you about my trip. It is about a hundred and thirty miles down the Sound, and the scenery will be great, I expect.

Good bye dear.

Lovingly, Will

Letter 13

Tacoma, Washington
Monday, June 16, 1890

My Darling Sweetheart,

Have just arrived from Fairhaven, Sehome, Whatcom, Seattle and Snohomish. I hardly know what to tell where to begin to tell it or where to leave off. I left here Thursday afternoon at five o'clock on the steamer "State of Washington" known as the "greyhound of the sound." She is a moderate sized vessel, but on the plan of a Mississippi steamboat of the stern wheel pattern. It takes all night to go up to Fairhaven, so that much of the scenery up the way is missed. But notwithstanding that I saw enough to satisfy the most exacting.

The first thing after going on board was to secure a berth. The boat was crowded so that there was a great scramble to get to the purser's office. I managed to purchase a piece of paper which gave me possession of the middle "shelf" in stateroom number nine. The staterooms are microscopic affairs and have three berths, no waste of space on the boat. I can assure you. When I got up in the morning we were a little less than twenty miles from Fairhaven. Right along there (at the place where I got up I mean) is the most beautiful scenery that I have seen anywhere. It was right at the entrance to the Strait of Juan de Fuca Islands, great rocky eminences rising way up out of the water clothed with a mantle of forest trees, like all the country out here. Twice I caught a glimpse of an arctic bird, the great auk skimming over the deep,[12] sometimes just wetting its wings as it flew. Here and there a porpoise would leap for a moment out of the water. I was told that sharks are plentiful at that point. I did not see any but they are said always to be around somewhere when a porpoise is seen.

Arrived in Fairhaven a little after seven o'clock. It is a struggling town, built among the stumps of the trees that have been cut down to make a place for the town site. Everything of course is new. They claim three thousand inhabitants, but if they have twelve hundred actual residents they will do well.

*In a little real estate office I found Mr. **I.C. Templin**, Mr. Henderson,[13] an early resident of Mt. Pleasant and **Det Bird**. In another office **Ross Sullivan**. Likewise another Mt. P worthy – I should say Kenworthy, otherwise "Dave" of lunch counter fame. Everybody up there thinks that Fairhaven is a great place. I confess that I couldn't see it in that light. The land company that owns the town site must have good faith in it though, as they are just constructing a $75,000 hotel.[14] A very handsome stone and brick structure.*

Part of the town is on a steep hill overlooking the bay. Right around a point is Sehome, a town about the same size as Fairhaven and blending with that, practically making them one town is Whatcom. Bellingham used to be a town between Fairhaven and Sehome but it has been incorporated with the former place so that there are three towns not more than two miles and a half from the commencement

Northwest Lumberman. Courtesy Gordon Tweit Collection.

11th and Harris Avenue. The Terminal Building at the Northeast corner (known as the Evans Fick Building in 1890) is today Tony's Coffee. Henderson & Templin was located next door, just east of the Terminal Building, which is the present site of outdoor seating for the Harris Avenue Café. Arrow notes the Knights of Pythias building under construction.

of one to the ending of the third. Whatcom is built on the tide flats a long stretch of Sound that are covered with water at high tide but are bare at low tide. The main business street is built on piles over the water and from the odor that arises I should think that a splendid crop of malaria and typhoid might be cultivated. The most interesting thing about Fairhaven and Whatcom is that there are no homeopaths there. There is one at Sehome who practices in that place and Whatcom but who does no business in Fairhaven. I think that someone with some energy might get business in all those towns.

I called on one of the allopathic physicians in Fairhaven accompanied by Mr. Templin who was showing me around. Mr. Templin introduced me as Dr. Gray. I didn't want to be there under any false pretenses so handed him my card showing which side of the medical fence I had climbed down on. You should have seen that man freeze up. He didn't address a direct sentence to me while there. I never saw a man so lacking in courtesy. He was a great gross man with cheeks hanging down and with a collar of flesh around his neck – in fact had I met him anywhere than in his office I should have taken him for a man whose business it is to stand behind a bar and draw beer and who was his own best customer.

Unless some better place should unexpectedly present itself I think I shall locate in Fairhaven for a time at least. If I do, Dr. Hathaway will not be a friend to say the least. Some of the small towns out here would astonish you; they look so rough and ragged. The trees have first to be cut down and burned. Then the stumps are blown pieces with giant powder and then they too are burned. The blackened remains of the forest lie scattered all around. Great stumps all over in the middle of the streets.

I only stayed in the cities of Bellingham Bay part of one day returning at night to Seattle. This place is the largest city in Washington and is a lively place. Fine business blocks many of them as fine as those of St. Paul have been built since the fire.[15] The docks are very extensive and a great deal of shipping, especially of coal, is carried on (as the geographers would say). It is too hilly for comfort however and I only had a short time there. I know that I didn't want to locate there so I didn't waste any time there. Saturday morning I made a run up to Snohomish, a short distance from Seattle to see Dr. T.F. Thompson of the class of '90 at State University of Iowa. In other words, a classmate. He is the queer genus I told you about whose wife came out here long before he did and picked out a location for him. I intended to come back the same day but he insisted that I should stay over Sunday and as it would only cost me a hotel bill in Tacoma if I returned. I stayed. He is getting along pretty well. He came right out here as soon as he graduated so that he has been practicing just about three months. His first months' business amounted to six dollars. The second about seventy and the third about one hundred, so that his business is increasing all the time. Snohomish is in a rich valley which when it is cleared will make a good agricultural county. The town has about 2,000 people in it. Thompson wants me to go up there and stay until my examination takes place and I don't know but I will go.

Returning to Tacoma I found your letter awaiting me and you can imagine how glad I was to get it. It is just a week ago since I had one and it seemed an age. And it came just in time for I was getting blue. It has cost so much more than I expected here, everything is so high that I have not been able to see my way clear and part of the time has just been in despair. I have tried to keep it out of my letters and think I succeeded in all but the last one from Ellensburg. I guess some of my discouragement erupted into that one. But that was a disappointment. You say in your letter that you think I am catching the western enthusiasm. I have been enthusiastic over the scenery only. That is grand. But about the country itself I have not known what to say. Everything is boomed too much. There is too much false enthusiasm. The pulse of the country is too rapid and the temperature is at fever heat. Prices are asked for property that are away beyond what the property is worth. Snohomish is a town that has no possible chance of being anything more than a nice little agricultural town. The town site is platted with lots for two miles out into the woods, and there isn't a lot that can be had short of five hundred dollars. In Tacoma there are lots platted twelve miles from the business center and there have actually been found people foolish enough to buy them. At Fairhaven I don't think there is a lot that can be had much short of a thousand dollars. There is not a town along the Sound where they will not gravely and earnestly assure you that that particular town is going to be the terminus of the Great Northern Railroad and is bound to be the greatest city in the country and they ask prices for lots accordingly. Residence property can be bought cheaper in Chicago or San Francisco today than they can in many of the towns along the Sound. Ask any of them what the resources are and the almost invariable answer is "unlimited mining and agricultural and lumbering." Well the lumbering is practically unlimited. But it will take years to develop the mines and the land must be cleared of trees before there can be any farms. What farmers there are raise nothing but hay. They can get two crops of hay a year or about six or seven tons to the acre and get from twenty to forty dollars a ton for it. In Iowa hay cost about four or five dollars a ton.

Everything that is eaten has to be shipped in. In summer eggs cost twenty four cents a dozen and in winter fifty to seventy five. Vegetables of all kinds are sold by the pound. Potatoes cost three cents a pound. Cabbages thirty cents a pound and everything else in the same proportions. But it is a great country. Where the resources are developed when the land is cleared they will raise immense crops. But it will take time and money. In the meantime the cities are developing faster than the development of the country will warrant. It cost five hundred dollars an acre to clear the timber off land for farming purposes. It is frequently costing twenty dollars to blast out one stump.

Well I guess this is enough about the country for a time. Now something about yourself (and myself). I am glad you are through with the school for you need the rest. I have said that before, I think but I feel it so much that I must express it again. But Anna, however much work you may have to do never sit up all night again to get through with it and especially under the stimulus of a nervine. It is destructive to the nervous system and you can't afford to lose sleep that way. I don't care anything about the wrinkles and crows feet. They will come with care and time but I do care for your health and it ought to be as important to you as to me. Now that's a nice bit of professional advice for which I shall make no charge, only you must pay attention to it.

I was delighted to hear you say that you wanted someone to take care of you instead of your taking care of me. That's the first time you have admitted that. Whoever it was that said they thought Mr. Gray needed you was a person of discernment. You can't imagine how much encouragement there was in your letter and how much good it did me. I have felt that things will go all right since reading it. It's hard being out here away from you, but do you know I believe it would be harder if I was out here in this strange land and could not reflect that there was some one who watched with loving heart all the good and real fortune that might come to me. It is a very consoling and sustaining thought to remember that Anna will rejoice with me in my success and grieve in failure and disappointment. I won't call myself any more hard names since you don't want me to and am about convinced that there is no need of calling myself what I did in my letter from Ellensburg because I have your love and that is sufficient for everything.

Was sorry to hear that Aunt May is having her old enemy rheumatism around. Hope she is well by this time. Enclosed you will find two flowers. One of them I don't know what it is. The white one is a blackberry blossom. Blackberries are thick all through the woods and will soon be ripe. I haven't got any of my books out yet and so have had no means of pressing flowers or I should send some more in better shape. I will have my books out soon though and I will have to study some and do some reviewing for the examination. I don't know where I may be when this reaches you, but write to Tacoma and I can have it forwarded. I will let you know positively in my next letter whether I will go to Fairhaven or not. I remain,

Yours devotedly,
Will

Letter 14

Tacoma, Washington
Saturday, June 21, 1890

My Darling Anna,

For the first time in my life I think, I have destroyed a letter that I had started Thursday. I am feeling just utterly discouraged and that's just the whole truth of the matter. Everything seems all wrong. The examining board is going to meet at Walla Walla instead of Olympia and that is way down in the southeast corner of the state, across the mountains. As railroad fares are high it will cost me including the examinations fee, fifty dollars to go before the board and that is more than I have at present. I had expected after the examination to work awhile and then commence practice. But it looks now as if I would have to wait until the first of next January before taking the examination and getting my license. The whole thing just makes me feel as if I wasn't intended for any use in this world and that the sooner I was out of it the better it would be. The last three days I have just felt desperate. I try to console myself with the thought that it will all come out right but it is present necessities that are making it hard and no amount of hope for the future will make them any easier. There, if that isn't laying my feeling and affairs before you, I don't know what is. And I feel all the time that I am doing it that I ought not to for it will only cause you to worry and I don't want to do that. But I must tell it to someone and you are the only one I could tell it to and I know you will forgive me for it. I know that you will sympathize with me, even if you do not say much.

Another thing that has made things go hard this week is that I have not heard a word from anyone since I had your letter Monday. For the last two days I have been expecting a letter from you and have commenced to wonder if it could be possible that you sent one to Fairhaven. I tell you a letter is a great thing to me these days. I think I could accept the situation here a little more philosophically were it not that there are three or four good openings in towns that started as fair prospect of becoming fair sized cities and the first man in them would have a great advantage over others that might come in. A delay of six months and these places will likely be filled to say nothing about what a delay of six months in getting fairly started may mean to us. I guess I would better stop now or there is no telling what I may say. I will write again soon and may feel better. I feel just too discouraged now to write anything.

One thing though I want to say and that is that the more dismal everything else looks the more precious your love is to me. I know that whatever else may fail me that never will. And as for mine that grows stronger all the same. So good bye now, my darling. Never so well beloved as now.

Yours devotedly,
Will

Letter 15

Tacoma, Washington
Sunday, June 22, 1890

My Darling Sweetheart,

Yesterday I sent a letter that I wish very much now that I had not sent. Not that the situation has changed any for the better. But I am feeling a little more hopeful. The fiends of despondency are not chasing me quite as fiercely as they were yesterday. Do you know why? I had a letter from you today. Just a dear good letter from the "sweetest girl in town." And that is enough to make a man feel better, no matter how deep down he may be. Is it for me to say that I enjoy all your letters? No, you know that without my saying it. But I don't believe I ever enjoyed any letter more than I did this one. I think it must be, because it came because I needed it so badly. (Now that sentence may sound just a little mixed, but you will know what I mean. I think you generally know what I mean.)

Harper's Weekly 1891.

Mt. Rainier from a Tacoma balcony.

If I had gone to the post office today and had no letter awaiting for me, I think I should have gone down on the dock and looked at the water and wondered if it was very wet and very cold and whether it was muddy at the bottom and how it would feel down there and a great many other cheerful speculations not to mention in this brief epistle.

Fairhaven Herald. December 29, 1890. CPNWS.

View of Mt. Tacoma, today known as Mt. Rainier.

This is a beautiful Sunday – the first really clear day that I have seen. Mt. Ta-coma shows up beautifully. By the way if you should look for Mt. Tacoma on a map you will not find it, but you will find Mt. Rainier. Tacoma is the old Indian name while Rainier is the name of the explorer who first discovered, so in the books the latter name is always given it. Tacoma people always call it Mt. Tacoma while Se-attle people never give it a name that is borne by the only rival on the Sound, but always speak of it as Mt. Rainier. You speak of it being hot in Mt. Pleasant. I have not seen a hot day since I have been here. It has been delightfully cool. It rained for about a week right ahead however. But it was pleasant rain. There was not a parti-cle of wind with it and it came down so quietly and gently that it was very pleasant. No one pays any attention to rain here.

Well I believe I will stroll out and see if I can't find some flowers for "the collec-tion." I don't know whether I mentioned it or not, but the last ones I sent are gath-ered in the woods near Snohomish. While speaking of flowers, don't fail to drop around to our house quite frequently and get sweet peas. There must be an abun-dance of them by this time. Sweet peas will always have a pleasant remembrance from me, for they played quite a prominent part in the doing of "our summer" – our eventful summer. And sweet peas from "Mrs. Gray's potato patch" can still be had only you will have to get them yourself since I can't be there to carry them to you. How carefully I used to gather them and how carefully I used to fix them up and then how (apparently) carelessly I used to hand them over when I reach the "stone house on the corner." Reminiscing yes, but I expect to do a great deal of that with-in the next "year and a half." Am going to get a great deal of comfort out of it too. Looking back at happy and pleasant days and looking forward to more pleasant and happy years in the future will be my chief recreation out here. Well I will be off now and continue when I get back. This will be a rambling letter but perhaps there will be something in it after all if you can sift it out. Can you guess what? It is in all my letters as well as all my thoughts. Now there's something for your imagination. Tell me what it is when you find it. Au revoir beloved.

6:55 p.m. *– Here I am back again after quite a stroll and it was one in which I saw much that was beautiful. With the exception of just a glimpse the first day I came, this is the first time that the mountains have been visible on account of the clouds that hung about them. The Olympic range in the west and Mt. Tacoma in the east are grand. Tacoma is one great mass of snow apparently and all the oth-er mountains of the range seem little more than hills compared with it. Then out on the water it was lonely. It has been very still, so that except for a cats paw that played over it – here and there the water is like a sheet of glass. Here and there a little sailboat glides along while off beyond just rounding the point where the bay comes a large steamer. Down at the docks lie a number of vessels. One of them loading lumber for Hong Kong, another a South American brig, loading coal for Valparaiso. The others for San Francisco.*

No use talking, I do like to live near the water. If I live on the Sound sometime I will have a yacht. This is one of the greatest bodies of water for yachting in the

*world. One can travel for three hundred miles in land locked waters that are abso-
lutely safe as far as storms are concerned. Just listen to the dreamer will you, talking about having a yacht when at present he is wondering how in the world he is
going to get a little matter of fifty four or fifty five dollars wherewith to pay an examination fee. Never mind. I'll have it yet, the yacht I mean. Yes and the examination fee. I came out here practically "broke" but I'll be worth something when the
State of Iowa sees me again and inasmuch as you and mother are there that must
be very soon.*

*Yes and there's another thing about this delay business. I had hoped by Sep-
tember to be doing something so that I could get **mother** to come out and not take
a Club another year. But I guess I'll have to abandon that project. I expect it will
take about a year anyway to persuade her to come. She has a prejudice against the
West. I am saying nothing about my discouragement to her by the way. She has
enough worry without that.*

*I enjoyed **Jessie's** and **Jeff's** addition to your letter very much. It was funny. I
was deeply grieved though Anna to hear of your conduct. I think it is a good thing
for Jessie that college is ended and Mr. Jeffrey is gone. Perhaps however Jessie would
not agree with me in that conclusion. Just think of giving Mr. Jeffrey pansies and
carnations and writing him notes and not going to tell me anything about the note.
I didn't think that of you Anna. But I am a very forgiving individual and so I forgive you. Well it strikes me that this letter has been pretty much devoid of flowers.
So while I am speaking about flowers I will call your attention to the enclosed specimens for the collection. If you will get one half as much delight out of the pressed
flowers as I shall, you will get a great deal. And when I go back to Iowa (after you)
I shall expect to see a great and interesting collection. You are right in saying that
the twenty-first of August (you said 1890 in your letter, but you meant 1888 didn't
you?) and the seventeenth of May 1890 are important dates, especially the first.*

*By the way Anna what kind of flowers did you wear that night? I was too much
excited all the time, too much embarrassed before, and too bewildered with happiness afterwards to know what kind of flowers you had on. I know you had on that
light striped summer dress with the great number of tails to the overskirt but the
flowers have escaped me, in fact I never knew. I know that once that summer when
I went to see you, you wore nasturtiums. Was that the time? You may be sure that
I will never forget it when once I know and that is a question that I have wanted
cleared up. About all I had any knowledge of that night was that all the long suspense was ended and that the one woman in all the world for me had promised to
come and make home a paradise for me. Anna, I pledge you my solemn word that
I will not go to lodge five nights in one week nor three nights. It might possibly happen once in a great while that I would go two nights but I hardly believe that. If I
have any practice at all I will have so little time to myself that I shall want to spend
it at home. I shall not want to go out much at night where my wife can't go. See my
dear we will have no fuss on that score. So you find me a satisfactory correspondent
do you, because I tell you just the things you want to know? Do you know that I*

am delighted to hear that? I am trying to improve about telling things and it's very gratifying to know that I am succeeding. You used to say that I was no good about telling things. You were right too (as you generally are). As you may see from this paper I invested in a new tablet and the paper is so thick that I have to write finer and get in fewer sheets. Especially when I have such a branch of flowers to send as I have this time.

So you are "fessing up" when people say anything to you now, are you? Do you know dear I like that better. And see if you don't find it much easier. For all of people's curiosity in such matters, I think most of it is a kindly interest after all.

Galen Biery Collection, Whatcom Museum.

The locket photo of Will.

There have been times when some pretty good friend of mine has said something about it that I should have felt was so much better if I could just frankly express my views. And you will find that many people will be quite comforting too, when they know how matters stand and can talk about it without feeling that they are on uncertain ground.

I'm boycotting the barber again Anna. You know the barber is my enemy. Anyway and I'm giving up grooming for sometime. Out here he charges twenty five cents for a shave. I will be a party to no such systematic robbery as that is so the beard will come again and I will once more look as I do in the locket picture. How will that satisfy you? Don't believe I will change again.

Oh I don't believe I told you (or did I?) of the victory homeopathy has gained in this state. The original object of the allopathic physicians in having the present medical law passed was to shut out the homeopaths as much as they could. Well the homeopathy, by the aid of the elections have obtained control of the examining board and elected Dr. Munson president. So that every doctor that practices in this state, allopathic or otherwise will have to have his license signed by a homeopath. But one thing is sure, Dr. Munson is a man that will grace any position. An intelligent cultured gentleman. Any school might be proud of him. In fact I have been very much delighted with the physicians of my school that I have met in this state and particularly with those of Tacoma. They are all thorough gentlemen and what is more of high principle.

And now I must close once more or there will not be room in the envelope for this. I have got to the end of my letter and haven't said much after all. But I have missed you so much, dear, all day. I can't tell you how much. If I could only see your *sweet face once I think everything would be all right. I close my eyes and can see you sitting in the familiar parlor, and then remember the one sweet caress you gave me as I sat in the dusk of the evening. I think of all the evenings we spent together and how we talked on indifferent subjects while the love was in our hearts and I think sometimes in our eyes, and I wish oh so longingly for another of those same sweet evenings. But I suppose there is no use calling up vain desires. It only makes it hard. But sometimes they will come up unbidden. When the love in the heart must have full sway to tell its longing and so tonight I long to see the one whom I love always, with such a deep affection all else in the world is nothing. And now good night my darling. I suppose I must go!*

Lovingly, Will

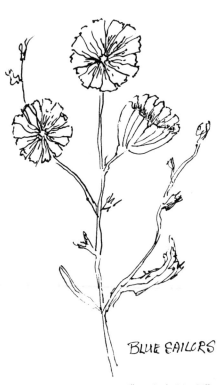

Illustration by Brian Griffin.
Flower picked along the streets of Tacoma.

Letter 16

Snohomish, Wash
Monday, June 23, 1890

My Darling Anna,

Have just a few minutes to write a few lines to you. Am up here at Thompson's to stay until the examination is on hand and do some studying of a few things that I feel a little shaky on. Yes, I am going over to the examination. Was up to see Dr. Munson a couple of days ago and tell him that I could not appear for examination at this meeting and would wait for the next. "Well" he says. "That won't do; we want to get all the homeopathic physicians practicing in this state that we can and as soon as we can. You go on to the meeting of the board and I will advance what is necessary for expenses." I hardly knew what to do. I took a day to think it over and finally concluded that the best thing to do was to get through with the examination. Six months is a long time to wait and inasmuch as I can do but little studying when I am working in an office, I would be better prepared for the ordeal now than I would be at the end of that time.

Another thought has been definitely determined that the Great Northern Railroad has purchased the Fairhaven & Southern[16] which means that it will go with Fairhaven. Where ever I have been I have kept my ears open and have heard a good deal of conversation about the cities along the Sound and the general opinion seems to center in a larger city – on Bellingham Bay. It may be Fairhaven or Sehome or Whatcom, but they are so close together that it will practically be one town anyway. And now is the time to get in there and be ahead. I will start for Walla Walla next Monday morning at seven o'clock and will be riding all day. It will take two days, perhaps more, for the exam and a day back so that it will be Friday of next week before I get back and know whether I pass or not. I will then go to Fairhaven at once I think and commence business. I will stop now and put in the next few days in solid "stuffing."

Will drop you a line or two Sunday before I start. One thing decidedly unpleasant about this exam business is that I will have to wait until Friday of next week before getting any mail. I will arrive in Tacoma Sunday after the post office closes and leave Monday morning before it is opened. Suppose I will have to stand it however. Well "here's hoping." With much love I am,

Yours devotedly,
Will

Continue to write to Tacoma.

Letter 17

Tacoma, Washington
Thursday, July 3, 1890

My Darling Anna,

Am just back from Walla Walla. Would have written a little sooner but circumstances have been such that I did not get time Sunday night – came down from Snohomish and had to leave at seven Monday morning for Walla Walla. But before I go any further I will tell the important fact. I passed the examination all right. Tell you what Anna, if my examinations are any indication as to my future success I ought to stand at the top of my profession, again. I stood highest on a general average. There were eleven applicants representing as many different colleges including Hahnemann of Chicago, Bellevue of New York and Long Island Hospital College of Brooklyn. My general average was 84, not as high as at college but the examination was about twice as hard. In fact to use a slang phrase it was a "stunner."

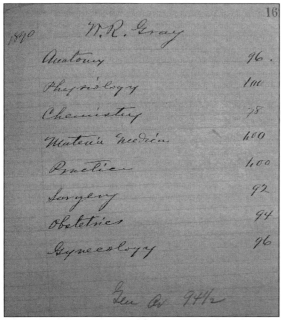

Records of the College of Homeopathic Medicine, University of Iowa Archives, Iowa City, Iowa.

Will's grades.

There were fourteen branches to pass in, (I had 8 at Iowa City) and an aggregate of one hundred and sixty questions. The Minnesota examination has been considered about the hardest in the country but at the last examination there were only eighty four questions. There the conditions under which the examination was passed were the most favorable that could be imagined.

Sunday night I did not reach Tacoma until twelve o'clock. Had to get up six o'clock next morning and travel all day. Had to lay over at a junction from five in the afternoon until twelve at night and did not reach Walla Walla until four o'clock Tuesday morning. Examination commenced at nine. Of course could not get any sleep. In addition the thermometer for the two days of the examination stood at 102° in the shade. (This is east of the mountains.) There were two nights without much sleep. Wrote until eleven o'clock Tuesday night. Had an inside room at hotel without any windows (102° in shade). So hot did not sleep any that night (three nights) commenced at 8:30 Wednesday morning and wrote until 3:00 in afternoon. Left Walla Walla at seven thirty at night and was traveling all night – until eleven o'clock (about twenty minutes ago) making four nights without sleep. This with the prostrating heat – and the ordeal of such an examination has pretty nearly exhausted me so that I am just taking time to let you know that I got through all right and then I am going to sleep.

Before I stop though I want to say that I stopped at the post office on my way up and got a bundle of mail (four from you, one from Ed Scott, one from Will Taylor and one from Dr. Baker my old roommate.) The needle case is all right – just the thing! And as pretty as it can be. That "G" is about right. I thank you ever so much. (Wish I could do it in person.) I am going to write to mother tomorrow. If you should see her within a day after you get this tell her that I got through all right. Will give you more detailed description of trip tomorrow.

Send my next letter to Fairhaven. That is where I am going. The census gives the three towns of Fairhaven, Sehome and Whatcom a combined population of 9,300. There only being one homeopath in the three places, that gives me a good field, if I can only work it right. I shall start tomorrow or next day and get my "shingle" painted. I am going to struggle through someway and believe that in six months time I can see my way out of the woods. Will stop now and write tomorrow. "Goodnight" dear. With much love I am so ever,

Yours devotedly,
Will

Letter 18

Tacoma, Washington
Friday, July 4, 1890

My Darling Anna,

This is the great and glorious fourth but I am not celebrating – it costs money to celebrate. Stop! I'll take that all back. Of course I'm celebrating – I am writing to you. That's about as much pleasure as I can get out of the Fourth of July anywhere.

For didn't we have a time on the Fourth two years ago? Didn't we wander around the park all forenoon, go to a baseball game in the afternoon and go out to **Anna Crane**'s *in the evening? I rather guess we did. And had a great deal of pleasure out of it too.*

Mt. Pleasant Beautiful 1909.

Cousin Anna Crane lived a few blocks down on East Washington Street from Anna Kurtz. Today the building is the home of the President of Iowa Wesleyan College.

Well now, I promised to tell you about my trip to Walla Walla. Don't believe I have much to tell after all, except what I have told you already. The trip over the Cascades of course was lovely and it was all in daylight. But after crossing the mountains it became insufferably hot and dusty. At Pasco Junction[17] had to wait from five in the afternoon until twelve at night. While there became acquainted with three or four of the other applicants for license. All of them very nice fellows, in fact the cream of the doctors that came up for examinations. We had quite a pleasant time talking on medical subjects of course.

The board of examiners was a great mixture. Six out of nine of them were from west of the mountains and all but two of the candidates, so that it was a regular outrage to have to go to Walla Walla. There were two homeopathic candidates (including myself) and I am sorry to say that one of them got "plucked" (the only one). Dr. Munson, the president of the board (a homeopath) was the most popular man there. Everybody liked him, and he commanded all the respect of everyone. I think I was more pleased at passing highest on his account than on my own, because of his kindness to me in regard to the expenses of the examination. I had more satisfaction out of this anyway at coming up as I did on account of the fact that except in materia medica I stood exactly the same examination as the allopathic applicants and also from the fact that all but two of them were men who had practiced over five years and therefore were of experience. Besides that they represented some of the best schools in the country while one of them had taken a seven year course in one of the best universities of Europe – that of Christiana Norway and there practiced for a year in one of the New York hospitals. Dr. Munson was greatly tickled over my success because it was a kind of offset to the failure of the other man. The other man, by the way, was a graduate of Hahnemann College Chicago. I begin to feel that the Homeopathic department of the University of Iowa is a pretty good one even if it is small.

Walla Walla is the oldest town in the state and looks more like an Iowa town than any that I have seen. It is surrounded by good farming country. The town is perfectly level and the streets are shaded with trees. The yards are large and well kept and taking it all and all it is a very pretty place. Did not have much time to look around as I was kept busy all the time I was there. So did not have a chance to get any wild flowers. But on the way back I gathered the enclosed little yellow flowers at Enumclaw, a little place in the Cascades. The little pansies came all right and will be kept along with the one you gave me the night I went away.

Well, I suppose that before long I will be able to tell you about "that first case." It has been definitely settled that the Great Northern Railway from St. Paul will go into Fairhaven, they having bought the Fairhaven and Southern. I suppose though that Clint Howard has told you all about it. In fact I suppose that if I undertake to tell anything about Fairhaven when I get there that it will be to a chestnut. No, we won't have any boarders when you come out to Washington. There have been boarders enough at our house for the last six to eight years to last a lifetime.[18] Tell Clint however that we will be delighted to have him build a house next to ours and have him and his wife for neighbors.

Elizabeth Gray (back row in doorway) with the boys of Gray Club.

So you think there was a great contrast between two of my letters to you? Well, I expect that there was. I am sorry that I wrote that first one of the two, but I couldn't help it. I couldn't see things any other way. But I guess things will come out all right now. Of course there will probably be a wait at the start before patients commence to come in, because that is inevitable. But I can stand that. It cannot hold out forever. But when that examination went over to Walla Walla and I didn't have enough money to get over there with a prospect of having to wait six months before getting started and falling behind in my studies all the time – well it looked a brilliant ultramarine blue and no mistake. But we'll have a tiled hearth and a fireplace with a hammered brass front yet Anna.

Don't forget that is now Dr. W.R. Gray of Fairhaven, Washington. The State Examining Board says so. And I feel certain that I can get a good advantage up there before long. I seem to be able to fool people about my knowledge out here as well as in Mt. Pleasant. Dr. Munson is going to give me letters to a number of homeopathic families in Fairhaven. Another doctor is going to give me a letter to a contractor there who employs a large force of men and who at one time had promised them all his work if he would go up there and the doctor thinks that I can get it. Well, I will stop now and write a letter or two for some of my goods that it will be necessary for me to have. Monday I will write to you from Fairhaven. We're over our muddle now and are going to win. With much love, I remain,

Yours,
Will

Will Has Selected Fairhaven!

WILL GRAY'S TWO MONTH ODYSSEY had finally ended. He had completed a three-week train trip to the waters of Puget Sound. Along the way he marveled at the beauties of the western mountains and the isolation of the barren plains. He investigated the possibilities of joining established medical practices in Ellensburg and Snohomish or of starting his own practice in Tacoma or Seattle, and he finally decided to cast his lot with the exciting prospects of Fairhaven on the shores of Bellingham Bay.

He had overcome the challenges presented by Washington State's new physician's licensing requirements, passing the rigorous exam with the highest score of those taking it. He rented offices on the third floor of the brand new Mason Block, just across the street from the Fairhaven Hotel, which was nearing completion.

He arrived in this booming town at the height of its optimism and growth. The streets were entirely mud, yet to receive their two-by-twelve fir planking. Most of the streets still had tree stumps standing in them awaiting the dynamite and horse teams that would clear them for travel other than by foot. New buildings were being hastily erected of rough sawn lumber to join the stores, rooming houses, taverns and brothels that already lined the main Fairhaven business streets of Harris, McKenzie and Mill avenues.

Away from the business center, small rude houses were cropping up along the platted but unfinished streets, and a few palatial homes were appearing on the hill rising above the town.

Dan Harris had sold Fairhaven to Bennett and Larrabee just two years earlier. Now, in 1890, their Fairhaven Land Company had succeeded in attracting thousands of believers to their fledgling town. The "Boom" was on and Will Gray was convinced that Fairhaven would prosper. The proof was in the very recent sale of Larrabee's railroad, the Fairhaven & Southern, to James J. Hill's Great Northern Railroad. The sale surely meant that Hill would build his transcontinental connection over the Skagit River pass to Sedro-Woolley, where it would meet up with Larrabee's former track, leading the commerce of the nation directly to meet the sea at Fairhaven. Fairhaven was destined to be the Northern route to the riches of the Orient and the greatest city north of San Francisco.

Will was alternately hopeful and despondent. He was almost completely without funds. In fact he was in debt, a fact that worried him greatly. His loneliness, the delays in getting his office set up and his medical supplies delivered seemed to force him to the edge of depression, but a letter from Anna always brought an upswing in his spirits and a return to optimism. His financial condition dictated that he must sleep in his offices. Of sheer necessity he arranged a cot for the office, taking his meals in a nearby restaurant. Will was urgently awaiting his first patient and the beginning of an income stream.

Letter 19

Fairhaven, Washington
Sunday, July 13, 1890

My Darling Sweetheart,

    *Sundays here are not such pleasant affairs, though today is as beautiful as any-
one could desire. It is perfectly clear, and that occurs so seldom that a perfectly
clear day is an unusually rare treat. But with nowhere to go and only a small room
in a lodging house to stay in, life gets very monotonous. I have written several letters and a little while ago took a walk down to the wharf. The thing that I get the
most pleasure out of, watching the boats and vessels. Was on board a large ship
that is unloading railroad iron here. She is one of the largest I have seen, and I went
over her and saw how beautifully everything is kept and then looked aloft at the
rigging and at the masts and spars. It was very easy to understand a sailor's enthusiasm for a fine ship. Out in the bay numerous small boats with Sunday pleasure
seekers were skimming over the water, dancing on the waves. Their white sails glis-
tening in the sunlight.*

    *On the wharf numbers of men and boys were fishing. I watched them for a few
minutes, noting the different kinds of fish that are being pulled up from the depths.
Many of them, in fact, most of them, were new to me so that I had to inquire what
they were. Others I didn't learn at all, because I didn't want to expose the density
of my ignorance all at once, and so kept still about some of them, preferring to remain in ignorance. Besides, you know, it wouldn't do to show too much curiosity
about fish caught on Sunday. Well, there were salt water perch, much like a fresh
water perch, bullheads, much like a catfish.*

    *Now comes up a crab. I won't undertake to
describe a crab this time. His anatomy requires
accurate study and very close observations before
attempting to portray all its points of interest.
Suffice it to say that it seemed to be a kind of triangular helmet – breastplate I mean – with claws
and legs sticking out in all directions and with a
great deal of fight in him. This is somewhat his
style. That is, that's about the way he looked to*

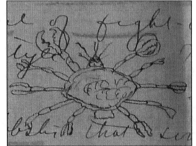

Crab illustration by W.R. Gray.

me. In fact he is a lobster that someway has grown out wide instead of long.

    *The next curious thing was a flounder. You know the expression, "as flat as a
flounder." That doesn't express it. It is the essence of flatness. What you might call
the essential principle of flatness. A flounder is a fish—that statement perhaps is
superfluous without going on to say what kind of fish. But to continue, a flounder
is a fish that looks as if the side of a house had fallen on him in infancy and he had
lain under there and could only grow in one direction. You could cut a very nice
looking flounder out of the cover of a shoe box. It is just about as thick. The funny
part of him is that he is not flattened in the same direction that any other fish is.
An ordinary fish you may remember is flattened at the sides. But the flounder to be*

contrary is flattened from above and below. His eyes are on one side. His back is mud colored.

Flounder illustration by W.R. Gray.

I will give you a top view and the side view of the flounder. As to speak of him architecturally I will give you the ground plan and the side elevation. This is the ground plan. This is the side elevation. By the way, what do you think of my illustrated letters? Don't you think I had better have my sketches published?

The next fish is a sea bass – a black bass. Well, he doesn't look much different from the ordinary black bass except in the markings. The color is a velvety black with bright blue stripes about a sixteenth of an inch wide running his entire length. Without any exception the prettiest fish I ever saw. Well I guess that will be enough on the subject of fish.

This time yesterday was out sailing on the bay. There was a party of about ten. Det Bird was in the crowd. It was a good sized sailing vessel almost a yacht. A good stiff breeze was blowing and there was quite a high sea which made it quite exciting. I never enjoyed anything more in my life in that line. In fact, it was the first good sail I ever had coming in with the wind. We made eight miles in thirty minutes – sixteen miles in an hour. So you may know that we were "scudding before the gale" at a pretty lively gait.

There is nothing new in the line of my prospects. I have not yet received my goods so have done nothing. Ordered some cards yesterday. They will be out tomorrow. Will send you one when I get them.

I thought I gave you the dimensions of my rooms too small in my last. They are 10 x 12 and 12 x 17.3. Those make very respectable rooms and can be fixed up very comfortably. I am now waiting for that first case. Hope I will get it this week as I am getting tired of waiting. They must begin to come in because I tell you what it is Anna, about one year of restaurant fare is all I can stand out here. My digestion will be ruined and you know a man can't accomplish anything with a ruined digestion.

Now I call that putting the material side of things with a vengeance. I find myself wishing all the time that I could see you. It seems a long time. I have traveled around so much and seen so many different places that it seems longer than it has before in the same length of time. I must close now or I will not get this off on tonight's boat. I am expecting a letter on tomorrow's mail. The mail boat does not come on Sundays, so I can not get any Sunday mail until the railroad is completed to Seattle.

Take good care of yourself dear and good bye, for a day or two.

Yours lovingly, Will

Letter 20

Monday, July 14, 1890
Fairhaven, Washington

My Darling Anna,

    I wrote to you yesterday to Mt. Pleasant I will be very glad when they get railroad mail facilities from here and do not have to depend on the boat which makes a letter about a week on the way between here and Mt. Pleasant. Am very glad you are taking the trip to St. Paul. I should say perhaps that I am very glad you took the trip to Mt. Pleasant for I suppose by this time you have left there. You have doubtless found both St. Paul and Minneapolis lovely cities.

    I wish I had known you were going to that I could have let Will Taylor know you were there and have him and Golda invite you to their house. Maybe you saw them however. I hope you did, for they would have been very glad to have done anything to make it pleasant for you that they could. Of course I know that Harry would. I envy him his good fortune in having the privilege of looking to your comfort and I wonder when I am to enjoy that same privilege on a more extensive scale. It seems a long time coming.

    I suppose that you have had my letters forwarded to you by this time so that you know the results of the examinations. It seems such a long time to me since it was passed that I can hardly realize that at the time you wrote you had not heard the result and my intentions as to the choice of locations. Do you know dear that it is a great comfort to know that you prefer my letters and there is so little of comfort out there that every one you get is a great boon. If you could only know how precious yours are and how I look for them and cherish them when I get them. And then if you could just realize how much comfort your faith in my success brings me and especially your belief in the good quality of the "stuff" that I am made of because I declare I lose faith in that sometimes.

    I have been feeling kind of blue for a few days past. My goods didn't come and I don't seem to get acquainted as fast as I ought to do anything here. You know that I am rather slow to get acquainted with strangers and I find it hard work. Then my office not being ready makes it difficult. I have no place to tell people to come to when I do get acquainted. So that it is difficult at times to take a very cheerful view of things.

    And then when your letters come each one containing something of encouragement – and a great deal of love – well you just can't imagine what a world of good they do me and I wish that they came oftener. You don't know how letters are valued here. All kinds of comforts are so scarce (except for those who have homes here) – that a letter from a loved one is the greatest treat that one gets. And pictures too! You can't imagine how pictures are valued. A few days ago I was in Henderson & Templin's where Det Bird stays and he was showing me his little bunch of pictures. Then he asked me if I had any. I told him I had a few and that sometime when he was over in my room I would show them to him. He walked the floor a little while and then said "Well let's go on to your room and look at your pictures will you?" So

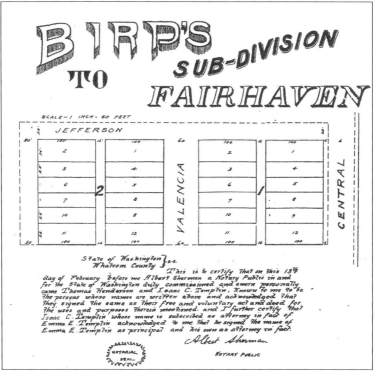

Det Bird was involved in numerous real estate transactions with Henderson & Templin. This plat was dedicated on February 13, 1890, by Thomas Henderson, I.C. Templin and his wife Emma Templin. Today, the Bird Sub-division is located close to Sehome High School, between 29th and 31st streets.

we came over and I showed him my little bunch of photographs. I have pretty near-ly reached the end of my paper, but I don't feel like stopping writing. I will get some tomorrow and complete the letter as it cannot go out until then anyway. But I feel like writing more now.

Ah, here is a piece of wrapping paper – it will have to do. I remember hunting up a piece of wrapping paper once before in the middle of the night – on which to write a note when I was leaving Mt. Pleasant for Iowa City. Do you remember it? And now that I have found it I haven't the least idea what I am going to talk about. I think I am a little in the same position that I was sometimes when I went to see you. It was happiness enough just to be there and see you if much talking wasn't done. And so tonight – I feel that I want to write just because it is communication with you. If I could just see you tonight, my darling, it would make the struggle of life seem bright. But without you it is very hard. I sit here in my room, away off from all who care anything for me and from where I have any love and think of the times when it was not so, of the time when loving eyes looked into mine and where the mere presence of one loved from was perfect bliss. We will repeat those days sometime Anna, and let us hope that it will not be so very long. You say true dear.

It is poor life indeed living away from each other. Our happiness is bound up in a happy life together. Someway there is no music in life when one voice is not heard. There is nothing really beautiful when one sweet face is absent. Love is all there is of life worth living after all. But why go on and say more when it is all summed up in the one wish. I want to see your dear face Anna. The dearest in the world to me. I want to see you, oh so badly. What more can I say than just simply that I love you and the one thought – tonight – is that I feel that you are dearer than ever to me and what a priceless treasure I possess in your love and your confidence.

I am glad to hear that you think you are getting better acquainted with mother. You won't have to try very hard to make her like you. She can't help it when she knows you. I am trusting dear that she may be a good mother to you some time and that time not so very far distant. That she may help make up for you the loss of your own. I will stop now and say goodnight, and finish this tomorrow. Good night my best beloved and may all peace and happiness attend you in the dearest wish of our devoted love. Will

Tuesday *– Here we are with a new tablet and a few minutes in which to use it before mail time. Have been out all afternoon with Det Bird along the beach. We walked along the beach at low tide for a few miles, about three, but on the way back the tide had come in and we had to take to the bluffs and climb about a hundred feet of cliff. Had fishing tackle along and did a little fishing but we should have been in a boat for that and caught nothing but crabs. I had the curiosity to catch a few star fish. But of course they were of no use and so were thrown back. They can be picked off the rocks almost anywhere just under water. They look decidedly different from the miserable dried specimens seen in the museum. They are of many different colors, but most common are purple and orange. Had my first bath in salt water this afternoon and it was immense. I came out feeling as if I could jump about ten feet in the air. The water seemed very cold at first but I soon became accustomed to it. Think I will have to take a dip in the sea every day as long as warm weather lasts.*

Yesterday afternoon went in to Whatcom and walked all over the town. Struck a real estate boomer from Ogden, Utah, on the way over and was with him all afternoon. He beat anyone I ever saw as a talker. He told me all about himself and a great deal more. And finally told me all about his love affairs. I got very tired of his talk but he was an endless source of amusement and was quite a character. He knows Bert Warren.

Well, I have to stop now and get this in the post office. The yellow flowers that are pressed flat I picked in the woods back of Fairhaven. The bunch with the sharp pointed petals are from a ledge in the rocks overlooking the bay.

Good Bye Dear,

Lovingly, Will

Letter 21

Fairhaven, Washington
Friday, July 18, 1890

My Darling Anna,

Have just finished reading your letter from Minneapolis, and was very glad to receive it, I tell you.

My hard medicine case came day before yesterday and I have been busy getting the labels on the orals and putting it in shape for use – though I have had no use of it yet. Today am going to visit a case with Dr. Lawrance of Sehome in Whatcom. It is for the purpose of information however. There will be nothing in it. It is the case of a poor girl who is sick with some form of fever that Dr. Lawrance can't make out at all. It seems to be a mixture of several of typhoid, malarial, menningeal and hectic. He described it yesterday. We discussed it together and could make nothing out of it. So I am to see the case today with him. It will certainly be instructive. I heard this morning that there had been a homeopathic physician practicing here for about a week past and that he had plenty to do. I can't find out anything about him, however and am inclined to think that it is a mistake.

Do you know I am more glad of my success at Walla Walla on your account than my own? One of the most tormenting thoughts that I had before going over was if I fail how am I going to tell Anna. I know that you have such confidence in me that I tremble for fear that I may not justify it. It's a hard thing Anna to have a reputation to support. But it is also a great comfort and support to know that someone has faith in my ability to accomplish something. And it makes me all the more anxious to be doing something. In fact in a very prosaic modern way. I would win the laurel crown for my beloved one to wear. You better look out though, dear, how you talk about my intellectuality or you will make me wonderfully vain. And if you should, just think how it would react on you to live with a man who thought that all he did was just about right. Imagine me going around the house with a very patronizing and superior air as much as to say: "Congratulate yourself my dear, on having such a very smart husband. Bow down before his superior wisdom, and tell all your lady friends what a really superior person the doctor is." Can you imagine that? No I don't believe you can. I don't believe you will ever make me vain, but I do know and believe that your faith and pride in me will always be a constant stimulus to make me endeavor to deserve it. And I know dear that there is nothing that will make a man so strong to do his chosen work as the belief in his strength that comes from a loving woman and believing that who ought to be stronger than I, for who lives a more loving heart than the sweet little woman who has entrusted her future happiness to my keeping. And don't you know dear that the great mystery of mysteries to me will be how I succeeded in winning and holding the one great treasure of the world – the great riches of your love. I never expect to solve it but will just content myself with the important fact that it is so. But see here my darling. I can't permit yourself to underrate yourself by talking about a lack of intellectuality.

Right there I play the part of the despotic lover and say "stop it – I won't hear it." I won't allow my future wife to be abused even by herself. Intellect. Who is to judge of intellect? Who is it, Emerson that says that there is only one wise thing in a silly world and that is love?

Fairhaven is rejoicing over the fact that we now get two mails a day. The through Eastern mail now comes through on the morning boat so that we get it about 2 or 3 hours sooner than formerly. I am glad you look for the flowers and like them. It is such a little thing to do. Do you know I shall be quite interested in seeing that botanical collection. I think that the notes accompanying the same will be much more interesting than those that usually accompany a herbarium – to two people in this world, at least. Two people there's another mystery isn't it? Two people with two thousand miles between them and yet nearer to each other than they are to anyone else in the world, by the close tie of affection which joins them closely together. The world is full of mystery, but there's none like ours, is there dear? That's all our own and no one else can have any part in it. They may speculate about it outside but they are not of it. We are the sole possessors and are not selling or giving away any subdivisions in lots, parcels or blocks. We hold title in fee simple, and the property is not on the market. Now there's a spiritual application of a material entity – how does it strike you?

Couldn't help it you know, when real estate is about the only thing talked about here. It would even be a relief, I think, sometimes if Bluff Park could be talked about once in awhile.[19]

Well I hope you will thoroughly enjoy your vacation for the rest of the time. I know you will at May – Williams (I was going to say Weir). Get those hollows in your cheeks that you spoke of filled up and then get a picture taken. The first part of that sentence is a command. The last part is a request, an entreaty, a strong desire, a consuming desire.

Well this has been a rambling letter. I wonder where it will ramble before it reaches you. As you said when you finished your letter that you were going to keep right on writing. I shall expect one tomorrow.

Good bye sweetheart.

Lovingly, Will

Chuckanut Bay
½ mile below Fairhaven
July 21, 1890.

My Darling Anna!

Am writing this on half fare
new book came out sailing
and have been becalmed so
that I am afraid we will not
get back in time to write Etta
as I intended so thought I
would write note and perhaps
would get back in time to
mail it. Your letter descriptive
of your visit in Minneapolis
came today. I was very glad to
learn that you were having
a pleasant time. I should say
that you have been doing well.
You have seen more than I
did all the time I was in St.
Paul. I am glad that you are
beginning to like the country for
that is one of the great sources
of pleasure out here. You should
see me now there are five in
our party and we came out
to have a boil, but wind and
tide have been against us. We
run the boat to shore and
jumped out to catch rope.
Just then a breeze came up

and carried the boat out again
so the boys had to make another tack, and I am sitting
on a rock waiting for them
to come in. All around is
very beautiful and very wild
Up the sound, just looking
into sight — is the finest
steamer sailing in the
sound — the "Eastern Oregon" Do
you know when I got your
letter this morning I felt
quite guilty for coming out
here. (Well here the boys
are with the boat) Sale. Have
just had our bath and am
back at Fairhaven, and have
just few minutes in which
to write. It took us four hours
to go down to our swimming
place, a distance of a little
less than two miles. We came
back in fifteen minutes in
a fair wind. If ever I make
any money out here I am
going to have one of the
finest yachts on Puget
Sound. Ed Robinson and
Clint Howard are expected
tonight on the steamer Premier
from Vancouver.

I managed to get a flower
while down the bay which I send
Will write you a letter to Red Wing
which will be an answer to
letter received this morning from Clear Lake. I have
sent two letters to Red Wing
and will send this there. I
judge from the date of
your last letter that one
of them might have reached
you at Minneapolis, but I
was afraid it would not
as your first letter from
there, written on the road
was detained two days at
Tacoma, so I thought that
Considering the time it
had been on the way and
the time it would take one
to get back from here, I
didn't know whether I
would even catch you at
Red Wing. I must stop now

and get this in the office
very quickly or it will
not go out tonight. I am
afraid that you will think
I am sending you some
pretty hard looking paper
lately, but it just happens
that I have either had to take
what was at hand or wait, and
I am just conceited enough to
think that you would rather
have the poor paper. This is
written with just as much love
as if on the finest paper in
my most careful style.
I must say good bye now, dear
until tomorrow.

Lovingly,
Will.

Chuckanut Bay before the Great Northern trestle.

Letter 22

Chuckanut Bay
½ Mile below Fairhaven
July 21, 1890

My Darling Anna,

Am writing this on a leaf from a notebook. Came out sailing and have been be-calmed so that I am afraid we will not get back in time to write a letter as I intend-ed so thought I would write a note and perhaps would get back in time to mail it.

Your little description of your visit in Minneapolis came today. I was very glad to learn that you are having a pleasant time. I should say that you have been do-ing well. You have seen more than I did all the time I was in St. Paul. I am glad that you are beginning to like the water for that is one of the great sources of pleasure out here.

You should see me now. There are five in our party and we came out to have a bath, but the wind and tide have been against us. We ran the boat to shore and I jumped out to catch rope. Just then a breeze came up and carried the boat out again. So the boys had to make another tack and I am sitting on a rock waiting for them to come in. All around is very beautiful and very wild. Up the Sound just looming into sight is the finest steamer sailing on the Sound – the "Eastern Oregon."

Do you know when I got your letter this morning I felt quite guilty for coming out here. (Well here the boys are with the boat.)

Later *– Have just had our bath and am back at Fairhaven and have just a few minutes in which to write. It took us four hours to go down to our swimming place – a distance of a little less than two miles. We came back in fifteen minutes in a fair wind. If ever I make any money out here I am going to have one of the finest yachts on Puget Sound. Ed Robinson and Clint Howard are expected tonight on the steamer "Premier" from Vancouver.*

I managed to get a flower while down the bay which I send. I must stop now and get this in the office very quickly or it will not go out tonight. I am afraid that you will think I am sending you some pretty hard looking paper lately but it just happens that I have either had to take what was at hand or wait and I am just conceited enough to think that you would rather have the poor paper. This is written with just as much love as if on the finest paper in my most careful style. I will say good by now, dear, until tomorrow.

Lovingly, Will

Letter 23

Fairhaven, Washington
Tuesday, July 22, 1890

My Darling Sweetheart,

I wonder what you thought of the miserable little note I sent you yesterday. It was such a poor little affair.

But I started to talk about something in that and never got to finish it. I was saying that I felt guilty about coming out here. I know, don't I know, only too well how lonely it is, but I thought it all for the best dear. One has to wait so long in old settled communities but sometimes I feel as if I have made a mistake. It has seemed as if everything had been against me. Here two months have gone by and I have done nothing yet. There was the delay of the State examination and now the delay about my office. I cannot get in for a week yet. It is all very disheartening. It all makes me feel that perhaps I would have done better to have settled in some of the small towns of Iowa. And the thought that it brings a moment's unhappiness to you is the hardest part of it. I hoped that by coming out here I could hasten matters was my reason for it all.

I have wished many times since I have been out here that I had not come, that I am here and must make the best of it. I will stay now that I am here until I make a success of it but I dread to think how long it will be if things do not change for the better before long. But why do I talk about this. It can only have the effect of making you feel blue and unhappy for I am appreciating more and more all the time how much you take to heart – all that concerns me – that concerns us. It fills me with joy to think you love me so well, but it saddens me to think that you are ever unhappy on account of my absence. I used to try to get you to say what you would rather have me do. I reproach myself now for any blindness in not seeing that you didn't want me to come out West, but were too proud to say so, and you were right in your pride because I should have been aware enough to see it for myself without asking any questions about it. I expect I was blind to a good many things when I was at home. But time opens a man's eyes to many things. But here I am talking along when I just simply want to say that I have wanted you, too. It's all so dreary away from you. There's no disguising the fact Anna (even if I wanted to, which I don't) that there is no use in or pleasure in life away from you.

You represent all there is in existence to me and I have your sweet confession to the same effect and yet we have to live apart. We ought to be two very happy mortals, Anna, when our time for waiting is ended and I doubt not we will be, but oh the weary waiting. How many times have I said that within the last two years? Yes it is very nearly two years. One month from yesterday will the 21st of August the one bright anniversary. I wonder what you are doing now and where you are and where you will be on the twenty-first of August. You must tell me all about it.

I am glad that you have been able to see so much in your short stay in Minneapolis. I know about all the points mentioned in your letters. I have never eaten at the "Delicatessen" in its present quarters but have when it was over on Seventh Street.

Minnesota Historical Society.

Construction of James J. Hill's home on Summit Avenue in St. Paul, 1891.

I worked in the old Pioneer Press building on Third Street. The new building was not completed when I worked there. There is one part of St. Paul that I am afraid you missed at least, you said nothing about it. That is Summit Avenue – the prettiest residences in the country.[20] *There is nothing to surpass it in the country. I have pleasant recollections of White Bear Lake. I think it the prettiest lake I know of. But do you know I am positively jealous of the three young gentlemen out there and of Harry also – no, not jealous either, but decidedly envious. I keep thinking, when will the time come when I may be around with you on those pleasant excursions and while I wouldn't deprive you of them in fact am grateful, especially to Harry for any courtesies shown you, yet I am selfish enough to want to do all that myself and rebel at the hard rate that makes it impossible.*

And so Harry thinks we have it bad, does he? Well, that's all right. I am glad he has that opinion. I am happy to state that we have. Ed Robinson and Clint Howard returned last night accompanied by **Mr. Woods** *and his daughter Alice. I have had no opportunity for conversation with them. Do you know I believe I will stop now and write again. Soon. To tell the truth, I am blue and haven't the heart to write. It is hard work to write a cheerful letter so I think I will wait.*

In the meantime, believe that I remain yours.

Lovingly, Will

Letter 24

Fairhaven, Washington
Thursday, July 24, 1890

My Darling Anna,

How your letters do cheer a man up especially when he is low spirited. Yes, to-day and the day before I was as glum as a man very well could be. Today I feel quite cheerful and why, just because I had a letter from you. This morning's mail brought a beautiful letter from my "best girl" and one from my best friend Ed Scott – so I could feel cheerful even if a rather unfortunate bit of news has turned up. And that is that there has been a homeopathic doctor here for a long time – only no one knew it because he was not practicing. He is part owner of a large saw mill and a pioneer of Fairhaven and just within the past week or so has commenced practice. Well it may not hurt me. It may be support for it will bring my system of medicine more prominently before the public. **Dr. Heacock**[21] *is a man well on in years having practiced for over twenty and will be very likely to shove a great deal of the night work off onto me.*

And so Harry is caught is he? Good! He will have a little appreciation of how it goes with other people now. But really Anna. You are quite a matchmaker to have had such an effect with one conversation. Your influence must be immense. I think I met the young lady when I took dinner once with Harry in Minneapolis and if it is the one I had in mind I should never had imagined that he would marry her. They were apparently on such free and easy terms that I should not have thought that he had anything more than a friendly interest in her. And so Harry is a great deal more practical than I am is he? Well, I suppose he is. I'm not a very practical individual especially where a lady's necessities are concerned. But then you know I never had any opportunity to know. I have been away from home so much and all that I know about girls personally is what I have seen of them in social gatherings, and you know that is not a very good place in which to learn what a girl really is. But then you know there is hope for me. I will know sometime and I may develop into one of the most practical and domestic men you can imagine. Certainly the life that I am living now is calculated to develop a very strong desire in that direction if I never had it before.

The restaurant where I board, and which is the only one in town where anything fit to eat can be had,[22] *has no tables but has a large semicircular counter with high stools for seats. Think of living at a place like that for a year or more. A nice boarding house cannot be had. I only know of one in town and that one costs seven dollars a week for day board which is a little above my resources at present.*

Brian Griffin Collection.
Heacock's Mill from 1891 Fairhaven Birdseye Map.

But I have been telling you very little of Fairhaven in my last two or three letters. I wonder what I can tell you that can be of interest. Well I'll

Whatcom Museum.

Charles E. Moody unloading rails for the Fairhaven & Southern.

first mention one little thing to begin with which may be of interest from its novelty but of which I can give no description because I was not present. The ship "Charles E Moody" which has been lying at the ocean wharf discharging a cargo of rails for the Fairhaven & Southern Railroad is the first large sailing vessel that has come into the harbor. She is a beautiful cargo ship, one of the largest that has ever entered Puget Sound. The captain's wife accompanies him in the voyage and their cabin is very handsomely, not to say luxuriously, filled up. Well, night before last a ball was given by the Captain and his wife and dancing took place on the deck of the ship, which was beautifully decorated with Japanese lanterns hanging from every yard arm. As the masts are about a hundred and fifty feet high you may imagine the effect. You will hear Fairhaven spoken of as truly beautiful but that is not so. It is potentially beautiful. Its site is beautiful and the city will be so, but it is not now. It is too full of half burned stumps and unfinished and unpainted wooden buildings but another year will change much of that and then it can make some pretension to beauty. I think it has the possibility of being the most beautiful city along the Sound. Its prospects also grow brighter all the time.

The Northern Pacific Railroad has applied for track facilities and right of way and probably in less than a year will be running trains in here. The Great Northern will be here within a year and communication with the Canadian Pacific will be completed in less then sixty days. It is only forty-five miles to the main line of the Canadian Pacific and track laying is well underway. Never fear, if we stay in Fairhaven you will have the pleasure of living in a large place. It is bound to be a good seaport. There were, as you know, four towns here. Fairhaven, Bellingham, Sehome and Whatcom in the order named around the bay. Fairhaven and Bellingham were incorporated into the one town some time ago.

Sehome 1889. Elk Street, now State Street, leading to Fairhaven. The Boulevard now departs to the right of the hill.

Next week Whatcom and Sehome will vote for consolidation with each other which will have two towns instead of four, thus concentrating their energies and it will certainly not be were those three years if it will be as long before Whatcom and Fairhaven will be united into one town. Two miles and a half around the shore of the bay includes all three towns as they now stand and the building tendency is toward each other. Fairhaven growing in the direction of Sehome and the latter in the direction of Fairhaven. Fourteenth Street in Fairhaven is now being graded and paved through to the main street of Sehome, making it practically one street. As soon as the paving is completed an electric motor car line will be put in running in all three towns. Gasworks are now being built which will supply all three towns.[23] You see they are so close together that they are bound to be one town.

Well I guess that's enough Fairhaven for this time. But I must tell you about my office. The building is built of red pressed brick trussed with brownstone. The woodwork is in red cedar except the stairways and railing which are ash and white oak finished in natural wood. I think that in time I can make the office look pretty nice but at present it will be a rather primitive affair. Just a table, a couple of chairs, a small washstand and a red lounge. The only thing in the way of ornament will be your engraving and I can assure you that it will add much to the appearance of the room. I am also going to put up the colored picture of Jessica that you gave me Christmas, for do you know that I trace some resemblance to you in that picture. When I get into the office I will tell you all about how I have everything.

Consolidation

FOUR SEPARATE TOWNS came into being around the shores of Bellingham Bay. First there was Whatcom clustered about the mouth of the creek of the same name. Next was Sehome a bit to the east growing around its early coal mine, then the town of Bellingham adjoining Sehome to the south and platted by Edward Eldridge and Erastus Bartlett in 1883. Finally the most southerly village of Fairhaven which Dan Harris named and platted in that same year.

The economic reasons for these four towns to consolidate into one were compelling and rather obvious but self interest and political considerations thwarted consolidation efforts for years. It came to pass gradually.

In 1890 Nelson Bennett, C.X. Larrabee and the Fairhaven Land Company purchased the Bellingham townsite from Eldridge and Bartlett and soon merged it into Fairhaven. The name Bellingham ceased to exist as a town name.

There were only the now larger towns of Fairhaven, Sehome and Whatcom.

In 1891 Sehome changed it's name to New Whatcom and shortly thereafter consolidated with Whatcom under the name of New Whatcom. The name was changed to Whatcom in 1901.

After several contentious elections the citizens of both Whatcom and Fairhaven finally voted to consolidate in 1903 into the city of Bellingham.

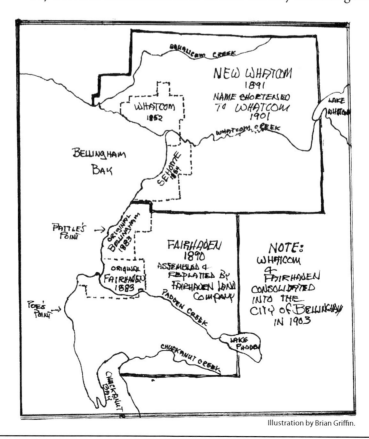

Illustration by Brian Griffin.

The Methodist Church[24] has just been completed and is one of the prettiest little churches I ever saw. Inside the ceiling is high and vaulted with cross beams finished in natural wood, as are most interiors out here. The wood work, except the cross beams which are of yellow fir, is red cedar. The windows are arched gothic and consist of the prettiest stained glass I ever saw except in a special design. By next year a good opera house will be built so that first-class companies can come here.

Yes Anna, I think you are right in supposing that I understood you in your lack of demonstrativeness. Sometimes just at the moment I was puzzled and at a loss, but that was only for a short time. Whenever I thought it over I always understood, at least I always thought I did which amounts to the same thing in effect and do you know Anna, I thought all the more of you for it. I think caresses can be made so common that they lose their sweetness and that very often those who are so lavish while they are lovers become very indifferent after marriage and the latter is worse than the former. I hope we can be lovers all our lives dear. You know I always flatter myself that I understood you a little better than anybody else and I think so yet I do not say that I thoroughly understand another without years of closest association and perhaps not even then. But I understood pretty well, didn't I dear?

But I say Anna dear, drive me wild with envy by telling about how pleasant other people are making it for you. I don't object to them doing it. I am glad they do it but then how could they help being good to you? Of course they couldn't. But I do get wildly envious by other people being able to do so much more toward contributing to your pleasure than I could ever do. You understand what I mean and what

I feel when I say that don't you? How can a fellow help it when somebody else is able to do so much to make life pleasant – pleasant to the one he loves most on earth while he has to be thousands of miles away and can do nothing. I think I have a fit of being envious anyway. Yesterday, no it was the day before I saw in the Journal that Dr. W.B. Hanna of Chicago had started on a three month's trip to Europe

1890 Fairhaven Illustrated. Whatcom Museum.
Methodist Episcopal Church.

Pat Wickline Collection.
Being used as a residence 2009.

as attending physician to a wealthy family who paid all his expenses and gave him a handsome salary besides. Now that's what I call luck and it will take someone with a more angelic nature than mine to avoid being envious, even if envy is a very undesirable quality. That's one of my many imperfections. However, I have talked on this line before and used Will Hanna as my illustration too, I believe so, I think I would better veer off on that tack and take the other direction. I always have one consolation and a very great one it is when I get to thinking this way and that is that other people may have their good luck – I have the best and loveliest girl in the world and that ought to be sufficient for one man.

I had heard of the accident on Lake Pepin during the storm[25] *but had thought it best to say nothing about it. At one time I was very apprehensive that you had been at Red Wing at the time and that the horror of it would be a great shock to you. This letter may not reach you before you leave Red Wing but I would advise you not to stay there very long. Such universal gloom as there will be there, and especially since you can do no good cannot be other than a very unwholesome atmosphere. It is not depression but pleasure and recreation that you want to enable you to go back to your school with strength and energy enough to be carry you safely through another year and to be thrown into an atmosphere of unavailing grief and sorrow will not contribute to that end. So get out of it as soon as you can. I am not urging you to a selfish act. If you could do any good there I should say stay as long as you can. But you can't and may do yourself injury.*

I will close now and will wonder where you will be when this reaches you. Good bye dear one.

Lovingly,
Will

Letter 25

Fairhaven, Washington
Monday, July 28, 1890

My Darling Anna,

Another of your welcome letters came this morning and consequently I am in the best of spirits today. A letter from you never fails to make things look brighter. They always contain promise for the future that is bright and helpful. I can't begin to tell you now much you are helping me out here.

Another reason why I am feeling good today is because at last I am going to get into my office. This morning I got tired of waiting and went around to the lessor of the building and told him that I had to get in there right away and no more delay about it. He said he would see the foreman and have my rooms fixed at once. I stayed with him until he saw the foreman and the result is that I move in tomorrow.

Fairhaven Illustrated 1890. Whatcom Museum.

Will would become the first tenant of the Mason Block.

I have ordered my sign – my "shingle" which will also be done tomorrow. It is to be a modest little affair of Japanese tile with gold letters on, bearing the legend "Dr. W. R. Gray, Homoeopathist." So that tomorrow the gentle breezes will cause that important shingle to flop around and will carry that little legend laden with its burthen of glad tidings to a genuine accursed and suffering multitude. It will proclaim to the long suffering public that a new era of enlightened medicine has dawned upon the beautiful city of Fairhaven. No longer will the morphine, the quinine and the little hypodermic hold its sway unchallenged. So now look out for that first case. I missed that first case by the way by being at church yesterday.

A gentleman called at the office of Messrs. Henderson and Templin where I have spent a considerable portion of my time and wanted to have me visit – his child is very sick. He said that if it did not get any better he would call in the afternoon. He failed to return so I suppose the child was better and I missed two dollars and a half. But seriously, I had a peculiar sensation when I realized that I was likely to be called into a serious case, and that a child. It made me feel that the great struggle is yet before me – the struggle with responsibility and the sudden sense of the gravity of the situation that came over me was absolutely oppressive and terrifying. I hope that I shall have no such sensation when in the absolute pressure of the danger. And it stirred me to activity too. I felt the necessity of having a place where my library and resources would be where I could avail myself of them at once.

I attended the dedicating services of the Methodist Church yesterday and heard a very able discourse by Dr. Harrington of Portland. The music was good and altogether it was a very nice service. There was something over three thousand dollars indebtedness in the church edifice and it was all raised so that is free from debt.

Do you know Anna that in your letter this morning you touched me very closely. You said that my love for you has stimulated in you an ambition to do good and do some good in the world. I think that I too have been feeling that more since I have been out here. Everything is so loose and the temptation to go wrong is so great that a man of any fine sense of what is right feels compelled in a spirit of self defense to ally himself on the side of the church. It is either that side or the side of the devil absolutely. It is remarkable how quickly a man can become tolerant of his surroundings and degenerate to the level of the people around him. As an example, I think of Clint Howard. I would not have club friends in Mt. Pleasant know it, but he is not what he was in Mt. Pleasant. I don't mean that there is anything bad about

Whatcom Museum.

Clint Howard.

him yet, but he has lost that fine and high sense of morality that characterized him before coming out here. His language used to be irreproachable but he uses much bad language now and I don't believe he realizes it at all. It is the power of association. That is the most characteristic feature of the change that has taken place. I know a number of men here who seem to be very nice fellows and yet, their language is frightful. Oaths with nearly every sentence, and that not in the heat of anger, but in commonplace conversations.

So I say as a matter of protection it is beginning to look to me as if a man must formally place himself where his face is set firmly against any contamination of this kind. I think I shall get on the right side as soon as I can decide where I belong. Mother would like to have me join the Methodist Church of course. My own inclinations are toward the Presbyterian. Doubtless you have thought that I have been very silent on this subject. But it is something I have not cared much to discuss but would to think it out for myself.

We will try to do our good together Anna. I like Det Bird first-rate. I never knew him very well in Mt. Pleasant but have been with him a good deal since coming here. I find him a more congenial companion than any of the other Mt. Pleasant people here. I will remind him of your trip to the dance with him. I will have to stop now and write a letter to mother before today's mail goes out. I will once more write on the envelope.

Good bye dear,

Your's lovingly, Will

Letter 26

Friday, August 1, 1890
Fairhaven, Washington

My Darling Anna,

 Another of your letters has just reached me, and I am of course quite happy. I am writing this in my office. Moved in yesterday, hung out my sign and had two calls – $3.00. I gloat over that three dollars to a great extent, for I thought that was doing pretty well for the first day. I can live if I arrange that each day and no more.

 My office looks rather bare just at present, but I have put in about everything that I can afford just at present. You need have no fears about my being extravagant to start with. I couldn't even if I wanted to. There would be a temptation to indulge in something rather fine if I could inasmuch as all the other firms going into this building have been here some time, have made money and are filling up their rooms quite elegantly. But, I will have to wait for that. I have only furnished one room yet and use the other for a storeroom and closet, not that I have much to "store" and everything is as cheap as I could get it. I have an oak table with a green cloth top – the only nice article of furniture I have ($12) – a small stand for a wash stand ($1.50) three wooden chairs @ $1.00 for $3.00, a cot-mattress and bedding at a total cost of $11.50 – an eighty cent lamp and that constitutes the furniture. On the floor I have a large rug – blue and gold ($12.50). On the walls I have your engraving and my university and medical society diplomas. The little things are what take the money though. As soon as I had to occupy my office as a sleeping apartment, it occurred to me that a little water for purposes of cleanliness would be a very desirable not to say necessary thing hence involving the expense of toilet bar soap etc. etc. Then came towels. In the evening I found that it would be necessary to have light at night. A lamp followed and so it goes. Window shades and curtains are a necessity as are also a bookcase and a medicine and instrument cabinet. How is this for the practical details? Have I done pretty well telling about it?

 My sign is of tin block with the name in gold letters. (This is on your praise of my former artistic efforts.) Say! Just wait till I draw you a picture of a skate. I presume that being a school marm you know that a skate is a fish. I haven't seen one

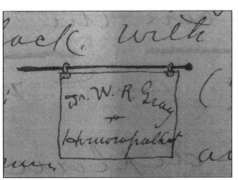

Will's shingle.

yet but from descriptions that have been given me the flounder is the very acme of true and beautiful proportions compared with it. When I see one I will make a faithful sketch. Just hold your breath till you see it. If you don't you certainly will when you do. Oh, I didn't tell you what those first cases were did I? They were a couple of men with common everyday dyspepsia. It was no trouble at all to prescribe for them. In regard to the girl in

Whatcom I should say that she had cerebral meningitis, differing slightly in some respects from the ordinary course of that disease which had the effect of puzzling the doctor in attendance. The leading drug store in the city is in this building[26] and they say that calls for homeopathic physicians are quite frequent, and that they will direct all who come there to me. It is a good thing to be in the same building with a good drug house as it is much easier for them to direct a person upstairs than it is to tell them to go up the street on the right hand side, third door from so and so store, on the second floor left hand side of the hall – you will see a sign on the door. That's a tremendous waste of good breath "you know."

Well I think I will have to leave you for a few minutes and occupy one of the high stools at the restaurant – so au revoir my dear. Will be back soon.

After Dinner – Here we are again. I suppose a man ought to feel good after dinner, but I believe that is the result of a good dinner but I haven't had a good dinner ergo I ought not to feel good. However that kind of logic is fallacious and notwithstanding a poor dinner I am still feeling pretty good.

I will write to Harry and will draw your enjoyment of your trip as strong as possible and will also more sincerely congratulate him on his sensible act in choosing himself a wife. I hope you set his mind at rest as to my openness of his being a "chump." I wonder what put such an idea as that into his head. And you can't imagine how glad I am that you are pleased with my letters. I have tried to write a little better since I have been out here than I did before. For one thing I have had more time, another is that there has been more to write about. But the chief thing is that we are so far apart and must be for so long that letters must take the place of everything else and be so much more to us, that there is every reason that we should make them as good as possible. And don't reproach yourself Anna for writing your longings with the idea that it may make me feel more lonely for it has a very different effect I can assure you.

I hope you will keep right on gaining in weight. You must have become pretty thin to weigh only one hundred and five pounds. Nothing would please me more than to have you send me the picture you received from Harry. Any picture of you would be more welcome than anything else but I'm sorry you can't bring yourself to have a new one taken because I am so anxious to have a picture of you taken since our engagement. I would be a great favor Anna, for my sake. Truly you would confer a great happiness on me. But I will say no more about it if you do not want to. I guess I will stop now and study awhile. I am getting rather rusty and must do considerable reading to be ready for the "large and constantly increasing practice."

By the way, I wrote a blue letter a few days ago. Pay no attention to it, please. Your last letter came through in five days. It will not take quite so long after we get railroad connection in about forty days. I wonder where you will be next.

Good bye dear.

Lovingly, Will

Letter 27

Fairhaven, Washington
Sunday, August 3, 1890

My Darling Sweetheart,

This is a beautiful Sunday afternoon and as I sit here beginning a letter to you that will probably be a piece cut off from the same style that I have been sending you for so long – it is long isn't it, it seems so to me anyway – it comes over me that there is nothing that I should like quite so well as to be in Mt. Pleasant today with the prospect ahead of seeing you this evening. That is about the brightest prospect that I could conceive of. We will also suppose that it is as bright there as it is here and also moonlight bringing to my mind visions of a walk out on East Washington Street. Of course I should not expect to be alone on that walk.

Oh, those old days! I know now how happy I was there. And it makes it seem so lonely here now. It is lovely here. It doesn't simply seem so – "Seems madam, nay it is. I know not seems." There isn't a place in town where I can go. I hardly know what the inside of a house looks like and oh how sick I am of the manners of life at a restaurant. It isn't on account of the fare that's reasonably good. But the daily going to a place and mounting a stool among a lot of strangers, everybody in a hurry, the waiters rushing around the clatter of the dishes, the shouting of the waiters to the cook. It is all distracting and I long to sit down quietly to a meal once more and enjoy it like a civilized person. About two at the table I think would be perfect bliss.

Yes, I think about one year of the life that I am living now will prepare me for domestic life. I think I will be ready to be the most domestic man you ever saw. I could draw quite a picture. I think a pen picture if I should give free rein to my imagination, but I hardly think it safe. There is no telling where it might carry me if I once allowed it to get a start. But of course you know that whenever my imagination gets started, you are the chief central figure around which it plays its antics and however it may vary in its detail the main theme is you installed as mistress of a snug little house. And it always makes a very pretty and satisfying picture too.

By the way, some time ago I wrote to mother a little in which I spoke of her coming out here and what do you suppose she answered? She said that when I owned some lots and had built a house for myself and another one for her she would come out. I wrote back and told her that she was becoming mighty proud and stuck up of late – to want a whole house by herself. You know I told you that she had a thing that she would never live with us – that young folks ought to live by themselves. But she has always said that she wanted to live near. I shall have to depend on you to change her views in that regard and if you can't why we will have to do it by strategy after we are married. How easy and natural it comes now to write those words – "after we are married." And they look pretty well after they are written though I think they would sound a great deal better if I could whisper them to you myself.

Later *– At this point I had a caller. Now don't get excited. It was just an acquaintance dropped in to make a friendly call. Since then the afternoon and* *evening have slipped by. Have just come back from church. Went to hear the Congregational minister at what is known as the tabernacle. It is a plain wooden building without any lath or plastering – just boarded up on the outside. But the preacher is the best in town. This morning Dr. Copeland a Unitarian preacher of Tacoma and said to be a very eloquent man was to have preached in one of the halls. I went to hear him, but he failed to arrive having missed the boat and it was too late to go anywhere else when the fact became known to the audience. Mr. George McAdam and Rick and Mr. Henderson and myself (now, there is a artfully constructed sentence to be evaluated by the late "literary geniuses" of the IWU" – were together at church.*

Mr. McAdam has bought a lot here and is building a residence to rent on it. Mr. Henderson is an old Iowa man who has passed most of his life in the West and a large portion of that time in Montana as an Indian agent. He is a man apparently over fifty years of age, a man naturally refined but with a little of the roughness of the frontier and an old bachelor. I must tell you of one thing that he has done in the world. There was a little Sioux Indian girl at the agency when he was, in a starving condition, dirty, half naked, in fact in about as low and wretched conditions as is possible for a human being to be in. Out of pity he clothed and fed her and took it on himself to take care of her. Finally he became attached to her, adopted her and educated her. He has given her a college education, one year of which was spent at Parsons. She is an accomplished musician and judging from abstracts from some of her letters that Mr. Henderson has read to me and also from her graduating oration in the college magazine, she has considerable literary ability. She is now traveling in the South but intends to teach at an Indian school. Mr. Henderson has photographs of her taken when he first took charge of her and at various times up to her graduation. They are a perfect study in advancement wrought by education. At first she is a rather stolid looking child with straight black hair hanging down her back. Each picture indicates the growth of mind over matter. In the last she is a very pretty refined intellectual and stylish looking young lady, not seeming to differ much from a white girl except that her complexion is a little dark. Mr. Henderson calls her "Puss" and is as proud of her as if she was his own child – and she is taking into consideration the fact that he made it possible for her to become what she has.

I will send you a paper which may have something of interest in it concerning Fairhaven. There is at least one compensating feature about the lack of comfort that we experience here, and that is the positive pleasures derived from watching the city improve. Every day adds something in the way of improvement. When I first came there were only two graded streets – the rest were all stumps. Now there are eight and others under way. The "Fairhaven Herald" which is now published bi-weekly will soon be issued daily. The plans are drawn up for a fine opera house. Machine and car shops for the Great Northern railway are now being built. It is quite a novel sight this building of a city. I wish you could see it.

Well, I am stringing this letter out pretty long and want to write something tomorrow, besides tonight I want to see you. Something new? Oh. No! I have that

Whatcom Museum.

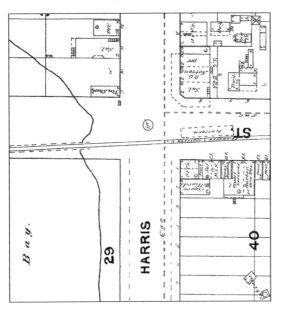

Grading and planking were going on throughout Fairhaven. This view looking east up Harris Avenue shows the building where Will took his meals, just above 9th Street. Brunswick Billiards, on the right is the current site of Harris Square.

Sanborn Fire Insurance Maps provide an invaluable record and give historians a "freeze frame" in the history of the city. In this instance, there is a photo to corroborate the accuracy of this map in 1890.

longing at least fourteen times everyday by actual count. Have been getting letters from you every Monday morning for the past three weeks. Wonder if I will get one tomorrow. How I do long for those letter days. If it wouldn't be so selfish I would ask you to write oftener. It gets so lonesome here you can't imagine it of course. I put in some time studying, but I can't do that all the time. And I have no social privileges at all as I don't know anyone – that is in a social way. Of course I have met a great many people but am intimate with no one. You would better look out. I will be a veritable savage by the time I get back to Mt. Pleasant. Are you not a little afraid of that? There is one thing that will save me from that fate though. Can you imagine what it is? No? Well then I will have to tell you. It is your love. I could not degenerate into the savage state quite with that face ever in my mind. So I think I am safe with that score. Wonder where this letter will wander to next or rather my thoughts. It is decidedly rambling up to date. You say you always like my letters for some one thing in each. Now tell me what is it you can find in this one. Perhaps I may get it in tomorrow. I may get a letter tomorrow, and that will start me off on a new train of thought that may have something in it worthy of consideration. I wonder what you will probably think, that I am in a chronic state of comedy if I don't stop pretty soon. But do you know, that while I am aware that I am doing little else than filling paper. I didn't want to stop. I want to keep on writing because you are the one to whom I am writing. You. I just think of you and our contact for the present – to think of of nothing else. When Sunday night comes around I feel as if I ought to see you. I just ought to and that's all there is about it. And when I feel that way I get rebellious at everything that separates. But there, if I get on that strain I will make it hard for both of us. But I can't stand it, so very long. As soon as I get to doing something. I feel as if it must come to end. We can't afford – WE can't afford to wear our hearts out repining for each other's absence any longer than it required by absolute necessity. There you see dear, I am always assuming that it is as hard for you as for myself. You will understand the seeming conceit in that assumption. If I don't stop this letter very suddenly I will hear myself worked into a state of the blues in my desire to be with you. So, I will say good night my darling.

Monday afternoon – No change in the situation today. Am still waiting for prescriptions. "They cometh not he said." (Excuse the paraphrase.) Have been pounding away in my books. Think that I will be pretty well informed if time continues to be such a constant possession of mine. "Time is money." I am the wealthiest man in town, just at present. Have just three dollars left. It is an absolutely necessity that patients commence to "get a move on" and "come early and avoid the rush." I can't very well cut my restaurant bill down to less than two meals a day while ahead of me looms the gigantic figure of a month's rent – seventeen big round hard dollars – and a half dollar added, and a millionaire for a landlord.[27] Such is life in the hard West. However "here's hoping" three dollars will last five days and there is no telling what may happen in that time. I will surely catch one or two enough to last two or three days longer.

Now is a good time for a display of sympathy. It would fit in exactly that right place. They say it is darkest just before the dawn – the daylight must be mighty close around here because Egyptian darkness was as the sun at midday compared with the clouds that envelop my material prosperity just at the present moment of my existence upon this terrestrial sphere.

Enclosed you will find an artistic gem. A cartoon – so to speak. I can do worse than this if this one isn't bad enough. As I will prove when I give you a picture of the festive skate. Please don't load your answer to this with dynamite.

West Shore Magazine. Gordon Tweit Collection.
Millionaire landlord, Allen Mason, 1888.

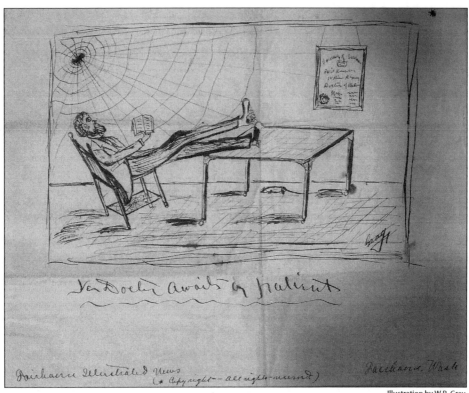

Illustration by W.R. Gray.

"Yer Doctor Awaits a Patient."

Well, I see this effort has consumed so much of my time that I will have to close this to get it in the mail. By the way, if this "cartoon" should be at all obscure, a chart will be cheerfully furnished free of charge accompanied by a guide book giving a complete description of all places of interest. Visitors will please not rub their fingers over the canvas or disturb the spiders. This is their time to sleep.

Well now I have commenced another sheet but think I will have to stop anyway. Did not get any letter this morning and so felt a little disappointed, but have great hopes for tomorrow. I hope you will survive this effusive of words. If it has any deleterious effect – just let me know and I will be careful in the future. I fear that it may have a narcotic effect. But perhaps the accompanying illustrations will have a sufficient stimulating action to modify and neutralize the soporific actions of the epistle.

"Well really I must go now." Will call again soon.

So good bye dear.

Lovingly,

Will

Letter 28

Friday, August 8, 1890
Fairhaven, Washington

My Darling Anna,

I wonder where this will find you – whether at home, at Bluff Park, the great and only Bluff Park or at May Weir Williams. You are on the move so much lately that I have almost quit trying to imagine where you are at any special time, but I am always glad that you are moving around that way because I think it will do you good. The time will come soon enough when you will be a prisoner once more with the festive kid as your jailer.

By the way are you giving "Normal" the go by this year?[28] I hope so for they are women-killers and ought to be abolished by the board of health under penalty of capital punishment to the instigators and their abettors. I would also pass sentence of death on the Mount Pleasant school board from whose villainous clutches I hope "someday" to rescue you. There I feel better now. There was no special cause for that outbreak just at the present time, but I would not be in normal condition if I couldn't belabor the school board about once every so often.

Things are moving along quite well with me, all things considered. I have three cases in hand and people are beginning to know that I am here and where I hold forth. One case is a child with tonsillitis which presents a few symptoms that may result in diphtheria. Another is a man with traumatic pleuritis – I give you these terms now because you may as well get used to them gradually as you will have to hear of them often enough as the doctor's wife. The third case is a young girl about a month married who has been traveling around a good deal and having a great deal of gaiety and excitement which has been a little too much for her and she is consequently rather exhausted and debilitated. She is a sister-in-law, by the way of Dr. Wisner, of Tacoma. He is Dr. Munson's partner and it was through hearing of me from him that I was called in. Speaking of the "doctor's wife," a few evenings ago there was a call for Dr. Heacock, the other homoeopath here. He was out of town, so his wife went over to look after the case which was a sick baby. There are just little hurts you know.

You accused me in one of your letters recently of not being very practical – that is, not as practical as Harry. How does that strike you? In this "practical" connection assure Mrs. Bassett for me – I suppose you will write to her – that she has my heartfelt gratitude for that "cookbook." That is a very "practical" way of manifesting interest in our affairs or your affairs, as she knows me so slightly. Not that I would for one moment insinuate that you stand in any great need of it for I know that you do not but as I said it is practical interest.

Well, I find even my two or three little cases give me considerable sense of responsibility and worry. I have made two calls on the child with tonsillitis and each time after I get back to the office I wondered if I had even the right remedy and if I hadn't made a fool of myself in the eyes of the parents. The next thing was a search of every scrap of information I could get. I read the Materia Medica, my old notes, my work on "practice and pathology" and finally concluded it was about right. The same way with the other cases. I had a letter from Thompson at Snohomish yesterday. He said he was getting over his worry about his patients and advised me not to worry over mine. Also he said he had been quite busy and was doing well. His first month's business was five dollars and I think I have before remarked I have been in my office and open for business eight days and done twelve dollars business. So I think arguing from analogy that my prospects are pretty fair. I have felt rather embarrassed when making a call, but I don't believe it was noticed. I think it was something like my efforts on the platform at home. I always felt scared half to death but everyone always said that I appeared easy. Perhaps I may have the same success here until that embarrassed feeling wears off, as of course it will in time.

I am studying pretty hard as is necessary in order to keep ready for what emergencies may come up. Did I tell you that Dr. Gray of Ellensburg sent me sixty of the principal remedies in one ounce bottles sufficient to last me for a good while

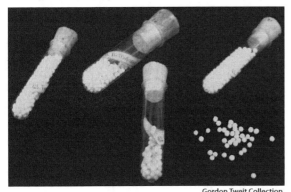

as they are in strong tinctures and will have to be diluted for use. All the remedies are commonly required, so they do very well until my full supply comes which will be in a few days now as they have been on the road nearly three weeks. My books from home, also carpets sufficient to carpet both rooms, are also on the way so that I will soon have all my personal property here.

Gordon Tweit Collection.
Homeopathic medicines in one-ounce bottles circa 1890.

Well this letter has been very largely devoted to the material affairs hasn't it? But then I thought you would be interested. Am going to keep you informed right along as to my monthly receipts – I may do so much business before long as to need a bookkeeper and as I know nothing about that very commercial pursuit – it is professional you know – I think I will have to get you out here to keep my books. There's another "practical" idea – please credit that to me, also will you? Well I must stop now. It won't do to give you another such letter as my last for at least a month or the shock might be too great. So good bye dear.

With much love,
Will

Letter 29

Fairhaven, Washington
Tuesday, August 12, 1890

My Darling Sweetheart,

Things are beginning to lighten up with me I think. I begin to feel a little encouraged over the trend of affairs. Have been practicing just twelve days. During that time my business has amounted to twenty six dollars of which I have collected twelve. For a new beginner that is all that could be anticipated – in fact more.

If this keeps up, I will be paying expenses the first month and that is all the most sanguine could hope to accomplish. I believe too that I am making friends, that is professionally. One family, where I had a case of a child which got along splendidly, have already sent two or three patients to me. If I can only get several families in different parts of town working for me that way I will have at least a living assured although of course expenses are quite heavy at the start. There are so many little things to get at the beginning and that keeps cropping out all the time. I got in a bill of goods this week accounting to fifty-five dollars and it does not cover the barest necessities of every day practice and now that I have the goods it necessitates getting some kind of a case made to keep them in and so it goes but will get them just the same. Have a case of protracted typhoid on hand which was in the hands of an old school physician. This is the fifth week and the patient does not rally though she says she thinks she feels a little stronger since I took hold of the case. She has been almost drugged to death, added to which the sanitary surroundings are wretched.

The people are very poor and live in a little hut and everything is dirty, bad air, poor food and no care. All these things retard recovery. I don't know whether I will get anything out of it or not but of course that makes no difference.

I have what I consider one compliment to my personality. A man came to me one afternoon (sent by the family I spoke of), and I prescribed for him and he went home and commenced to feel so well that he ate quite a hearty supper before he had taken a particle of medicine. At supper he remarked that just the visit to that doctor had made him feel better and he thought that if he saw him once more he would be all right without taking any medicine at all. Now don't you think that was doing pretty well? That doesn't look as if I "glance" at my patients does it? I have the same man on the string now for surgical operation that may bring from fifteen to twenty dollars. He came in this morning and paid what he owed me.

All my patients so far have been among the poorer class of people. Of course the better practice is of slow growth. Saturday Mrs. Rena Howard was visiting at Mrs. Templin's. She had been spending a few days outing at Lake Whatcom and has bought an acre of land on the shore of the lake for a seasonal residence. I called on her in the afternoon and had quite a pleasant talk with her Sunday night. Clint Howard and I went up and spent the evening with Ross Sullivan. He has a very pretty little house and one of the most conveniently arranged I ever saw. Everything is arranged sans steps and labor and there is scarcely a square in the house that goes to waste. Mrs. Sullivan says that Ross lost several nights sleep worrying over the fact that there are three or four inches on each side of the fireplace that are of no use except as wall. I haven't seen anyone for a long time that seems to get quite as much solid comfort out of a house as Ross is getting out of his. But say Anna, I know two people who will be able to give him points on that in a year or so. Dr. Smith is going to be here next week and very like John Fitzgerald and then Mr. Sullivan says he is going to have a Mount Pleasant reunion at his house. If he does there will be about twenty seven people there. I wonder where you are by this time. Suppose you will be at Bluff Park soon and then at Centerville. You have been having a good time this summer and I am very glad of it. How many times have I made that same declaration since you left home? Well, it makes no difference how often I have said it, I am so glad of it that I want to you know it.

Yesterday Whatcom and Sehome took a vote for consolidation with each but it was not carried in Sehome. A great many people in Sehome do not want to unite with Whatcom unless Fairhaven is included at the same time. Whatcom is opposed to Fairhaven and I would not be all surprised if Sehome and Fairhaven should unite with Fairhaven now and shut out Whatcom entirely, or at least they would be in a position to dictate to Whatcom and make her come in as a suburb of Fairhaven and taking the none of the latter.

However I suppose this is not very interesting to you as it is difficult for one not on the ground to understand the full situation. Iron will be laid on the road between here and New Westminister, B.C., on Thursday of this week so that trains will soon be running into Fairhaven from the Canadian Pacific and then we will look out for "boom."

Time for reading with me is quite plentiful at present and probably will be for some time. When I get so busy that I have no time to read I will be making a fortune. The flowers are getting scarce. I guess I have sent you about all the kinds that grow around here. In the spring there will be a number that you have not yet received. If you have added very many to the collection while in Minnesota the herbarium must be quite large. Will be quite anxious to see it, and the owner. You can't imagine how I enjoyed the evening at Mr. Sullivan's just because of the appearance of home life. It was the first time I had been out anywhere in the evening for a long time and it was a great treat.

Well, I must stop now and do some reading. That typhoid case bothers me a little. Will write in a day or two again.

Good bye dear.
Lovingly,
Will

Letter 30

Fairhaven, Washington
Friday, August 15, 1890

My Darling Anna,

The last two days I have been feeling like a fish out of water and just because I have had no letter from you. Everything has been very quiet for the past few days. Practice has been very light; real estate has been very quiet. Building has not been very brisk and in fact everything seems to be taking a rest.

I get quite discouraged sometimes when I think about things quietly and seriously. Everything comes so slow. Surely after waiting so many years I ought to accomplish something after awhile. Then it seems as if it takes such a great while to get acquainted. I get to know some of the men on the street doing business down town but have not become acquainted with any of the families in town. I have set my heart on getting squarely and solidly on my feet this year and if I don't I will be bitterly disheartened and discouraged.

All around me I hear men talking about their property and how much it is worth and still considering themselves poor and then I have the exquisite pleasure of reflecting that what they consider themselves poor on would be better short of a fortune to me.

There is no disguising the fact, Anna. If I thought this separation was to last more than a year longer, I just couldn't stand it. There is no life without you and so I say I must get straightened out inside of a year, or I must pull up and be where I can see you occasionally. You are too much a part of my very being Anna to be able to stand it any longer than the length of time I mentioned. It's all so hard without you dear. I could be twice a man with you by my side. Why should we be apart instead of together giving each other help and courage and love? We have been apart for thee months now and it has seemed an age and it is no easier for me to be here now than at the beginning. In fact, it grows harder all the time. Maybe I am not making it any easier for either of us by talking this way but I must talk as I feel about it. And I know from your letters dear that it is no easier for you than it is for me, so can you wonder that I should wish to end it as soon as possible – and that consequently that I should feel a little blue when things don't seem to be moving off as I should like to have them.

I suppose I am really doing as well as could be expected under the circumstances and so to that extent ought to be encouraged rather than otherwise. I can't stand the present indefiniteness much longer and we will be cheating ourselves of much happiness if we delay any longer than is dictated by common prudence. This will probably reach you about the 21st – the ever memorable twenty first – the anniversary of the greatest day in our calendar to be the great day until changed for another – our wedding day.

It is two years since we have been engaged. It will be another probably before we can be married. But Anna it ought not to be any longer. Three years is a long engagement for anyone and nothing but the most extraordinary circumstances and soundest reasons should prolong it any longer than that. I state positively that I can and will be ready in that time and I am sure that in a year you can get what "duds" are necessary. I want a wife. We can look out for the trousseau afterward. Life is short at best, my darling and the last of the days are gliding by. Let us pick our blossoms while they are fresh "you and I together love." Saw some fine pansies and carnations for sale today. Wish they would keep so that I could send you some to reach you by the 21st. There's another disadvantage about the long distance. We can't send flowers except pressed ones. Think I will get some pansies and press them anyway and mail them the 21st. They won't be like fresh flowers but they will be a remembrance, at least.

Last Monday as I told you, Whatcom and Sehome voted in the question of consolidation. The vote in Sehome went against it and Fairhaven is consequently jubilant and Whatcom not. The next morning the newsboys went around calling out "Fairhaven Herald! All About the Whatcom Disaster!" I think Fairhaven was responsible for the defeat of consolidation, too.

The Saturday night before the election there was to be a last big mass meeting and hoorah in Sehome on the question at issue. Whatcom was there with a band. While the band was playing outside, the Sehome anti-consolidationists, supported by half a dozen Fairhaven men who were there for the purpose went into the hall and organized the meeting and elected one of their men Chairman. When the others came in the meeting was in full blast. Well things went along smoothly until finally it was noticed that there were some Fairhaven men in the crowd and they were asked to give their views on the matter. One after another the six men got up and poured forth their eloquence against the scheme working upon the sympathy and patriotism of the people of Sehome, until the whole Sehome crowd got up and yelled for Fairhaven. The Fairhaven men would make a point against Whatcom and then ask "Now do you want to go in with Whatcom?" and the crowd would yell "No, No!" The F men represented that Whatcom had over four thousand population and Sehome not quite 3,000. If the latter went in with Whatcom, Whatcom would have a majority on any future vote and would keep Fairhaven out and that would injure Sehome.

The Whatcom men were so hot they could do nothing but swear. One of them followed a Fairhaven speaker down into the audience and shaking both fists in his face said to the Sehome people, "So you want to go with Fairhaven do you?" And the crowed yelled, "Yes! Yes!" "Then go!" shouted the Whatcomites. "We're going!" responded the Sehomes. The result will be that no two of the towns will unite unless all three are in – the way it should be. But it was a beautiful piece of campaign work on the part of Fairhaven.

Well I need to stop now. Hope for a letter tomorrow.

Goodbye dear,

Lovingly, Will

Letter 31

Fairhaven, Washington
Monday, August 18, 1890

My Darling Anna,

Once more the sun shines and the earth looks bright because the mail brought me a letter this morning. Do you know Anna I am glad to learn that the "old independent spirit" is leaving you. I hope it is. That independent spirit used to worry me a good deal. I don't mean by that that I wouldn't have a woman independent but I thought it was not looking at the matter in quite the right light to consider that a woman is dependent on a man when she married him. In one sense she is of course. He (usually) is the one that provides but on the other hand is he not dependent for comfort and for advice and because it seems to me that man and wife become a complex organism with a division of labor, each dependent on the other.

Another thing Anna, you said in your last letter that you did not think I was a bit jealous. But I have been and of what do you suppose? Why of the school. I have been fearfully jealous of the school at times. Now there's a confession, but you can see it wasn't quite unfounded after all was it since you thought you would rather teach school than have me do things for you. But we're getting to understand things better all the time dear. The matter of living is a small one. It is how we live, and if we can be of mutual help to each other enabling each other to live right – better than we could by ourselves, that is the thing to be looked at.

And I believe firmly that we can. And I'm glad you took it for granted that I am just as much in love and want a home just as badly as Harry Grahn, if not a little more so, and I'm glad that you want to tell me when you change about things. And when you don't change as well. Why are we all in all to each other if not to tell one another what we think? I always think a little more of myself and feel better when I have told you about how I feel about different things. Although I guess you will have found out long ere this that my feelings and thoughts on different things all center about one bright object – yourself.

There is a building association started here and in a month or so if I can possibly afford it I intend to take some stock in it. Then the sooner we begin to talk about our house from a tangible practical standpoint, the better we will understand each other's views and the more complete we will have things without having anything superfluous. That house is beginning to be a very real thing to me, but I want you to understand that it will be the presence of the loving heart of my little sweetheart in it that will make the home more than anything we have. I too have been planning about that house in a material way. I enclose a plan that I was amusing myself with a few days ago. Of course it is a little more elaborate than I could hope to have for a time, but it struck me as a pretty good plan anyway, but the fireplaces are the bright particular ornaments of it. That is an idea I absorbed from Dr. Munson's house in Tacoma. In the hands of a good architect that little plan could be made into a very pretty cottage. But there is one more room to this than in your plan. Let me see yours. My slow mind has hardly got around to the decoration yet that is not in such shape that it could be put into words. I have a confused image in my mind but nothing tangible. But your plan will be all right anyway as I know it will please me why shouldn't it. And why should I be amused over your purchases in Minneapolis. Four pictures, a fruit plate and a cup and saucer are a pretty good start to be acquired in a week or two. Those little things that are picked up here and there are what go to make a place cozy and comfortable.

About my office, I must tell you I am going to move today. I remain in the same building but will have a little more desirable room as to location. The ones I have are down a long hall and a little hard to find and inasmuch as there are three old school doctors in the front of the building who would think they were doing a meritorious action in intercepting a patient. I want my rooms where they can be more readily seen. Otherwise the rooms are about the same except that the inside of the new ones is a little lighter and more desirable from that reason than the ones I occupy at present.

Do you know I have thought that I should like to hear you make something for my office, but didn't like to ask you to, and yet I don't know what I want, any little ornamental thing that will add to the beauty of the rooms.

No, I have no "splashers" and allow me to state Miss Kurtz, that my ignorance is not quite so dense that I didn't know what a "splasher" is. To prove what I say – a splasher is a business made of any material that the maker may see fit to use in the construction of the same. To wit: oil cloth, toweling, canvas, muslin cotton, linen, oiled silk etc. etc., ornamental and decked out in such design as may seem pleasing under the aforesaid maker (or under the recipient of the above-mentioned "splasher") and tacked, nailed screwed or secured into the wall, said spashers being tacked, nailed screwed or secured as above mentioned on the wall immediately back of and foremost a wash bowl and pitcher or other ablutionary apparatus. (Note: I consider "ablutionary" a good word – Ed). Am I not correct my dear? To this just let me add that nothing would delight me more than to have a splasher

Weekly World, 1890. CPNWS.

Mason Building ad. Shown below is the door of Room 34 as it appears in 2009.

made by your beloved hands, and if made I will promise not to "splash" it any more than I can possibly help.

Say Anna you don't know what a lot of trouble you may be getting yourself into by offering to make something for this room. I won't make any very heavy call on your time for the decoration of the office and why? Because I don't want to cause some time that may cause a delay in your getting you own things ready. See? That would never do. Do you know I think we are beginning to get a good deal of pleasure of a discussion of our future affairs and planning for them. So just tell me all you think about in regard to it because you may be sure that nowhere will you find such an interested reader as I will be.

I am very glad (I guess I have had a good many things to be glad over in this letter haven't I?) that you are happy about what I told you about the Church. I thought you would be because though I have said nothing I never forget how deeply interested you are in that subject but it is hard to talk in a letter. I wish I could talk with you. I have not made any decision about the church yet, as to what church I mean. It is a hard question to decide. A man wants to be sure that he can honestly subscribe to all the articles and as for the personnel of the church here that makes it a little more difficult. The Methodist minister is a young man whose intellect and ideas are very crude and not formed as yet – not one that I could in any way feel at home with. The Presbyterian is a rather reserved and distant man – hard to get acquainted with. The man with the broadest views, the most winning and with the greatest amount of understanding of the weaknesses and perplexities of humanity here is the Congregational and his people have about the same comparison with others in the town. Rest assured that I will tell you as soon as I decide, which I don't think will be very long. I must get acquainted with the people first and see where my likings take me.

Now I want to correct an idea you derived from my letter. You said that you felt that it contained something of reproof. I did not intend any. I have never intentionally uttered a word of reproof. I hope I never shall. I tell you what I feel sometimes, but never in the sense or meaning of reproof.

And now that I think of it there may have been something in my last letter that may possibly sound like reproof or complaint. I spend considerable spare time thinking about not having had a letter and since reading your last letter it occurs to me that it may sound reproachful. But it is not dear. I was just simply telling how I felt because it did not come. You understand don't you, Anna?

I was quite amused over Lollie's letter. I knew as soon as I saw the commencement of it, before I read a word further, that she had in some way gotten a hold of one of my letters. I have made this one pretty long now or I would enclose an answer. But I will answer it. I want to thank her for the recommendation she gave you. Really I was quite glad to get it Anna from a third party. That brings us around to the subject of dinners. I want to say

Ruth Crane Looker
Collection

Lollie Crane.

that today I had a dinner that I actually enjoyed at the restaurant too. And it was something that ordinarily I don't like – and you don't either by the way – it was fish – boiled fresh halibut with egg sauce. And right here I want to protest against an insinuation, an insinuation that I may be given to growling about my meals, and giving me a sly warning that there will be a fuss if I do.

Allow me to say that I never "growl" about meals, except those furnished by cheap restaurants and that I claim that the weakest – mildest – most long suffering of men would growl about, and very vigorously at that. Nor will I accept your statement that your dinners will be poorly cooked. That is one place where I must have the privilege of differing with you. I know that your meals will not be poorly cooked and moreover, I think that even granting for the sake of argument that they might be, that I will be enough in love with the cook to be willing to eat anything you may set before me and think it is the nectar and ambrosia of the gods. Now Anna that considering that I am a man, is the greatest profession of love that I ever made. Don't you think so? At any rate I here now pledge myself that I will not growl at the cooking unless it is done by a Scandinavian from Cork who never cooked anything but potatoes and mush.

But stop, a fearful thought came to me! Why did I never think to inquire about it before? Anna tell me, if you love me, that you don't like mush. For that would be cause for divorce at least if you should insist on my eating it. Don't keep me in suspense on that subject. And let me see, you wanted a promise from me. My beard, please your ladyship, is prospering nicely and I have quite a fine professional appearance and I promise that for your sweet sake it shall not come off until I see you again and you pass judgment. I place my beard in your hands and give you power of life and death over it.

What next? I am trying for once to answer a letter to the very end. Oh yes! The climate of Puget Sound agrees with me nicely though I don't think I have gained any flesh as yet. You see I have worried a little from time to time over different affairs and that has kept me down but when things get to going nicely I expect to gain some. Am sorry to hear that you have not gone above a hundred and eleven. I ought to be about one thirty. But if you feel well that is the great thing and I hope you will have no need of the doctor – that is professionally. I hope that you will have need of one doctor. You won't find any cheaper doctor out here than I am. There is a regular scale and all adhere to it – $1.50 for office prescription, $2.50 for visit to home, and $5.00 for night visit. As to the regular rates I did not think of your inquisition about the price of things in my office, but I wanted to assure you that I had not been extravagant. Am glad to be assured that Miss Clark was not the young lady I met. I hardly thought she was, for to tell the truth I thought better of Harry's judgment than that and am glad to have that belief verified. Well I think that I have given a pretty complete answer to your letter this time and I shall await with great impatience your answer to this as I shall look for your views on the house question – write down practical views, you know Anna. Oh, if this practice of "ours" would only hurry up now, we might begin to put out ideas to the test. That's about as large a subject as I know of at present. And I think I expressed some views that I hold quite fully in my last letter. I think of you and it seems to me more and more all the time and I actually don't believe I shall ever feel that I can do my best work until I have you right here with me. Several of the other young doctors were married almost as soon as they graduated. Their wives are here and the doctors are doing better than any others in town. People will employ a married doctor eight times out of ten – there's the hard practical side of it once more.

Well I must say good bye now dear, and don't forget I want those plans of yours. I am in earnest about this – very much so.

Lovingly,
Will

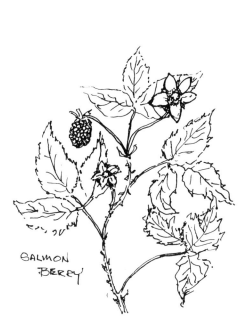

Illustration by Brian Griffin.

Letter 32

"Anniversary"
Fairhaven, Washington
Thursday, Aug. 21, 1890

My Darling Sweetheart,

Two years ago tonight I marched my way to "the stone house on the corner" with fear and trembling and some hope in my heart and there heard the sweetest word that a man ever hears in his life. The end of the two years finds me with much accomplished that I had hoped to do, my college course finished and struggling into a practice in a "far country." The years have but strengthened the affection that I then felt toward you and I know it to be deep and lasting, beyond any power to change. It has become stamped into the very fiber of my being. What a wonderful power it is that can make one person out of the whole universe all in all one to where every thought, every ambition is dedicated. The best that is in me must be brought out by you Anna. Oh, you need have no fear of anything that you expressed in your last letter. You need have no fear that I will not be good to you after we are married, dear. I only wish that I could commence to prove that to you right away.

Courtesy Mount Pleasant, Iowa, Public Library.
"The Stone House on the Corner."

You know I told you once that I used to amuse myself around home by putting on a very cynical air and saying that I should never be so foolish as to fall in love. Well, I fell in deep, deep, so deep that I can never get out and so deep that I never want to get out. I also used to hear myself talk in a very grandiloquent manner about how I was never going to do any work around the house. I would always have it done. I would have a fine cook, a coachman, a valet and I know not what all besides. Of course I was not going to do anything around a house, because I never intended to get married, but would have luxurious bachelor apartments, or if I did get married it would be a pure calculation and the lady should be wealthy – there would be no such mythical thing as love about it – poor foolish thing wasn't I?

Then I went to work and fell desperately in love with the sweetest girl in town – and was very happy in doing it and obtained a great deal more pleasure out of planning for a very humble little house than out of my luxurious fancies for I felt that the one could be a reality and the other but talk. I want you to be happy Anna, that will be my study. Say Anna, if you are really in earnest about that school business

– the private school you know, why all right. I want you to understand that I don't believe in a woman giving up everything that her ambition cherishes when she marries just to please a whim and the selfishness of her husband. As I cannot assure you too often, I want you to be happy and if it would give you pleasure to take a few pupils why all right, if it doesn't interfere with the house life. And you will find that I will work for you dear. Never fear on that score, and be glad to do it.

Say, Anna, since you have been thinking along such a practical line, there never will be a better time for a private school than right now in this place. The public school opened this week and is utterly incapable of accommodating the children. They have adopted the plan of having part of the children attend in the forenoon and part in the afternoon and that isn't sufficient. When the present school building was built, it was thought to be two or three years ahead of the town, but the growth of the place has been so rapid that it is far too small. So I think you would have a regular picnic with a private school. It's kind of hard luck though for a man to have a school for a rival. Don't you think so yourself now, if you just consider it for a moment. Say, I'll be with you on the garden scheme, Anna. A garden is a pretty nice thing to have in the family.

Fairhaven Illustrated 1890. Whatcom Museum.
The 14th Street School, on the northeast corner of 14th Street and Douglas Avenue, present site of Lowell School.

Well my office is beginning to look pretty well. My books and carpet came a day or two ago and I put the carpet down yesterday. I tell you it was a great job and I feel pretty sore today. It is an old carpet and has lost much of its early strength of character. Mother instructed me to stretch it tight but I had to consult the carpet on that matter. A very little pull and ... zip! ... there was a tear a foot or more in length. But with some care and a good deal of patching it was finally put down and it looks quite respectable. Am going to have one of my patients make me a book case. He is a carpenter, very hard up and it is probable that it is the only way I will ever get anything out of him and the bookcase will do me as well as the money as I will have to get one made anyway. As soon as I get my bookcase and get a table and few chairs for my reception room I will be fixed for a while at least. But some way the patients don't increase. Only made fifty cents yesterday, nothing so far today. The whole week has been very light. Was figuring up this morning and find that my business thus far has amounted to forty-two dollars with two days more to complete the first month. Well I suppose that is not doing so badly but it seems very slow. I guess that I am very impatient. Another doctor has come to town (old school) and has taken the rooms that I had, so that there are five of us in the same building. There is a drug store downstairs and there are four law firms on this floor. If there were just an undertaker in this building everything would be quite dandy.

Big pardon for that villainous joke.

Found some pansies in the fruit store this morning and bought a dozen of them, a few of which I send. It's a small thing in honor of a great occasion but perhaps you will give them a place in our collection. Am very sorry that I can't send a nice fresh bunch of flowers, but the distance prohibits. I have been wishing especially all day to see you and will wish it still more tonight if that is possible. I long to see you sometimes so that it seems that I can't stand it any longer and it is always worse at some of these times that are especially rich in memories. (I stopped there to prescribe for a Norwegian that could hardly tell his symptoms and about all I could get out of him was "I feel so sick.")

One year more of this is about all I can stand, Anna. If you could only realize how fearfully lonely I get and could realize how lonely I have been all my life. You would agree with me that it would better end in our marriage as soon as in the least practicable. I expect you to think that I have been talking about this a good deal lately but it is the thing nearest my heart and so will seek utterance.

You don't know how impatiently I shall await the arrival of your letter telling me of your plans about our home. And you know there will be good practical reasons for my knowing sometime ahead what your views are and how you want things. A woman generally dreams more about such things than a man – at least I know that you know more than I do about it. I could define perhaps many of the things that I should want in a house but as to arrangements for convenience I know very little about it. Then by knowing where someone intends erecting a small house to rent, it might be arranged just to suit.

Whenever I think of that home, and especially of the one who is to share it with me and make it lovely by her presence I get quite excited. It is in my mind all the time. Shortly expressed it is; I want Anna; I need her, and want her now. I don't make it harder for you do I dear by dwelling on this so often. I don't want to but I want to keep the fact impressed on your mind that you are necessary to my happiness. Now that is the selfish side of it isn't Anna. But I will be so good to you, my darling. I will keep away all trouble and pain and labor from you that it is within my power to do and watch over you with such loving care when once you have placed your happiness in my keeping. And now before I close I want to review the vows of two years ago. I love you Anna with my whole soul, and will be a good husband to you and care for you and minister to you all the days of your life, and dear it will be a proud day for me when I can promise in the presence of witnesses to "love you and care for you and keep you in sickness and in health."

Good bye, my darling.
Yours devotedly, Will

Letter 33

Fairhaven, Washington
Sunday, August 24, 1890

My Darling Sweetheart,

Your letters continue to come and bring joy to a lonely man. Had another from you yesterday on the small sized paper for which you apologized – something that was entirely unnecessary since anything that passed through your hands is rendered precious from that simple fact.

A letter from Ed Scott came in the same mail in which he said he had been to see you twice in one day. He said that he had a delightful time and obtained a good deal of information. Also that you did not find out all you wanted to know and therefore he supposed that you did not have as delightful a time as he had. Also he informed me that you were looking well – which of course is always welcome news, whomever it comes from.

Ed confessed that he wanted to talk. He is much interested in this country and I expect that when he gets through with his law course will come out here somewhere. Of course I shall try to get him to locate in Bellingham Bay. As an inducement I have offered to give him all my legal business – the collection of bad debts etc. I wrote to him today and rather broadly hinted to him that I thought that it was about time that he told me whether there were anything to the rumors that were being circulated in regard to him and a certain young lady. I said a "very nice young lady."

Fairhaven continues to improve. New buildings going up every day. Two fine brick and stone residences each to cost about $10,000 have been commenced within the past week. The railroad continues to go ahead. Of course we are all interested in that railroad because it is to make this town a large city. The northern branch which is now being pushed will be the first connection with a transcontinental line and means much for the place. It means that by a traffic arrangement with the Canadian Pacific that the Great Northern can send passengers and freight direct from St. Paul to Fairhaven until its own main line is completed and thus it can compete at once with the Northern Pacific to Tacoma and Seattle.

The practice I suppose improves a little, though it seems very slow. It will be the end of the month soon and then I will send you a statement of the month's business. I have a patient on hand now that is exercising all my knowledge as to a diagnosis. It is a German woman about fifty years of age who is down with a fever that seems to be typhoid, though it is a little too early to say yet but the puzzling part is pain in the stomach which I am afraid is caused by cancer of the stomach. If so, the fever probably arises from that which means that it is nearing the last stage, and in that case of course there is nothing to be done. I have succeeded in reducing the fever and subduing the pain to some extent, but cannot tell whether the improvement will continue. Am making two visits a day. Including tonight's call today's practice will amount to six dollars. It seems as if I get more calls on Sunday than any other day. Had a call just as I was going to church this morning which kept me from going. That seems to be a doctor's fate to be called just when he is going some place, even if he has not had a call any other time during the day. I have not had my slumber disturbed as yet however for which I am very thankful, although a few night calls at $5.00 each would help out the month's receipts considerably.

I hope that mother and you will not begin to misunderstand one another. Mother is not very demonstrative, in fact, we have accused her sometimes of being too dignified for anyone and I think besides that she has had an idea that you felt rather sensitive and diffident about going to see her or talking with her very much in company for fear that it would be talked about and so has wanted to respect that feeling on your part. But you need not fear that she disapproves of you, because that would be a great mistake. I know that sometimes she appears rather cool and indifferent just when she feels the opposite – a trait which I guess I have inherited. But you need not fear that she does not or will not like you. The fact is, you have neither of you seen enough of each other to thoroughly understand the other's character.

I will send you a paper tomorrow which contains something that may interest you. Last week six young fellows among whom was Clint Howard, took a trip to Victoria in a small yacht. They had a little rough weather outside and Clint was pretty badly frightened, I guess. The paper contains a humorous account of the trip which you may get a little fun out of.

Say, Anna, I really think that I shall have to drop a line to Ada Sharpless and tell her to keep an eye on Will Stutsman. I never got even you know for the good time that you and W. S. had at Bluff Park last year. I am afraid that my opportunity has been lost forever and think I shall have to write to Jessie too and find out what it is she has to tell me. I would like to keep informed of all these little things. I did not quite understand from your letters whether the things she had to tell were uncomplimentary to you or to me, which is it? After having Lollie's letter though I fear that it must be me. If it is, tell Jessie to draw it as wild as possible. Say, Anna we will have a good deal of visiting to do when we come West. There is Mrs. Bassett, Aunt Rosie says of course we will have to stop at Minnewaukan and **Aunt Jennie** insists that we will have to go to Victoria. They say that Victoria is a beautiful place. I hope to get over there in a month or so for a few days. What a trip that will be anyway – our wedding trip I mean. Well I must stop and get this in the post now.

Good bye dear.
Lovingly, Will

>〜◎〜

Letter 34

Fairhaven, Washington
Friday, August 29, 1890

My Darling Sweetheart,

I have just finished reading your anniversary letter and still continue to admire the souvenir. Looking at the latter I have been thinking that it was a kind of a mean trick to outdo me that way. But then that's the way a woman generally gets the better of a man. You see the man like the great awkward animal that we are usually just takes the plainest roughest way of doing a thing – for instance I send a few pansies put loosely into a letter and what do I receive? Why a lovely little souvenir that has all the gracefulness and beauty that a woman always casts about a thing. That's just the difference every time. But therein it always delights the man to have it that way. And didn't I enjoy your dainty letters – the back, the writing, the contents, in fact everything about it. How experience does change a man's views of things.

A few years ago when I was ignorant of how a man touched by cupid's arrows felt about things. I used to smile at the idea of the "old story that never grows old." It was at the latter part that I used to smile the most. It seemed that like every other pleasure it must grow old sometime. But I didn't know much then and I didn't know you. How different the reality however. Now it seems always new, always bright and sweet and never grows old and I realize more and more how little I knew in the days gone by. And so you think it will be a long time before we can make a definite plan of the future? Say, just wait until I send you my report for my first month and I'll astonish you. I am going to astonish myself. I want you to know my dear that my business in one year from now is going to be not less than $2,500 a year and I believe will be $3,000. That sounds rather sanguine doesn't it? But this town is going to astonish the nation in another year and my prosperity is going to increase with that of the town. And I want a little wife to make the earth bright and I am going to keep right on hoping that we can be united as soon as I have said before. As I see it, it might not be any other way. We will get along better and be happier together and I know that we could manage all right. Why according to your Aunt Carrie's theory, just think how necessary you are to me as an advertising medium. There's another practical remark!) Oh, I'll surprise you with some more of these from time to time.

And now what did I mean by "duds"? Well what is ordinarily meant by duds? Clothes, of course, wedding finery, white dressing sacques etc. etc. The thousand and one things that a lady always thinks she must have and which of course a man knows nothing about. As to my knowledge of the word, I think I am indebted to Mrs. Lulu Ambler Officer, through Miss Anna Kurtz. Now you know or if you don't know, I will disclose it unto you that manlike, I cannot see the necessity for any delay on account of those things. Maybe that is a peculiarly mannish idea, but of course being a man, I could scarcely be expected to hold any other. And I shall repeat a statement made formerly, that in these months I shall know definitely enough as to my business success to ask you to set some day within a certain prescribed time for our marriage. Then if there is any good reason why in your account it should be delayed we will discuss that fairly. The first of December A.D. eighteen hundred and ninety I shall submit that question to you, in the meantime keeping you informed as to the increase in my practice so that you may understand that part of it as well as I do. I think by that time we ought to set a definite time, whatever that may be and then we can labor to that end. We could get along very soon, dear. I look around me and see so many young people doing so nicely and in fact, accomplishing so much more than they could otherwise that I long to join their ranks. In a new country the young married folks are the people.

In a former letter you said that we all seemed to be greatly interested in that railroad. Of course we are because that railroad is to make this town a very large city. While you were in St. Paul and Minneapolis you perhaps heard something of the Great Northern or Manitoba Railroad. When it is built to the coast it will be one of the greatest railroads in the United States, and Fairhaven is its western terminus. The Great Northern will build up Fairhaven as the Union and Southern Pacific built up San Francisco – as the Northern Pacific built up Tacoma and Seattle. It is generally conceded that in the next five years no town on Puget Sound will make such strides as Fairhaven. Her population has increased about one thousand since the census was taken, that was in June. If that isn't growth, I don't know what growth is.

Oh, if I stay here about two months longer I will be as good a Boomer as there is in the country. This is the country. Det Bird, Hugh Templin and Ross Sullivan have just returned from a few days outing on Orcas Island, one of the fruit islands of the Sound[29] and they brought back specimens of fruit the likes of which I never saw before, apples, peaches, pears and plums. They brought a small twig of a plum tree only about a foot long which held thirty nine egg plums and which weighs something over five pounds. The plums are so thick that they almost hide the branch. And in Whatcom I saw trees that were propped up all around to keep the fruit from breaking them down.

Today, Sehome and Fairhaven hold a joint meeting by representatives with reference to consolidation. It is not known whether Whatcom will be represented or not. When it was talked of some little time ago she would not send a committee or have anything to do with anything with which Fairhaven is connected owing to her jealousy of the latter place. The mossbacks over there can't see that instead of Fairhaven being an injury to Whatcom, it has been of positive benefit because all the growth here on the bay has been caused by Fairhaven money and enterprise. Some time ago Whatcom tried to entrap Sehome into consolidation with herself leaving Fairhaven out. By doing that she would have had a majority of the votes and so could have shut Fairhaven out on a future vote. But Sehome voted against it and Whatcom blames Fairhaven (perhaps not without reason) for her defeat. Just after that election, the present movement for the consolidation of the entire

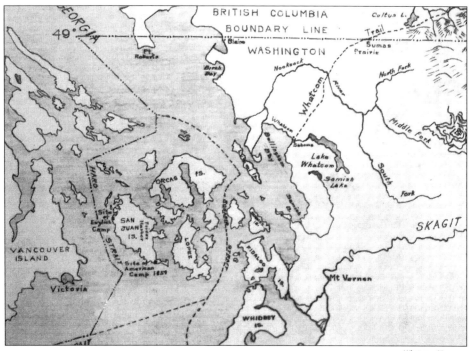

Whatcom Museum.

Sketch by Lelah Jackson Edson based on an Immigrant Aid Society map of 1880, before Fairhaven and Bellingham were platted. Orcas Island in center.

bay was inaugurated and Whatcom chooses to stay out. If she does, she is a goner. Fairhaven and Sehome will unite without her, under the name of Fairhaven making a population of over 8,000. The territory of Sehome almost surrounds Whatcom so that with Sehome and Fairhaven united, the latter could grow right around Whatcom. In the future in self interest Whatcom would be forced to unite with Fairhaven on any terms the latter might dictate, which of course would be that she should come in under the name of Fairhaven.

If she chooses to come in now, probably a compromise would be made in the name which would probably be Bellingham, so Whatcom will only be "cutting off her nose to spite her face" if she refuses this consolidation. Sehome has nothing to lose in name as some time ago she changed to corporate name from Sehome to New Whatcom and has not had the latter name long enough to lose anything by changing it. While she will gain by taking that of Fairhaven, as the latter has been so extensively advertised. The final outcome will probably be that Fairhaven, the youngest town in the Bay will absorb all the others. She has already taken Bellingham, next will be Sehome and Whatcom last. If Whatcom wants to save herself from taking the hated name of Fairhaven, she would better consolidate now because there is no doubt but Sehome will vote to unite with Fairhaven. Well this is a good deal of Fairhaven for one time isn't it?

Say Anna, you couldn't have made a better agreement with mother than the one you did. Just keep on and I know you can bring her around. If you can once

Alice Long Taylor, "Aunt Alice."

convince her that it would please you to have her live with us I think she would consent. Her theory has always been that an elder woman in the house is always a source of unpleasantness to the younger one. That is the point to attack. I agree with you that she has had her share of taking care of people. If **Aunt Alice** is going to need taking care of, it is Will Taylor's duty to do it. Let him look after his mother. I will take care of mine. Mother has had enough of it. Much as I like Aunt Alice and bright as she is, I don't want mother and her to live together as it would be a one sided affair. In the past, without going into any particulars, I will say that much of the expense and all the work of keeping up that large house has fallen on mother. I say nothing but truth when I say that Aunt Alice has had the advantage and comfort of a large establishment together with no work at less cost than it would have taken her to board in one small room, on very plain board and I don't want mother to be subjected to such arrangement for the future. So I think Will Taylor would better take care of his mothe.

I don't know whether you know how mother has been rewarded for all her care of grandmother or not. I presume mother wouldn't say anything about it, but grandfather died in England in June and left all he had to Aunt Rose and Aunt Jennie, leaving mother and Aunt Alice out. It must have been a pure caprice on the part of the old man. But at any rate, that is the way it stands. It is doubtful however if anyone ever gets any of it as each legatee would have to apply in person under the law of England and I don't believe that either Aunt Jennie or Aunt Rose would cross the ocean for the whole of England. Mother and Aunt Alice got most of the courage that was going around in the family.

By the way, you wanted to know how Rena Howard liked the country. I asked her that question and she said yes, and no. She likes the climate and the beauty and picturesqueness of the country but she doesn't like the newness and crudity and doesn't like the almost universal atmosphere of money getting and real estate. I think she misses the interest in literary pursuits that is so prevalent in Mt. Pleasant and yet, she says that nothing could induce her go back to Mt. Pleasant to live. There is not enough of the intellectual to suit her here. She says that even in the pulpit there are no brainy men here. Well that is in a measure true. But that is more true of Seattle than it is of Tacoma. While Seattle is perhaps a little the larger place, there are more brainy men and women and a greater degree of culture and refinement in Tacoma. Rena says it was very noticeable just during the short time she was visiting in Tacoma. I quite enjoyed my call on her. Can you imagine why? Because she talked a great deal about you. Like everyone else she just simply assumed as a matter of fact that I heard from you, knew all about you etc. and just *candidly talked as if I did too so that without any confidences we understood each other pretty well. I find that Rena understands you pretty well and so you may readily understand that I enjoyed the talk because it was the first opportunity I've had since I left home to talk with anyone about you and it was right good to be able to do so. It is a great comfort sometimes.*

I will have a good idea of work and study cut out for me for a week or so one of my cases. It is so obscure that it will probably take considerable research. There are two days more in the month so that in my next letter I will give the result of my first month practice and as I say prepare to be astonished – not very greatly. Don't get your excitement so high that my news will fall flat –but we're coming along. Anna we're coming along.

You may be sure that I will keep that letter. That was a pretty nice letter and certainly it was on unique material. And besides the fact that it was written on our first anniversary makes it doubly precious. We will keep that anniversary regularly.

Well I have made this pretty long already, so will close and permit you to rest which you will be ready to do by the time you reach this place.

Goodbye sweetheart. I am awaiting those plans of yours.

Yours lovingly,

Will

Letter 35

Fairhaven, Washington
Sunday, Aug. 31, 1890

My Darling Sweetheart,

This is the last day of the month and it is the last day of my first month of prac-
tice and it is a month of some experiences, notwithstanding that my cases have not
been many. But they have been numerous enough to prove to me that it is going to
take a constant study and a good deal of courage to practice medicine and also em-
phasizes the fact that I have pretty nearly everything to learn yet. Sometimes cas-
es don't run the same course and present the same series of symptoms that are set
down for them in the books, or proclaimed from the lecturer's desk.

But before going ahead to enlarge on the experiences of the month I must tell
you what my first month's business is, for I am going to be conceited enough to
think that you are as anxious to know as I am to tell you and that is pretty consid-
erable. There is really one day more than a month as I commenced on the 31st and
want to get straightened out, so that my business will run from the 1st. The sum to-
tal, including a call to be made yet tonight is $101.25, $43 of which has been done
during the past week. Isn't that somewhat better than you expected? I wrote to Ed
Scott last week and told him that I expected the month to run a little over sixty, but
had no idea that it would touch the one hundred mark.

Another little fact, or coincidence. The first twelve days practice was $12, the
last day's practice was $12. If I should average that for the rest of the year it would
go above $4,000. Don't you think that would do for two people to start life on in a
humble way – in five rooms?

I have three quite important cases on hand, one of which I am quite worried
about as I am a little afraid that he is not going to recover. Was called early yes-
terday morning to see a young man suffering agonies from extensive inflammation
in the abdomen. It was so excruciating that nothing short of morphine would qui-
et it. The serious part of the case is that he had a severe attack of the same disease
about three months ago from which he was never fully recovered. The physician
who treated him told him that if he ever had another attack it would kill him. The
effect of such unwise information is that it renders the patient very despondent and
of course decreases his vitality and resistance just that much.

***Later** – I feel encouraged. Patient seems to be doing well. Has made consider-*
able improvement since morning. Another case is remittent fever – which seems to
be taking a tendency toward typhoid. Here too I have had a little new experience.
The patient is a comparatively young married woman who has never been sick in
her life and while her case is not at all serious – seeming to run a mild course, it is
tedious. Yesterday some of the neighbors had been in and one had told her one thing
and one another and one or two had said that doctor was no good or he would have
had her up before this until the woman became quite dissatisfied and wanted to
call in another doctor in consultation, or get someone else to take the case.

The husband came to me and told how the matter stood, said he was perfectly satisfied but thought he would better accede to his wife's wishes so that in case she did not get well, he would not have anything to reproach himself for. I said all right. I was wishing to have Dr. Heacock (the one they wanted called in consultation) but that the case was not critical and that the Dr. would probably charge a good stiff consultation fee. Well he said we'd better see

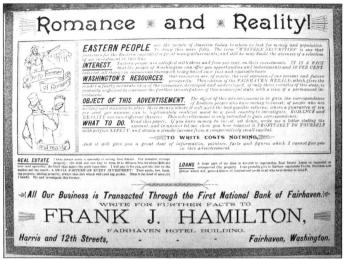

Fairhaven Herald, December 29, 1890. CPNWS.

Mr. Hamilton was one of the real estate men who helped to "boom" Fairhaven.

Dr. Heacock and find out what his fee would be. Went up to the Dr.'s house and couldn't find him. Then he concluded that I'd better go and see his wife again alone anyway. So went over and every thing was all satisfactory. But I don't know how long that will be.

The third case just saw today for the first time and while of course from the point of view of doctor and patient I am equally entrusted in all three. This last is of the most importance for my future success. It is a little boy (another case of fever) in one of the nicest families in town where it will do me lots of good socially and professionally. I have quite a responsible place to fill, owing to the fact that I get this case through Dr. Munson of Tacoma. (I think my three or four weeks in Tacoma did us some good if I was doing nothing but spend money.) The father of the boy and his wife were down to Tacoma a few days ago and were guests of Dr. Munson. During their visit the Dr. took occasion to recommend me very highly to Mr. and Mrs. Hamilton. (I give you their names so that you may remember them as you may know them sometime. Mrs. Hamilton is a lovely lady.) In fact I judge from what they told me and from the way (they) treated me that the Dr. laid it on pretty thick and now the question is to come up to the standard of the reputation he gave me.

I think my cases are all that keep me from being vain after the success I have had in making intelligent people believe that I know something. But when I come into the sick room all the conceit is knocked clear out of me by the fact that here is something that I am not certain about and my inexperience and liability to error stare me in the face and make me severely conscious of my own ignorance.

I played a policy act a few days ago. Subscribed ten dollars toward the erection of a Scandinavian Lutheran Church, and you should see the deferential bow that the pastor gave me when I met him in the street. He can do me some good among the members of his flock. There, you see, is a cold blooded calculation. Did you *believe that of me? Well, this is a pretty good dissertation – on my practices and I expect that you have had about enough for once. But I thought that perhaps you might be interested and of course now at the close of my first month my mind is naturally kind of full of it. I feel quite encouraged and from a financial standpoint think I have a right to be as it is so far beyond my expectation. But I never wanted to have some ready money so badly as I have this week. Dr. Heacock wants me to go in with him and establish a homeopathic hospital. It would be one of the most paying things that we could get into, as the hospital receipts would make quite a profit to say nothing of the prominence such an enterprise would give those engaged in it. Dr. Heacock would want me to do most of the surgical work and he the medical which would satisfy me as I should like the experience. But, alas 'tis but a dream. The Dr. would want me to "put up" half the money.*

I have another old story to tell – wonder if I dare mention "of it." It simply is that I'm mighty lonesome. I don't like this lonely life a little bit. While today has been the busiest day I have had, it has also been just about as lonesome as any I have put in. I suppose you know my dear that my loneliness is for one person. It's about time for a letter again and I'll not know what to do now until I get one. I am looking for one tomorrow morning. Think it is about time for the letter with your domestic plans enclosed. Guess the quickest way to get it is to wait oblivious in sleep so as to bring the morrow all the sooner, so think I will say good night sweetheart.

Monday morning *– Well, feel all upside down this morning. Having had a little experience that a physician has to meet with quite often, but it's my first and it goes hard. Yesterday afternoon the case of remittent fever that I spoke took a turn toward typhoid. I told the lady's husband that it seem to be taking that turn. Left the remedies necessary and left. It was pretty soon clearly define typhoid so last night they called in an allopathic physician, who pronounced it typhoid and said it had been from the start. Of course it was safe for him to say that and throw suspicion on my diagnosis of the case. While of course this is something that will probably happen again and again in practice. Yet I must confess that the first time comes with a sense of shock. If I had been retained and the typhoid symptoms continued to grow more serious and the case should grow critical I would not mind being discharged. I should think then that I had better study harder, but to be superseded by another physician just at a junction where there was no danger and when I stood just as good a chance to pull the patient through as another why I feel a little as if I had hardly had a fair show. Because as I look back over the case I feel that I have made no errors and that the present turn could not have been avoided.*

However the case may turn out now it will be to my disadvantage if she recovers it will be through the skill of the second man. If not why the other man will say that if he had been called at the start everything might have been all right. Well, I suppose I must reconcile myself to a hard cold fact that I will meet again and again. But what do you suppose my first impulse was after I had been informed that another physician had been called? Not exactly an impulse – that doesn't express it, it was a longing for you to be right here, so that I could go to you and forget my disappointment. *You can't realize how that longing came over me as the first thing that would make it easier. Does that give you an inkling of what you are to me and what you will be in the future? A solace and comfort in time of trial and discouragement as I hope to be the same to you. So you see I need you, really need you now in these early days. I expect you will think that this letter is my well mixed intermingled elation and discouragement.*

Mr. Hamilton's boy is better this morning so hope that everything is going well in that direction. I suppose there is no loss without some small gain. I was paid in full this morning for my services up to day for my "lost" case and as I was in need of money to meet bills for the current month, it came in quite handy. Then though I couldn't go to you, you came to me by letter. Your plan for a room suits me to a T. Of course I like yellow and I can't conceive of anything nicer for a room or more artistic. It meets my approval exactly, so go ahead with your little "fixings" and as to painting the furniture, I'd like to get a bucket of white paint – a few tubes of gold paint and start in right now – if you were here to watch me. That's where the fun would come in. But say Anna, you won't be too dictatorial while you are watching me do it will you? I tell you Anna, I think we will agree beautifully on the question of household decoration. And what a paradise I will think myself in when I get where I can sit down to a pretty table and have a pretty wife to preside over it. You ask me if I would like to entertain company. Why my dear, that's been one of my dreams, to be in a position when I could occasionally entertain a few good friends. I don't want a large circle but I do want a few good ones and nothing will be too good for them. There again we are one. By the way, I wonder if I made it emphatic enough that I liked the plan for the room. I just want to add something to it for your approval. How would it go to have in addition to a colored rug or two a couple of good sized white fur rugs? And for a dash of deeper color to bring out the delicacy of the yellow here and there a little royal purple. How's that. Then of course a little red would be wanted to give an appearance of warmth. Say, about that plan of mine, let me suggest some changes. Say knock out the fireplace in the bedrooms, leaving one in dining room and sitting room and put closets between the two rooms so that each bedroom will have a closet. Then have a very large arch between the back bedroom and dining room, so that ordinarily it can be left open thus giving abundance of light from each end. With a combined book case and folding bed in back room it can be used commonly for a library and on occasion for bedroom. Now, isn't that a practical arrangement. Now the entry can be large enough so that in the absence of a stairway, it will do very well giving room for nice hat and umbrella rack, a leather curved settee and a chair or two.

How do the alterations strike you? Say Anna, this is a lot of fun. But by the way I have quite a scheme. There has recently been organized here a Building and Savings Association. I think I shall join it in about two or three months – just as soon as financial affairs are a little less strained. The shares are $100 each. They are issued to members, as many shares as they want for which they pay 5 cents a month on each share or as much more on each share as we may want to until the stock is *paid for. If any member wants to put up a house coming within the amount of stock held by the member, the association builds the house, the owners of the house simply paying the regular monthly account on his stock. When the full amount is paid he gets full title to the house and his stock is cancelled in payment. By this means a man can live in a home, paying per month less than it would cost in rent and at the end of a certain length of time the building would become his. For instance suppose I take ten shares, $1,000, paying therefore $5.00 per month until the shares are matured. After a time I wish to build a home costing $1,000. The association puts up the building and I take possession still continuing to pay the $5.00 per month and 8 percent interest per annum on the cost of the house. During this time until my house is paid for I am entitled to whatever dividends there may be from loans made by the association which are applied in payment of my stock. When my stock is all paid for the association takes possession of it and I come in full possession of the house. In this way for five dollars a month I become the owner of a house which I have had the use of all the time by practically paying a very cheap rent and besides having the house built the way I want it. Every member has one vote for each $100 worth of stock and is thereby a controlling factor in the arrangement of the company. It is a sort of mutual aid association for the purpose of enabling men to build houses.*

Well, I've spun this out to some length. I wish I could have been with you at the picnic to have made the number even. But then that's nothing new for I wish to be with you on every occasion. In fact I wish that oftener and oftener and you just hit my case exactly when you say that sometimes two letters a week seem like no letters at all. But say, Anna you hit me rather hard in this last letter. You say "I intended writing Sunday but … I was so disappointed at having a letter from you that I felt decidedly blue." Do my letters have such an effect as that? But my inordinate egotism came into play there again and I concluded that you meant the word "not" in there somewhere but that your mind was working faster than your pen and that little word was dropped out. Am I too egotistic in my construction dear? Every once in a while you drop a word out that way and I complacently go ahead and put the construction that my love and faith deems the right one.

Do you know Anna that I count more and more and almost certainly on your being with me next year. I feel more and more and more that another year without you would be another year out of life unnecessarily. We need to be together to strengthen each other. Well guess I'd better quit or you'll be so prostrated that you can't commence school. But I wish you were here Anna. I would feel then that if I failed to inspire confidence in anyone I could go home and meet one who would believe in me and in her love forget all the troubles of the outside world. Hasten the day when that can be!

Goodbye dear.

Lovingly, Will

Letter 36

Fairhaven, Washington
Wednesday, September 3, 1890

My Darling Sweetheart,

That title seems to me to gain more and more significance as the days and months glide by and to become dearer and dearer day by day and will continue to do so until I can change it for a still dearer title.

I believe I am in the mood tonight to write a veritable love letter. Why? Well, because for one thing I haven't written one for quite a while and am about ready to overflow again.

And so tonight – I just feel full of you – so full that there is room for nothing else, and so I reach out to you in spirit tonight with infinite love and tenderness across the geographical gulf that separates. But that physical gulf is all. Someway, Anna, I feel that not withstanding the distance that separates us we are growing more and more together, more at oneness with each other. It seems to me that in your letters we are all the time growing into greater accord and unison I wonder if there is anything of the same nature in mine, or if they present themselves to you in that light. I want to put myself into my letters, but I suppose that the cold words fail to keep me there.

I ran across two or three little things today in the September "Century" that just struck me as very beautiful.[30] *One of them is the description of the perfect love between Baron and Lady Kelder, in their old age, in Amelia Barr's beautiful story "Friend Olivia." Another touch of the same kind was given by Joseph Jefferson in his auto-biography where he tells about the visit made to him in Linden by the Rev. Joseph Jefferson. The third touch is in the "Bric-a-brac" department and is so short I quote:*

> *"I wish you sweet dreams she said on the stair,*
> *As he gently bade his good-night.*
> *Thanks for permission to dream of you dear*
> *He replied as she vanished from sight."*

Those three little things are worth all there is in the whole number, and is especially worth the very unsatisfactory ending of Harry James's story "The Anglomaniacs." But that has nothing to do with my being lonely and missing you has it? Do you know I think I can tell why I have enjoyed your letters so much lately? It is because they have made me feel quite hopeful that we will not have to be lonely quite as long as we had decided probable. Now what do you think of the conceit expressed or at least implied in that "we." Isn't it somewhat colossal? But you see in these days my belief in your love makes me capable of almost anything.

I want to thank you very much dear for that splasher, and you may be sure that I prize it very much. How could I help it? Every stitch in the embroidery is dear to me because your fingers have touched them. And I believe I like it better because it was originally intended for your own room than if you had made it especially for me. But it is almost too pretty to put up in a doctor's office. However I happen to know your views on such gifts – and will put it to the use intended even if I would rather put it away and keep it.

This has been a gala day in Fairhaven. The Washington Press Association meets here for three days[31] and the city is doing her best to entertain them, for the people know that it will mean a great amount of good advertising for the town. The buildings are hung with bunting and flags. The main streets have been lined with evergreens and a huge arch constructed of evergreen with coal, iron and timber, Fairhaven's three great resources, used for decoration purposes. There are several boards that would make eastern people open their eyes. They are two inches thick, fifty-two feet long and four feet wide. How is that for a plank?

A band and orchestra from Tacoma are in attendance. Tomorrow night a grand ball will be given at the Hotel Fairhaven[32] which was opened today for the first time. I am fortunate enough to have an invitation and think I will go up for a little while simply to get acquainted with a few people, but not to dance. You know I have given that up.

My patients are coming along very well. My severe case of inflammation is convalescent, I think. I feel quite proud of him because it was a very serious case. I think it will do me some good. Have another case of typhoid on my hands now. There is a regular epidemic of that here now.[33] My business for the first three days of this month amounts to twenty-eight dollars. About the end of this month Dr. Heacock expects to be gone to Kansas for about two months and will turn all his practice over to me. As his practice is larger than mine, it will keep me pretty busy for awhile. It will also give me an opportunity to get acquainted with a larger circle and that of course means more business. A very little more would keep me quite busy as I have to study my cases quite closely.

I haven't come across that married lady yet that I expect to make a confidential friend. Maybe I will meet her tomorrow night at the ball. Think I will have to keep an eye open for her. But about the young lady that you so kindly give me permission to call on, I don't know. There are a great many very pretty young ladies here but they are mostly girls – young girls, you know – buds. I am although too "grave, dignified and serious minded" to please them and of course that would be necessary. I don't want to be a hermit but after all it's hard to be anything else. A man has to be one of two things here to cut any figure. He must either be a gay young fellow in for all kinds of fun, or he must be a young married man – and inasmuch as I don't fit that bill either way, why "I'm not in it." But let that pass. I suppose that your play day is about over and that the little Willowbank tyrants will soon be holding high revel.[34] Take it as easy as you can Anna. I hate to have you start in there again with the long walks through bad weather. But I suppose it can't be helped. I wish that about next month I was going after you to bring you out here, instead of your starting in to teach in the public school for another year.

Whatcom Museum.

The Washington Press Association Arch, in this view looking west on Harris Avenue. The Mason Block is on the left, Fairhaven Hotel on the right. Note the wooden street and sidewalk planking.

Just as soon as I think of what I want in the decorative line, I'll let you know. I'll have to get some more furniture first, I think. My "reception room" has nothing in it yet but the carpet so in a little time will have to get a table and some chairs and then I presume will want a table cover. What do you think of that? But come to reflect, don't believe I'll tell you what I want on it – will take time from what you want to do for yourself during the year and that won't do, you know.

Say Anna, I believe I am acquiring quite a faculty for writing long letters. Do you think I can stand it right along? Next time I'll tell you about the ball. Am going in style. Think I'll dress up to the extent of a new fifteen cent bow tie.

Must stop now.

Good bye dear.

Yours Lovingly,

Will

Letter 37

Fairhaven, Washington
Sunday, September 7, 1890

My Darling Anna,

Here we are again, right side up with care, as usual, but still rather lonesome. I suppose on the theory that a man always feels good when he has had a good dinner, I should be in quite a serene and complacent frame of mind for I have just partaken of the best dinner I have had since I have been in Fairhaven. Half of a broiled chicken on toast with some mashed potatoes and stewed corn preceded by a bowl of oxtail soup and followed up by a piece of plum pie and all quite well cooked for a wonder and made a very acceptable dinner. But someway that isn't what I want. I feel alone all the time and that isn't comfortable.

Well, I went to the ball, but didn't find my confidante. When I say that I went to the ball I mean that I went over for a little while and stood around and watched them dance. It was quite a brilliant affair. The music was furnished by the Tacoma theatre orchestra of eleven pieces and was very good. But such a jam! There were about two hundred couples to say nothing of the young fellows like myself who were not "coupled." There was hardly room to get around on the floor and the quadrille sets were decidedly cramped for room.

About one-third of the gentlemen were in evening dress, while others were dressed – so so. Some of the ladies were beautiful, some were plain, while some were – I forbear to say. Some were beautifully dressed, some tastefully while with others gorgeousness seemed to have been the main object. Some were gray haired ladies while others were mere children, all hair and stockings. There were a great many young girls, and many young married ladies. There were fat women with puffed dresses and sleeves and there were three women with no sleeves at all. Some were dressed as primly as Quaker maidens, while others were décolleté as far as the law would allow. In fact it was quite a mixture, and yet taking it all in all, it was about as nice a crowd as you will often see. It was a little too large however for me to make any effort to get acquainted so I contented myself with watching the kaleidoscopic multitude for a time and then went back to the office. I don't like large crowds.

Well, business increases a little and I do some worrying over my patients. Have two cases of fever on hand now that I don't know what the outcome will be. My case of inflammation is all right – up and around town in just one week from the time he was taken. I had a conversation with him as to the cause of his former attack and after questioning him pretty closely as to his manner of living am fully convinced that he was poisoned by taking canned beef. Six others were taken at the same time that he was, they all boarded at the same place, and all died but him. I feel quite proud of the way he got along. But we do meet some queer people. Was called in to see a man connected with the variety theatre here a few days ago. As soon as I went in it was a case of fever he says, "Now I want you to understand right from the start that if you cure me I'll pay you, and if you don't you won't get a d__m cent. I don't pay for anything that does not good." Then he wanted to tell me how I should treat him. But I knew my man, and decided to be as firm and independent as he was. So I said "If I'm going to treat you, I'm going to do it my own way. I'm not going to lose my pay just because you want to treat yourself. I've got to be boss of the job or I won't undertake it." He laughed a little and says "all right, go ahead – you're the doctor." In three days he was out, but I haven't seen him since. Think I shall just stroll down to the wharf tonight and see that he doesn't get away, as I think his company closed their engagement last night.

Monday morning *– was called out at that point – another case of fever. Your letter came again this morning and so I didn't feel quite as lonely as I did yesterday. Yes, I think you are right. My letters lately have been full of our home and our union and I expect they will be full of it until they become a reality (excuse the mixed plural and singular – I get excited on this subject, and good grammar has to become of secondary importance).*

Say Anna your talking about those moonlight nights – is an awful aggravation. I immediately long for your front porch and back porch and for the long walk out on East Washington Street and then the town of Fairhaven seems like solitude. I am counting more and more all the time on our being married next fall or summer. If we get married next year I want it to be early enough so you can see something of one glorious summer before the rainy season sets in. We can make it. I know.

Listen my dear, just hold your ear while I whisper, the first week of my second month figures up $66.00!!!!!! A rapid mathematical calculation on your part will show you that that means $3,432 a year if my practice remains just where it is. Just as a matter of conservatism, say that it will not quite keep up to this point and drop off the $432 and we will still have left a sum large enough to live on quite comfortably even in this country. I am fully convinced that four rooms will be sufficient to start with. I know quite nice people here who seem to be very comfortable on three rooms.

Rents are up and houses scarce. A house has to be rented as soon as the building is commenced. A six room house will rent for thirty dollars a month. Mr. Mc-Adam is building one with six rooms and a bathroom for which he is to receive thirty dollars as soon as it is finished. For such a house as we would want we would probably pay twenty five a month. But then as I wrote in a former letter I could go into the building association and the monthly rent would apply on the cost of the building, which would become our own after awhile.

Furniture is very costly on account of high freight rates, but still it is higher in proportion to the cost and after freight is paid than it is East. I expect it would pay to purchase at home and ship it out here. Besides we could then get something nearer what we want. This is being practical isn't it? I believe you my dear that it will be great fun, and great pleasure too, doing things for each other and don't go on feeling ashamed about what you asked in regard to my actions about the house. Those were very proper and pertinent questions and I so took them.

All the cases that I have at present are fever. One, a little four year old girl took symptoms of typhoid today and will require very close attention. My theatre man came around and paid his bill today like a little man. He was quite satisfied with his treatment. I find that the cases I have now, together with the study I have to give them keep me reasonably busy. If I had just two or three more, I would be quite busy, especially having no horse and buggy. The cases are considerably scattered and the city limits are rather large, so that it takes considerable walking and that consumes time and sole leather. But it costs more to keep a horse here than it would to feed him for three months. I can buy a Cayuse or bronco for twenty four dollars but hay cost from twenty five to fifty dollars a ton. I can board myself for less than it would cost to board a horse.

Well I must stop now and will write the next chapter very soon. Will have my new book and medicine case tomorrow which will add to the appearance and convenience of the office.

I suppose that today you commence the school again. Well, I hate to think of your doing it but I wish you all the pleasure and profit that you can get out of it.

Good bye dear.
Yours lovingly,
Will

Letter 38

Fairhaven, Washington
Tuesday, September 9, 1890

My Darling Anna,

I expect that my last letter was a day or two behind time. I was on my way to post it near mail time when I was stopped by some inquires with reference to one of my patients and so was delayed until it was too late. I was very sorry as I know by my own experience that letters behind time are always productive of much restlessness and uneasiness. Had another letter from you this morning and a delightful one – like all of them only a trifle more so.

I will try to write a letter that your **Uncle Hervey** *and* **Aunt May** *may read with the personal element left out, but say, Anna, it will be hard work. What you term "complimentary" remarks belong in letters from me to you, and it will be difficult to keep them out. But I will try and hold myself down for once – but not in this one – you must judge that letter by what I say in this one because I feel that I am full of those same complimentary remarks today, and so they will probably be found scattered through this letter quite profusely.*

I have been trying to write a letter for the Journal for some time, but someway it doesn't come easy. I don't write essays and correspondence as I used to do. It seems to come harder. But say, Anna, I would like to see your patchwork correspondence. I don't doubt but it would be well put together. But I wonder how it would read. You know I don't make any effort or pretense to literary style in my letters to you. I just try to put down impressions and feelings and thoughts, and what I think will interest you alone, just as I would in ordinary conversation and so I wonder how a piece of correspondence made up from extracts would read to the general public, and if there are parts of my letters you would like to have Aunt May and Uncle Hervey have or see, why not read extracts to them after you have read them yourself to see where the personal remarks are? I don't believe I could write as naturally as usual if I know I am writing a special letter that is to be seen and read by others. That's the way I feel in reference to the correspondence for the paper. In my desire to have it read well, I am afraid that it would be artificial. However, I will do the best I can and try to write something interesting and you may be sure that Fairhaven and Bellingham Bay will occupy a prominent part of any letter I may write.

The Great Northern will probably have its line completed to the coast the latter part of next year. It is now being pushed from Fort Assiniboine, Montana, to the summit of the Rockies. In the meantime, the branch connecting with the Canadian Pacific is nearly completed so that they can bring out iron and supplies by that road, and so build eastward on the main line from here, meeting the other end somewhere on the plains of the Columbia in Eastern Washington sometime the latter part of next year. Skeptics who have hitherto disbelieved that the Great Northern had possession of the Fairhaven & Southern only need to see Great Northern cars and locomotives running on this line. Fairhaven continues to grow.

The latest addition to the city is a sash and door factory that will employ at least fifty men. One of the leading saw mills has passed into the hands of a Scotch firm, who has moved here, one of whom has built a beautiful residence on a point that has a perfect view of the whole semicircle of the bay, with all three towns in full sight. A large part of the lumber cut in this mill will be shipped direct from here to Glasgow, Scotland. Among the most recent discoveries of minerals in the Cascade mining district are asbestos of fine quality, graphite and sulphur. The variety of mineral wealth all tributary to Fairhaven is wonderful. Marble, sandstone, iron, coal, sulphur, graphite, asbestos, silver, lead, copper, gold and mica, all exist in paying quantities. One of the mills cut a few days ago a log 32 feet in length and five feet in diameter, which measured, board measure, 6,000 feet of lumber. The cut was made in less than an hour.

Tom McAdam and Dr. Smith arrived here this morning. I have not seen either of them yet. They are guests of Ross Sullivan. Ross says he is going to have a Mt. Pleasant reunion while they are here.

You and Jessie will have a good deal of fun with your white and yellow arrangements. I want to state right now and emphatically that I don't care about anything fine in the way of finery for a wedding outfit. I suppose that is the man of it. I want you and don't like to think of anything extrusive delaying the time. And perhaps it would be as well to let you know right away something about the dress worn out here. As to style, I can tell you nothing because it is about the same as elsewhere as far as I can see. The same variety – and individual taste. People are not particular. But clothing will need in the main to be warm. People wear pretty much the same weight material the year round. Light or white dresses are not in much demand except during the middle of the day in summer. The evenings and nights are always cool, and to a newcomer seem chilly. And I'm "granny" enough to believe that with the dampness of the climate flannels should be worn the year round. You need not fear that anything you may have will not be in style because people are coming in here from all parts of the country and bring the style prevailing in the place they come from with them. And it gives a delightful freedom of taste. So you may indulge yours to any extent you may see fit. Will state that gusset shoes are worn by ladies a great deal here. It is often quite dusty in the summer and they always look nice, no matter how dusty the street is. So there again you may indulge your penchant for yellow. That's all I think of at present in regard to the dress. Have I done pretty well? When I get acquainted with a few ladies of fashion I will take notes and then quietly find out how to describe them correctly.

So for the present we will close the fashion column of this great family journal, and proceed to fill up the building and house decoration department. About that first house of ours, I suppose that the four rooms will be about enough. They will be enough to furnish sufficiently for our comfort and a very important consideration enough for you to take care of. I like your idea of a library immensely but dear, isn't that looking out for my comfort a good deal and not taking enough thought for your own? As you will use that as a place to send me to when you don't want me around

– the kitchen for instance, or where I get to be considerable of a bore. What's the matter with having a very pretty, dainty and cosy dressing room or boudoir for your own private use? Just listen to us, will you, talking about libraries and dressing rooms, when we expect to have three or four plain rooms. No I won't say plain rooms because I believe that between us we will have taste and ingenuity enough to make four rooms look quite handsome, with a few little inexpensive things that can be picked up here and there – an etching or two, a little water color, or a good photogravure. A rug or curtain here and there. A nice little bit of china or two on the mantel – for we'll have a fireplace and mantel or we won't play. And it will be easy enough to get it because the house will probably be rented before it is built. So you see even if we have a rented house it can be made to suit us. Consequently we must know what we want ahead of time.

Am glad to learn that Jessie and "Jeff" will be married as soon as next fall. There will be a great clearing out of Willowbank again for I feel pretty certain that we will be married in the fall or late summer unless something unforeseen should intervene to prevent and I don't anticipate that such will be the case and with you on the ground to work up the case, I think we can get mother to come and live with us inside of a year after we are married. You will settle the whole business by taking mother out riding, but I guess it is pretty well understood by this time. I am making no secret of it and I don't believe that you are now. Oh, I didn't get out the town crier, but just of things as a matter of course. I suppose that by this time you are nearly through the first week of school and don't doubt that Friday night you will be tired, as the "kids" will be restless enough the first week.

I will try and fix it so that you can get letters on Sunday. I will mail a letter every Monday and then you can let me know whether they reach you Saturday or Sunday and in that way perhaps it can be regulated. Well I must stop now and go out and see some of my patients. I wish I had my "ten dollar horse" and fifteen dollar cart. Will have some more medical news next time.

Goodbye sweetheart.
Lovingly, Will

Letter 39

Fairhaven, Washington
Saturday, September 13, 1890

My Darling Sweetheart,

Today was one of the times that I have wished more than usual that the distance was not so great between us, so that a letter could be answered and the answer reach its destination at the time it is needed. Your letter of the 7th came today and I never wanted to be with you more than as I read it because I know that you were unhappy and I was so fond as to believe that perhaps I could make you feel less unhappy. I certainly had the desire to do so at any rate. And now, perhaps it will be all over (your unhappiness, I mean) before this reaches you. I hope so anyway. But if this letter can't do any good I am very glad that one of mine did reach you in time and had something in it to bring comfort to you.

There are so many things I want to say that I hardly know where to commence. Perhaps the best way will be just to start right in and say them and let the thought speak for me. I suppose that after you had talked with your Aunt May about getting married next fall that she thought it was perfectly proper to discuss the matter with my mother. While the latter, while she always appears quite cheerful about her own affairs, is rather prone to look on the dark side of things. Mother is inclined to think that I am a little too sanguine about things, and so I suppose considers it her duty to keep you duly apprised of that fact. But this time she obtained her information from the wrong source.

I would like to pay my respects to Mr. Woods for his opinions as to my financial success for my first year. I will next fall, too. Mr. Woods' statements must be taken contrary always. He is always sure to take the side that nobody else is on. He knows, that is he knew, if he considers my word good for anything, that I made enough to keep me my very first month, which, as a business man he must know is a very good guarantee of doing more in the future. As a matter of fact, I made more than my expenses the first month. My expenses are about sixty four dollars a month and I made a hundred, or as I can't be sure of collecting more than ninety percent, ninety dollars. I have included in these expenses everything – medicines, etc. Had I stayed in Mt Pleasant and vegetated there, I don't suppose that I should have made more than enough to keep myself the first year. Hence Mr. Wood's remarks are entirely gratuitous and superfluous.

So much for that – perhaps I am foolish to say anything about that, and yet I feel that I have been sufficiently successful to be a trifle sensitive on the subject. I am sorry that anything occurred to call to your mind your old fears on one subject dear. I don't fear that there is any danger on that point. You say that you are over fearing anything for yourself but that you fear for the one you love. You fear to bring misery on that one. I wonder sweetheart if you fully understand that the greatest misery that could come to me would be to have anything occur to you, and I have no right to care for you and provide for your comfort. Loving you as I do, no greater misfortune could befall me than that I should not have the sole right to bear your burdens, your sickness or health, your worry or your happiness.

Do you understand that Anna? If you do, you understand that nothing, absolutely nothing shall stand between us. And I want to say here that mother knows nothing about your father's death – I won't say insanity in the family because he was the only one – at least I don't think that she does. And you mustn't think that she has not been cordial. The fact is that mother is about as shy as anyone I know of and very proud too. So that what has seemed coolness is simply reserve, I feel quite sure.

But Anna, your letter made me see one or two things that makes me more determined than ever that we shall be married next fall. I see now one of the reasons that I never saw before, that you want to get away from Mt. Pleasant and it is a very good reason. You are right in believing that you cannot forget with the hospital so near you[35] and it will be best that you should forget as much as you can. Do not reproach yourself or regret that you made anything about this and you need not promise to say nothing about it when we are married. I want you to talk about that or anything else that worries you. For will you not be telling it to one who loves you? Will not a loving construction always be put on everything? You know that such will be the case.

Oh my darling, if you only knew how willingly I would take every trouble from you if I could. I will be so good to you dear. I don't say that I will be good to you just to use a lover's phrase, but I know. I have a conviction that I will be good to you as no one else will. How can I tell you this to make

Courtesy Mount Pleasant, Iowa, Public Library.
Iowa State Hospital for the Insane, Mount Pleasant.

you believe it? Never mind if I haven't language to express it adequately. I'll prove it by deeds some of these days. The more I think of it, the more I feel that we must be married next fall, at least. I'll prove that I can be ready and I believe that you can. And we will both be strangers together dear. I feel more and more that we will be cheating ourselves by waiting too long for purely material reasons. We could get along all right and we'd be together. That's a great thought to me – together. And I have a fair amount of health and I believe some energy and know that we could live in comfort, if not in luxury. And I want you so badly dear. I want to get you where I can be good to you. Know I am going to stop on this now and will finish tomorrow, but I don't want to stop, and yet if I should keep on it would simply to be repetitive one theme – my love for you and desire for your happiness. I feel full of it tonight and I'm hungry for a glimpse of your sweet face. There's no use talking Anna. I couldn't exist without you longer than a year. You have become my life, my ambition, everything. You speak of the night out at Mr. Lewis Baugh's when I told you of my ambitions. Well I have them yet. But they have changed a little. I want you to enjoy them with me and nothing but your love and faith will make them possible. Without you I don't believe that I could or would accomplish anything more. Good night, sweetheart. I am going to sleep and dream of you which of course will be pleasant dreams.

Sunday Afternoon – I have but a few minutes now in which to write before the mail closes. I have actually been kept quite busy today. Did not even have time to go to church. Have been called in to see two of Dr. Heacock's patients, as he is out of town for a day or two. There are many more things that I want to say but as I want to get this off today, I will write again tonight and tomorrow. I want to say something about recent impressions in regard to people and patients – something of how the patients are getting along, a few words as reminiscences, and a great many as to ambitions for the future, and then of course a few remarks about Fairhaven. Tomorrow I will send you some papers containing something about consolidation and comments of various papers in the state concerning Fairhaven. What I want to say on the subjects above mentioned will each require a chapter so I will save them for the next letter.

About the financial side of my practice I will speak here as it will not take up much time. I think I told you that the first week of my second month amounted to $66. I now want to say that the second week closing today amounts to $91.50 and as this is being written in the afternoon there may be a call or prescription or two yet today. So much as to whether I can do more than keep myself the first year. Now as to collections, will just say that I have collected $77.50 of my first month's practice, and that without presenting any bills. You see it is scarcely thirty days since the most of my business has been done so that it is a little premature to formally make an effort to collect. But of the $101.25 for the first month, I don't believe that I will lose more than six or seven dollars and that you know is doing very well. If a doctor ordinarily collects eighty-five per cent he is doing unusually well and is usually satisfied if he collects 75%.

Just a little more practice and I will have to have a horse and buggy. Fairhaven covers a good deal of territory and with patients in different quarters of the city it keeps me running around. Nearly all the practice here is outside work. There is little office practice. There are so many young people that there are not many chronic complaints. Acute diseases are the order, requiring visits to be made.

Well I must stop now. I suppose that by the time this reaches you, you will be pretty well settled down to teaching again. This letter is just the prologue. The main work will follow divided into its proper chapters in a day. I have read over what I wrote last night and find that it is weak – that is, it doesn't convey what I wanted to say – doesn't make it half strong enough. Just add the proper vigor to it will you? Good bye dear (till tomorrow).

Lovingly, Will

Letter 40

Fairhaven, Washington
Monday, September 15, 1890

My Darling Anna,

Did not get to write last night as I was kept out quite a while in the evening and when I got back was too tired to write. Yesterday was the first day that my practice has really kept me busy enough to be tired. But I just felt used up. Did a great amount of walking in addition to which I am having a struggle with a pair of new shoes. Tried to get a wide squared shoe and couldn't find one in town so had to take what I could get. Well where shall I begin with my work in the practice of medicine – my continuous history as it were? I think I will commence with the patients themselves and then the people one meets where the patients are.

Chapter One

This history will first enumerate the characters with which it has to deal. At the present writing they are as follows: (Some of them you have met before.) There is the young wife of one of the merchants in Bellingham. Blue eyes, brown hair, nervous temperament, rather inclined to worry over things, but in a mild and sweet tempered kind of way. Her husband has a large store and they live in three rooms over the store. The husband is one of those men whose whole lives are devoted to debit and credit. His brain is a ledger. His sympathies are all bound up in stoves, crockery and groceries. His greatest fear always seems to be that his business will "go to the dogs." When he dies and goes to St. Peter the first thing he will ask when he gets to the Pearly gate will be whether he can have a general store in a bustling street and have his wife keep books for him and when St. Peter tells him that he can have the store but that he will have to hire a bookkeeper as his wife is going to enjoy herself, he will think the place isn't quite what it was represented to be. This was a case of remittent fever lasting about two weeks and a half. Made my last call yesterday. The lady is not quite well but they thought well enough to dispense with the doctor. This is the case I spoke of being quite low. She has come out much better than I expected.

Another case is a boy thirteen years old. The son of a butcher who has grown so fast that he is principally made up of length and weakness. So I suppose I ought to have a fellow feeling. Think this will be a case of typhoid and if so will probably be a severe one. His bedroom is in the back part of the butcher shop and his bed the lowest one of a tier of three bunks, one over the other where he and his father and the bookkeeper sleep. His father is one of the self-sufficient kind of men who think everything that he has anything to do with is a little better than can be done by anyone else. So, notwithstanding that the boy is in the worst kind of place from a sanitary standpoint, he won't have him taken to any better place. Insists that the ventilation is good and care excellent and that he is better off where he is.

The third is the little girl I spoke of – such a pretty little thing and very good. She has had an attack of typhoid, but is getting well and I don't think that I will have to see her more than once or twice more.

Then there is the German woman again. She had been well for some time but ate some grapes and brought on another attack of gastric fever. Her case worries me. Her stomach is so sensitive that it won't retain anything. Even a teaspoonful of water containing the medicine will not remain in her stomach and even a slight movement, as of a hand or arm, is sufficient to bring on nausea and vomiting during which the pain in the stomach is terrific. Then the worst feature of the case is there is no one to take care of her. Her husband is away at work all day and he is a regular turtlehead around the house. He can't do the first thing, either for himself or for anyone else and early in the evening he goes off to bed by himself and his wife is left to do the best she can for herself. (I want to remark parenthetically that such a man is encumbrance of the earth and ought to be killed.)

The fifth case is one of Dr. Heacock's to which I was called yesterday morning. She is the wife of a stonemason here and is very low with typhoid complicated with pneumonia and inflammation of the stomach. It is hard to tell what the outcome will be. The husband is greatly worried over the case from his standpoint but it is a very low one. Confound it (beg pardon, but I'd like to swear at some of the people I meet.) He was in the office this morning and was explaining why he wanted every effort made to save his wife's life, and I declare it seemed to me that his great trouble was the financial side of it. He had figured that it would cost less to have the close attention of a doctor if his wife could be saved, than it would be to send his little girl to relatives in Arkansas in case she died. Not a word as to the sorrow it might bring to him. A man would feel like disclaiming any relationship to his kind.

The father of the little girl with the typhoid talked about selling four horses that he owns and has working on the streets so that he could have money and time to take care of her. He said if he could dispose of his teams he would let everything go until "his baby" got well. They have been a little unfortunate since coming here and are living in a little shanty of two rooms but are real nice people and there is lots of love scattered around in the family. There are only three of them. The father, mother and baby, though the grandmother has come up from Tacoma to help while the baby was sick. It has been quite refreshing, and I shall be sorry when my visits cease there. A love that manifests itself in deeds is about the only thing of worth in this world anyway.

Dr. Heacock's wife is visiting his patients while the doctor is away. How do you think you would like anything like that sometime when I have to be away? The crying need here is for nurses. Nearly every place to which I go, the sick can't have proper care. The only case that I have had where the patient was properly taken care of was in the case of the young man with the inflammation of the bowels. His aunt took care of him and did it in a very capable and intelligent manner. I think if some of the good ladies of the churches who spend their time making garments to send to the heathen would visit some of the sick in their own communities they would be doing an infinitely more praiseworthy deed and would appear like angels of mercy to some of the disease racked patients.

Well that's about the end of the list that I am visiting. Of course there are some that drop in and get a prescription now and then, but I don't see enough of them to know much about them.

The undertaker here made a remark today that I wish he would repeat around town a little. It was to the effect that I was the only doctor in town with whose patients he had had nothing to do. Of course I haven't been here long enough for that to really cut much figure as to my success with the cases I have had. And yet there have been four doctors come since I have and they have all had a death or two among their patients.

Well this has been pretty much filled with "shop" hasn't it? Well, you have a chance to get even now that you are teaching again. I will resume the continuation of this history in my next ("To be continued in our next"). And in closing I will just say that Fairhaven still continues to advance towards her ultimate destiny of being the greatest city on the Pacific Coast and that you are still the light of my eyes. Come to think of it – I believe I will postpone the history in my next and make an eloquent and touching appeal for all of those pictures that you and "Mrs. Williams" had taken together – because why – they are going to be good. I like that one you have chosen to have printed better than any picture I ever saw of you. Well I must stop now. Goodbye dear.

Lovingly, Will

Letter 41

Fairhaven, Washington
Thursday, September 18, 1890

My Darling Anna,

Your letter written in school, or to be more accurate at the school house, came today. You failed to tell me whether in addition to that trouble you have the redoubtable James Drumin to manage and placate this year. If you have I think you would better resign at once and come out and start "Mrs. Dr. Gray's Select School for Girls." I suppose it is to be girls – No? Am I mistaken? And I suppose that now you are in school I will have to content with short letters once a week. I have enjoyed your long letters so much this summer and hope that once a week at any rate that I will get a long one. Long letters are always acceptable, and I am glad that mine have been enjoyed from that reason.

The magazines arrived yesterday for which I want to thank you. I had read the Scribner but had not seen the Harpers. You are always safe on Harpers as I never get it. But the Century I take regularly and Scribner's occasionally. Has it struck you in regard to the fashion or "fad" in story writing in the magazines? Some time ago it was the dialect. Now it is the pathetic or tragic and especially the simple pathetic as for instance "The Portiss" in the Harper you sent – "The Basket of Anita" in Scribner. Every month there is something of the kind in nearly every number of the different magazines. The story of "Jerry" is also somewhat on that order. I had not read that, as I did not have the first number, but at your suggestion I read it, and was so interested that I got the September number at once. It is very fine, I think. While we are talking about books, if you get time look up the back numbers of the Century and read "Friend Olivia." It is one of the most beautiful stories I have come across for many a day. I read a story by the same author last summer, "The Bow of Orange Ribbon," a story of the revolution that was very good. This story of Jerry is unique in one particular – in having – at least thus far, no female character. I feel that I must begin to read a little more than I have for a long time. But I have had so much in the line of medical reading to do it seemed to take all my time.

Had a letter from Ed Scott yesterday. He spoke of having been to see you, and evidently he hadn't recovered from the shock of that hundred dollars at the time he wrote. He fears that my success will make him impatient if he doesn't do as well the first month. In a letter some time ago Ed had said that he was coming out here next June, as soon as he gets through College. I wrote back and told him that I wished he was not coming out until fall as there was a possibility of our marriage at that time, and that if we put on that much style I wanted him for "best man." Ed writes in answer that his affairs will be in such shape that he will be obliged to get out and "hustle" as soon as he is through school, so that he could not wait, but he said that we would agree to another proposal. He will come out here in June and if I will wait until October he will go back with me and make up a party of four, coming back, to start two new homes. Miss Libbie Nix to be the fourth one in the party. How is that for a scheme? Their engagement is a secret in the same way that ours has been – no "official announcement," but suspected by everybody. Ed became quite poetic – quoted Jean Ingelow, in fact his letter was full of it. Ed said he had wanted to tell me about it before but had hated to "cold bloodedly" put it down on paper. That amused me somewhat. If Ed and Jeffrey and myself all commit matrimony next fall, all the old wheel horses of the Phi boys will be disposed of except Jay Kirkendall and Charley Blakeney. I think those two will be the only ones of all that I have known while in college except the boys that are still in. Oh, yes there's Laisy and Coddington – but then Laisy is as good as married as Elbert Smith once said about me.

I have written to Ed and told him that I was highly pleased with his proposal and would mention it to you for approval. Was that all right?

The consolidation committee has about finished their work, and it is safe to say that no consolidation will take place for some time to come. Whatcom and Sehome want every public building located in the latter place and then want Fairhaven to give up her name besides and take that of Bellingham. Inasmuch as the citizens of Fairhaven have spent $200,000 in advertising alone and as the name of Fairhaven is known all over the country, it would be folly for her to give up everything and get nothing in return. So Fairhaven will just work out her own destiny and after awhile the suburban towns of Sehome and Whatcom will be glad to come in on any terms, and under the name of Fairhaven, too. I will send papers containing reports of the committee meetings, and also an editorial on the subject which is pretty good I think.

Practice has been a little dull this week. Dr. Heacock is back from a few days trip and has taken the case I spoke of off my hands for which I am very thankful as I don't think she can recover and am selfish enough to want the case in someone else's hands. I must go out now and make a call. Will write again tomorrow. The fact is that I don't feel much like writing today. I'm not blue but most awfully lonesome. I sit in my office all days except when I go out to make my few calls, seeing no one I know and it gets very monotonous. I suppose there is no use complaining however. It can't be helped. Goodbye dear.

Lovingly, Will

Letter 42

Fairhaven, Washington
Monday, September 22, 1890

My Darling Anna,

Another of your letters reached me this morning and things are looking a little brighter than for two or three days past. For a little while I will feel quite elated over everything – my practice, the growth of Fairhaven, the picturesqueness of the country – in fact everything. Then will come a revulsion of feeling and I think of nothing but the loneliness of living here, the newness of everything. I get disgusted with the everlasting talk about real estate and real estate values. The constant boasting about the resources of the place and its future greatness – it all becomes very tiresome.

You inquired particularly about the weather in Fairhaven. During the time that I have been here the weather has been very fine. Through the middle of the day it is quite warm and very pleasant. The nights are quite cool. These fall days, early in the morning there is always a mist coming from the Sound, which is dispersed by the sun between eight and nine o'clock. A stranger would think each morning that it was going to be a rainy day but it is surprising to see how imperceptibly and quickly the fog disappears and how delightfully bright it is for the rest of the day.

I wonder often how you will like the climate and whether it will agree with you. If it doesn't we'll seek green fields and pastures new for there is no use in people suffering in a climate that is inimical to their health, if they have the means to get away at all. If this doesn't agree after a year or two we'll try the South – Virginia for instance is a good place for an enterprising man to go in these times. You ask me not to talk about next fall for awhile. Well I won't, any more than I can help, but you know I have my heart set on it so much that I can't help talking about it to some extent. To say the truth my sole object in coming so far west was that I could get in faster, so that we could be married sooner. If I thought it would be two years I should feel like pulling up here and going back east – and work up more slowly in some town there. I couldn't wait that long without being where I could see you occasionally. There I won't say anything more about that now.

Arrangements were completed Saturday for an enterprise that will be of more real benefit to Fairhaven than anything that has been started here since I came. It is a foundry and machine shop, the plan of which is to cost $75,000. It will employ a large number of men and will produce something that can be shipped away from here. In fact it will be a producer instead of a consumer and so will be of actual benefit to the town.

Ad for foundry.

Whatcom Museum.

St. Joseph Hospital, 17th Street and Adams Avenue.

The Sisters of the Sacred Heart are going to build a hospital here[36] *that will cost $30,000. Work is to be commenced in a few days. This will be a good thing for the town, though it will not do me any good. Anything that the Catholic Church is connected with clings to that which is ancient and medieval and so they will probably have nothing to do with anything that is as progressive as Homeopathy – with a big H.*

Later *– Have just returned from Whatcom. Saw Dr. Henderson over there and remembered you to him. He sends kindest regards to you. He has just returned from a trip down into Oregon where he was married. Only had a few minutes to stay as I wanted to catch a certain boat back. Dr. Henderson asked if you were coming out in this country before long. That Mrs. Howard had told him that you were engaged to a Dr. out here – perhaps I was the doctor. I told him that I expected that I was the doctor but didn't know when you would come out.*

Business is dropping off a little. The fever is subsiding somewhat, so that my real struggle for practice is yet to come. However, that has given me a start that would have made it harder had I not had it. It enables me to meet some obligations that otherwise would have been hard to meet. I am glad that your Uncle Hervey is pleased with the success that I have had so far. I want your friends and relations to feel that you have not taken up with a crooked stick or a good-for-nothing. I believe I said in a former letter that I was going to make a touching and eloquent appeal for one of those pictures. I fear that I can be neither touching nor eloquent unless earnestness can be so. But I do want one of the pictures. It is the best one of you that I have ever seen and it looks as you do now which makes it doubly valuable in my sight. When I playfully made a little fun of the other one you sent I had no idea of offending you so deeply that you would never give me another and I can hardly believe that you mean to deprive me of what would give me so much pleasure. You know how I would prize the picture. You don't know how much I prize the other, even if I did make fun of it. It would grieve me deeply to think that you would not give me one of your pictures. There. I won't say any more on that subject, except that you know how desirous I have always been to have a good photograph of you. I leave it to you to send one or not as you think good. If you made the resolution seriously I will not ask you to break it, but it will make me very unhappy.

I am thinking of going over to Victoria for a day or two this week to see Aunt Jennie. It is very pleasant now and may not be later in the season.

Don't regret that you sent me the letter in which old trouble had been recalled. If they worried you why should you not tell them to me? And thereby get what comfort you could from the telling. They are things not forgotten – if it is possible to forget; but when it is not why not tell them to me. Where love is we need not fear that telling troubles will ever prove tiresome. If you didn't tell your troubles to me I should feel that you lacked confidence in me to just that extent. Well, I must stop now and make a call. Would like to say more on the subject but can't now. Goodbye darling. Think of me always as,

Your Loving Will

WILD ROSE

Illustration by Brian Griffin.

Letter 43

Fairhaven, Washington
Thursday, September 25, 1890

My Darling Anna,

Have just invested in a new tablet and inasmuch as this is very expensive paper and as you are an advocate of economy, you can't have as much paper as I have heretofore been sending, but I will "try" and see that you get as many words as usual as you will see by this.

I have not yet gone to Victoria. I had made arrangements to go last night but yesterday afternoon was called to two more cases of typhoid fever and so cannot get away for two weeks at least, now. Had to invest in a new stove yesterday as the mornings and evenings are becoming decidedly chilly. It hurt me awfully to have to buy a stove but it had to be "did." However it was the cheapest little coal stove that I could find, costing, including pipe – I put it up myself – just the small sum of eight dollars. Just reflect over this page and see if I am not dwelling on the practical side of things.

By the way, must mention another little bit of experience (of the unpleasant kind). My case of inflammation that I spoke of and took so much glory in has "skipped" for green fields and pastures new, leaving numerous creditors to mourn his untimely skipping. I will have to take it out in glory and put twenty six dollars from the profit to the loss department and so the world moves on and the longer we live the more we find out. However I was able yesterday to meet a note for fifty dollars that came due at that time, and thus wipe one debt off the record. I wish to state parenthetically that I have been able to keep myself during the month besides and still have a few round silver dollars rattling around in my pockets to keep each other company.

Have also ordered an operating table made and bought a work on "Fevers" for my library out of this month's practice and the end (of the month) is not yet. Seemeth that like boasting? Well, may hap it doth a little smack of that unseemly quality but then you see I want you to know that I am doing pretty well. But – ah! That unfortunate "but" that always comes in to cast a moistened flannel over every good thing! I am still lonely and always will be until I have your sweet presence to chase away the loneliness. That loneliness is the one hard thing to control against. However I mention that so often perhaps I would better not dwell on it very long. I was rather looking for a letter this morning to dispel the clouds but it came not and the clouds are still hovering around, with the leaden side surely visible to the naked eye. I suppose that somewhere within those aqueous confines is an argentic interior that in course of time will suffer itself to shine with a silvery sheen – (if any of your little scholars are suffering from a severe attack of lisping just give them that last sentence to practice on). I will make not any charge for the honorable school plank to meet yet. I say plank because all the timber that I see out here is so large that it would not seem right to use the word board. Besides a plank is thicker and contains more wood than a board. Sabe?

PUBLIC IMPROVEMENTS

Our Street Work, Sewerage
and Fire Depart-
ment

More Miles of Streets Graded,
Planked and Side-
walked

In the Past Six Months Than in
Any Other Pacific Coast
City

About $400,000 in This Great
Work and More Pro-
jected

A Perfect Sewerage System
Constructing With All
Possible Vigor

A Model Fire Department
and Its Efficient
Officers

Fairhaven Herald, December 29, 1890. CPNWS.

Fairhaven still continues to grow (think I will have that remark electrotyped as it will be necessary to use it for a great many years.) It's a way Fairhaven has of growing. Now that the consolidation agony is over the people of this enterprising burg have settled down in earnest to build up the greatest city on Puget Sound. And then after awhile the moss backs on the other side of the bay will be glad to attach themselves to something living and have their bivalve existence prolonged by having some good warm live blood infused into their molluscian veins. (That word "molluscian" is my own, but as you are my other half you may use it if it ever comes handy to do so.)

You may think from these remarks that I have been engaged at a large salary to write double headed editorials for a lively boom newspaper. Nay, nay, not so but this morning I was down on the ocean wharf from which a fine view of the city may be obtained and whence I shall be delighted "someday" (soon) to show you the city and there were so many new buildings in course of erection that I have been prompted to utter these few eminently conservative remarks.

Tell you what Anna, you don't know what you are missing by not being here to watch this town grow. I really feel guilty for not going right after you and bringing you out at once to see the marvel of it. And say my dear, if things keep on unless we hurry we will miss the three room era altogether. Some beautiful residences are being put up now. I am afraid that by the time you get out here it will be a "metropolis" with all "modern improvements." So that you won't see the wild western town in all it's glory of stumps and unpainted houses. Never mind, I am hoping that by the time you come they won't have Mt. Baker fenced in and built to the summit or have Puget Sound planked over, but verily you will have to hurry. The latest scheme of the Fairhaven and Southern R.R. is to run a line up into

Alaska, bridge Bering Strait and run a line up into Siberia and Russia and thence to other European countries. However I expect they will wait until next week.

Well I have to bring this to a termination and go out and make some calls. There hasn't been much in this letter but there is a great deal more in my heart than I can give utterance to on paper. I wonder sometimes if I did not make a mistake in cutting myself off from all I hold dear by coming out here. It is worth the sacrifice – sacrifice it is. There is so little in life where you are not that I often think that I would better have plodded along in Iowa somewhere where I could go to see you every month or so. I am a miserable man away from you dear and that's all there is about it. I have to write "boom" words sometimes just to keep up my spirits but there isn't any pleasure in it when it is done. You have become knit to me so closely dear, that disguise it how I may, there is nothing in life away from you.

Goodbye sweetheart.
I am always,
Yours Lovingly, Will

Letter 44

Fairhaven, Washington
Friday, Sept. 26, 1890

My Darling Sweetheart,

Your letter of the twentieth came today, and though I wrote yesterday I feel that I must write a few lines to tell you how thankful I am that you were not severely injured in the accidental overturning of the carriage. I fear, however, that you were hurt worse than you would have me believe. You cannot imagine my feelings as I read your account of the accident and thought what might have happened. I fairly felt cold for a moment as I imagined the position you were in, and I cannot conceive that you could get out without being at least severely bruised. It was a sweet thought to me though to know that in the midst of danger your first thought was of me. Talk about life being of little value! It would be worth nothing to me if anything serious should happen to you. Your life and safety and health and happiness are more to me now than my own, so what would I do if they should suffer. Mr. Warrick has my thanks and gratitude of helping you out, but I wish if it had to happen that I could have been there to do it myself. How I long for the time when I can do something for you myself!

I have read the story, "A Birthday Letter," and agree with you that it is very prettily written – it is more than that – it is beautiful. I have been wondering how much of that you have applied to me? She speaks of her love as a "Wiseacre wrapped up in musty books." You don't think of me that way do you? I am rather afraid you do, by one paragraph that you marked – that one wherein she has been reading his work on psychology and regrets that he was above her in her reading. You can't intend that for me. There is one thing sure whether he was above her in reading or not, he was so far below her in loving that the plummet cannot sound the depth.

I smiled over the question, "Do you suppose every board will creak as I pass my uncle's room? Methinks I have heard tell of a particular board that creaked when a certain pair of little feet went over it – at six or seven minutes past nine at that. But say Anna, I never "smothered" you did I by the style of my reading, by my choice in literature? If I have, I'll try not to do so any more. At least I never asked you to read a work on psychology and I am quite sure that I will never ask you to read a work of mine on that subject.

And I know another thing – and that is if you send that story as containing a sample of your own thoughts and feelings, why I have as loving a sweetheart as ever had a love – but then I had felt certain of that long ago – and how gloriously I will revel in that love someday! Speed the day! We'll have the roses blowing in at the door sometime, Anna and enjoy the twilight together. I don't believe that I think of much else these days so if you want me to make that medical reputation that you are ambitious of why you must set my mind at rest by coming to be my companion very soon.

Street scene in Mount Pleasant (postcard).

And don't get bruised anymore. Just think of the state of a man's mind when he knows that the one he holds dearest out of the world's millions may be suffering. And just confess when you get this Anna, that you were pretty severely bruised, but wanted me to think that it didn't amount to much.

Well I must stop now but will write again soon. Good bye dear,

Lovingly, Will

Letter 45

Fairhaven, Washington
Monday, Sept. 29, 1890

My Darling Sweetheart,

Was on the lookout this morning for a letter but none came. Ah, those little white winged messengers, how I watch for them! And how the fog seems to take on another layer or two when they fail to make their appearance at the expected time. I think as time goes by that I look for the letters more and more and miss them more when they come not. I become more and more convinced that with me it is "un grande passion" that sways my life. I have been wondering how you are feeling now, whether you have recovered from the accident, you see I cling to the idea that you were hurt more than you were willing to confess, but I try to console myself by thinking that I am mistaken. Tell me that I am and I will be at rest.

Everything is moving along at about the usual rate. The real estate man complains that things are a little slow, but then they would like to see every lot in the city change hands every day – it would be a fat commission for them. Just at present the town is agog with curiosity around certain rumors that have been set afloat by members of the Fairhaven Land Company.[37] They say that inside of thirty days an announcement will be made of an event that will be of more benefit to Fairhaven than anything that has yet happened. No one can conjecture what it is unless it is that the Northern Pacific RR is coming in here. It can certainly be nothing less than a railroad project that can do more for the city than the Great Northern's purchase of the Fairhaven & Southern.

Notwithstanding the real estate agents complaints the published reports of transfers show that the market is pretty active while there is more building being done than at anytime since I came. The Sister's Hospital was commenced today. A temporary building will be put up until the main structure can be completed. The latter will be three stories of brick and stone and will have a length of one hundred and sixty five feet. It will be situated on an entire block of land overlooking the bay. The grounds will be terraced and planted with trees and flowers making a very beautiful place.

Was up on the hill Saturday taking a view of the bay. There was just enough smoke around the horizon to hide the point of meeting of sky and water. There was not a breath of air so that the water was as smooth as glass and the sun shining through made sky and water look like pearl. While I was looking a large steamer came out of the smoke and slight fog looking like a phantom, with a streak of radiant glory trailing behind it as it left a rough wake on the otherwise motionless waters, which the sun made appear like a wave of fire. The effects of the smoke and fog are sometimes strangely and wonderfully – I might say weirdly – beautiful. The sun will be seen quite high in the heavens appearing like a great crimson ball while all around is that peculiar pearly color, tinged with rose. Through this haze objects appear indistinct and yet bright and gradually fade away in the distance. But why try to describe something that must be seen to be appreciated.

Saturday Ed Howard and his wife were here visiting Mrs. Templin. I called on Mrs. Howard and had quite a pleasant talk with her. They have been camping and fishing at Lake Whatcom where Mrs. Howard has bought an acre of on the shore of the lake. Rena has become very enthusiastic disciple of Isaac Walton and tells some very interesting fishing stories. The trip has evidently done her good as she is looking so well, that you would hardly know her. And on one of their fishing trips she and her husband tramped 23 miles in three days, stopping and fishing at various points along the Nooksack River and some of its little mountain tributaries. The fish caught were lake trout, brook trout, and salmon trout. They are going to build a cabin at Lake Whatcom, which is about five miles from here, a very beautiful body of water, about six to eight miles in width and thirteen in length – a little larger than White Bear near St. Paul.

Tomorrow will be the last day of the month and with two calls that I have to make tomorrow the month's business will be $252.75. How is that for a start? I anticipate however that next month may fall off about a hundred dollars as the fever is somewhat subsiding. Collections of this month will probably not be as good as they were last. Including the fellow who took unto himself wings I will probably lose about fifty dollars. The little epidemic has helped me out at the start very materially and made things come a little easier – has set my mind at rest somewhat about bills that I had wondered how I was going to meet, but I will come out all right – I "guess."

Was quite surprised Saturday at being hailed on the street by an Iowa City man – one of the graduates of the dental school this year. He and his wife and baby boarded at the same place with me this year in Iowa City. He is opening a dental office here and I don't doubt will do well as he was one of best in his class both in theory and mechanical skill. I think we will enter into an arrangement by which I will have the job of administering anesthetics whenever they are desired by his patients. If so that will amount to quite a little sum in a month as soon as he gets to doing any business.

I am debating whether to go to a nice boarding house. Mrs. Sherman, the wife of one of Clint Howard's partners, is taking boarders, and I have an opportunity to go there, but the question with me is whether I can afford it. She wants twenty dollars a month for breakfast and dinner, lunch to be taken downtown. It is costing me about five dollars a week now so that it will not be much more. Am inclined to think I will take it as it will be so very much nicer than boarding around at the "lunch counters," besides offering a little social advantage. The table is small and select (?) Well I must stop now, and permit you to rest. I am still striving to get my trip to Victoria, but had another case of fever today – that's a doctor's luck – never can make arrangement for anything.

Goodbye, dear.

With much love,

I am Yours, Will

Letter 46

Fairhaven, Washington
Friday, October 3, 1890

My Darling Anna,

    Have been looking for a letter from you all day and was disappointed at last. The mail boat was six hours late today. I went to the post office several times this forenoon, but each time the answer was "The mail not in yet." Finally when it did come – there was no letter.

    There may be one yet in the afternoon boat, if that is not late also. The fact is that I have been too lonesome for any use, added to which I have not been feeling at all well. Have had all symptoms that precede an attack of fever. I have seen enough cases in the last two months to know what they are. I am going to try and circumvent it by going to Victoria for a few days. The sanitary condition of that city is good. It gets the full sea breeze from nearly all directions, and besides I will see some of my own people.

    Had a short letter from Ed Scott yesterday, dated from Mt. Pleasant in which he said that he started that night for Boston, and was going "to take tea at Anna's." I forthwith thought, "lucky fellow" and therefore grew envious. I know he enjoyed himself. How could he help it? How I wish I could see you once. I know I would be all right then. I hope you have recovered entirely from the effects of your "tumble."

    Fairhaven is rather quiet, but building goes on. President J.J. Hill of the Great Northern Railroad has been here for several days looking over the different branches of the road. Work has been commenced on the extensions of the main line eastward to connect with the other end of the line at some point in eastern Washington. It will only be a short time now, before the northern line to the Canadian Pacific is completed and then Fairhaven will boom, as "Jim" Hill announces his intentions to send passengers and freight through to Fairhaven over the Canadian road. This City will have a population of not less than 10,000 by this time next year. There is a movement on foot to build a fine opera house so that Fairhaven can have the benefit of the best attractions that appear in San Francisco, Portland, Tacoma and Seattle. There are four things that a city needs to put on metropolitan airs – a good daily paper, first class hotel, a good club and a first class opera house. Fairhaven has three of them and will soon have the opera house.

    I am going to cut this rather short today as I must go out and collect some bills, and make my preparations to go to the dominions of the queen tonight – on the palatial steamer "Eastern Oregon." Will write from there and then when I get back will give you a description of the place. Hoping to get a letter this afternoon before I do. I remain,

Lovingly Yours, Will

P.S. Enclosed pansies grown in Mr. Templin's yard.

Victoria, B.C., Birdseye, 1889.

Letter 47

Victoria, B.C.
Tuesday, Oct. 7, 1890

My Darling Anna,

Here we are spending our time in the Dominions of her Majesty. I am in Victoria and you can't imagine the difference a few short miles across the water makes in the appearance both of town and people. There is as much difference as if one crossed the Atlantic to England. This is said to be the most English town on the continent. It is a quaint old town, full of all kinds of odd nooks and corners. The streets are crooked and full of jogs. There are only a few streets in the town that pursue a straight course for three blocks. Some of them are two hundred feet wide and then suddenly they narrow down to no more than thirty feet while some are not more than twenty feet. Hardly room for two carriages to pass each other.

There are some spots in the business portions where I could imagine myself back in Stratford-on-Avon[38] or Belleville, in Ontario where I lived when a boy. As we enter the harbor which is reached by a narrow winding channel which might pass for the Thames, the city presents some such an appearance as pictures I have seen of London. Just such square turreted church towers rise up in the air. But you never saw such narrow provincialism as exists here. Most of the people here either came by ship from England around the "cape" or came directly from Canada by the Canadian Pacific R.R. and the only idea they seem to have of "America" as they call the United States is that it is a little place given over to blow, bluster,

Victoria Harbour. Water to the right of the road is the present site of the Empress Hotel.

froth, excitement, and filled with rascals and sharpers. To them Chicago is a much smaller place than Victoria (22,000 inhabitants), Philadelphia and Pennsylvania are both small towns. If you mention St. Paul they put on a vague look and say: "St. Paul – that's quite a little town isn't it?", and they have no idea of where it is. If one modestly undertakes to set them right – regarding the importance of some of the American cities they regard it as "Yankee brag."

And yet, they are very nice people, and the city is beautiful. It is almost hid in trees and shrubbery. There is a large natural park that has been beautified until it is very fine,[39] and the strangest thing to me is that it is filled with native oak trees, notwithstanding that right across the straits of San Juan de Fuca on the Americas side an oak can not be found, but everything is cedar and fir. I enjoyed the trip over very much on the "Eastern Oregon" to Port Townsend, then there was a crowd of people talking potatoes and medicine! I stood by and listened to their arguments and heard many new(?) and useful(?) facts. At Port Townsend had to stay overnight until the next afternoon. Was even entertained by the two Homeopathic physicians there. The ride across the straits was a quiet one. There was little wind, so there was not much swell coming in from the open ocean. Last night Aunt Jennie and her husband and myself went out to spend the evening – played whist – "quite English you know." Will tell you about it later.

Sunday night went to the Methodist Church and heard a very fine sermon, a good organ and a splendid choir. On each occasion was provided with a very nice and very pretty young lady, a Nova Scotian, who has some common cause and would like to visit "America." Am going out tonight to hear Frederick Archer, the organist and tomorrow night am going to take my two small cousins to hear a performance by a company that has been highly spoken of by Seattle and Tacoma papers. (They have to depend on America when it comes to anything of music and drama.) Enclosed please find some Victoria flowers. By the way believe I forgot to put pansies in my last – will do it as soon as I get back to Fairhaven. Paper has given out, so will have to stop.

With much love,
am yours Lovingly,
Will

Illustration by Brian Griffin.

Letter 48

Fairhaven, Washington
Sunday, Oct. 12, 1890

My Darling Sweetheart,

   I returned yesterday evening (Saturday) from Victoria. I must confess that Fairhaven, with its burnt stumps and many unpainted buildings looks rather bare and dismal after the beauty and trees of Victoria. I have in my mind a dozen places that I want to show you in that town "next Fall." The park over there is one of the prettiest places I ever saw. Aunt Jennie, my little cousin Nellie (she won't be my little cousin very long, she is fourteen) and myself went out to the park Friday. It is laid out with artificial lakes, stone and rustic bridges and nice drives. At one side is a hill which gives a view of the city one side, of Mt. Baker over in Washington on another, and across the straits on a third while beyond the hill is a white beach.

   Tuesday night I took Nellie and Jennie to the theatre. You should see that theatre. It was built only five years ago and yet if you should look at some old prints

Courtesy Victoria City Archives (MO8322).
Stone Bridge at Beacon Hill Park, 1890.

Stone Bridge, 2009.

of fifty or sixty years ago you would see just an interior. Dark, gloomy boxes and loges. The latter are ranged around the back part of the parquet and look just like a lot of dark closets. It is the old English love of exclusiveness. One could go into those boxes and watch a performance without anyone knowing you were there. They would be great places for a fellow to take his girl when he didn't wish to be interrupted. This English love of exclusiveness is also manifested by the high board fences and walls around beautiful grounds. Through a crack in the fence or half open gate (when the latch isn't locked) glimpses may be had of finely laid out grounds and beautiful flower beds, which it is arrant selfishness to thus keep hid.

But the curiosity of Victoria is Chinatown. I suppose that at least one forth of the population is Chinese and perhaps more. They have a quarter to themselves. There is a theatre and a Joss House.[40] I wanted to go to the theatre but didn't get an opportunity. Aunt Jennie and I and the girls – the four of us were together most of the time. Went through Chinatown.

Courtesy Victoria City Archives MO5580.

Victoria Joss house in Chinatown.

I saw some things there that I think you would be interested in. Particularly the china sets. There were complete sets of table ware (cream pitcher, sugar bowl, spoon holder, teapot, cups saucers, plates (1 dozen of each) of the most exquisite and delicate china for $7.00 to $10.00. All kinds of fancy decorative ware at very low prices. As it was nearing your birthday I picked up some embroidered handkerchiefs in the Chinese quarter, which I send you, together with a photograph of Fairhaven. The latter I have had for over a month and have kept it expressly for the purpose of sending it to you on your birthday, which I hope will be a very happy one. The yellow handkerchief is sent by Aunt Jennie. I told her what I wanted them for and she said she wanted to put one in herself.

Courtesy Royal B.C. Museum, BC, Archives, (Image D-04747).

Chinese quarters, Victoria, B.C., 1886. The King Tye Co. (in background) was located at the south west corner of Store and Cormorant (now Pandora) streets.

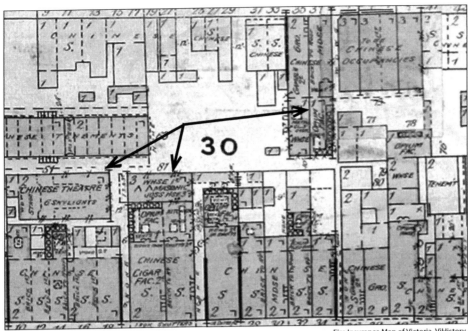

Fire Insurance Map of Victoria. ViHistory.

Chinatown 1891. Arrows note location of Chinese Theatre, Joss house, and opium factory.
Bordered by Store, Fisguard, Government and Cormorant (now Pandora) streets.

But say Anna, how I have lived for the last week, and how I have enjoyed the home cooking! It is kind of hard to come down to the restaurant again. And do you know dear, that I never go into a happy family circle anymore that I don't renew my resolve to be ready for our own wedding next fall – and I will be ready too, so just go on with your preparations.

I had heard rumors that the engagement between Anna Crane and **Leigh Woolson** was off[41] but of course knew nothing as to the truth of it. Leigh Woolson is a fool. I say that advisedly and think I can prove the proposition – that is if it needs proof. I don't believe it does because it is a self evident fact that anyone who is fortunate enough to win the affection of as lovely a girl as Anna Crane is a fool if he forfeits this by his own folly, if it can be called by as light a term as folly. Secondly he is a scoundrel, as his actions for the past four years will fully demonstrate and is devoid of moral principle. If Anna could live it down, it will be a fortunate escape for her as I believe firmly that he would have caused her a great deal of unhappiness if he had married her, but unfortunately often such things cannot be lived down. If we could make her life any happier by having her come out to see us I would gladly do it and the next time I write will give the invitation. There is just one trouble about that scheme of yours and that is that while it will be an easy matter to find someone worth a dozen of Leigh Woolson it will be a difficult matter to find anyone

Courtesy Iowa Wesleyan College Archives.
Leigh Woolson.

Ruth Crane Looker Collection.
Anna Crane 1893.

Courtesy Iowa Wesleyan College Archives.

Clara Cole.

worthy of Anna Crane. As you probably know she is one of the girls that I admire.

I should think from your description that your party was a very pleasant one – of course it would be for hasn't it been a saying (among the "boys" at least) that everyone always has a good time at Anna Kurtz's? And don't I wish I could have been there? I am glad it was my best friend that was your "special" company. Allow me to state that I think you did just right in regard to **Clara Cole.**[42] *I believe it must have been a mistake on Clara's part not inviting you, but such mistakes should not be made in social life.*

I am anxiously awaiting that picture of yours. By the way, how about that picture you got from Harry Grahn that you said you would send me if I wanted it. Of course I want it, as I can't have too many of you. And now, my darling I want to tell you that you have put new heart into me by your assurance that you are willing to come with me whenever I am ready! It makes me feel that on me depends everything and you know how it strengthens me. I am another one who is fearfully in earnest, and regard love and wife and house as the things worth striving for. So I am going to go to you next fall for my wife. This has taken firmer possession of me than ever since my visit to Victoria and after seeing Aunt Jennie and her family. Aunt Jennie's husband is government assayer in the department of mines for British Columbia and his salary is not large, and they sometimes find it hard work to get along but I don't believe there is a happier family in the country than they four are.

I never pass a house now that looks all cosy and comfortable within that I don't wish that I had one too, with the sweetest wife in the land to occupy it and again I mentally resolve that another year and I will have that same sweet wife. That resolve is further strengthened when you finally "fess up" that the school work injures your throat. I am going to transplant you to another school where you will have one big pupil to take in hand and train and you will find him quite a task.

I will send you something tomorrow for your throat. I send this on a routine for you to take until you can tell me your symptoms exactly, as you know that is important in homeopathic practice. Tell me all you can about it – just as near the exact sensation as you can describe it. When it is worse and when better – whether any particular circumstance renders it better or worse, whether in tremors or in paroxysms – and especially the time of day, and then I will send something on that basis. If you do this I ought to be successful as Dr. Swan for that is just the basis on which she made her prescription. When a throat is "just a little inflamed," and that lasts for a considerable length of time, it is of importance enough to prescribe carefully. You say that sometimes you can hardly speak in school. Tell me if at that time you are hoarse or if the power to speak seems to be gone without any particular hoarse-ness. Also whether it is brought on by using the voice a good deal or from mental emotion of any kind. I would like to cure that throat of yours if I can. Don't omit telling me anything you may think of because it may seem unimportant or not connected with the throat trouble. Sometimes something remote may have great influence so let me commence to be your physician, surely no one could be as interested in your case as I will be and the more complete you make the first clinical history of the case the quicker I can prescribe the right remedy.

I must stop on this now so as to get it in the mail but I will go right on with the letter. I have not said half of what I want to yet. I want to again wish you a very happy birthday. When that day comes remember that there is one who regards that day as a great one in his life's history as being the day which brought one into the world who is destined to fill his whole life with sweetness and love. My beloved I hope that some day – and all the days of your life that I may prove to you by actions all the love that I feel for you which I must now express in words – that all your days may be joyous and that you may never regret that you allowed your heart to go out to me in trust and affection and that the blessing that your love has brought into my life may return a hundred fold to yours. Good bye sweetheart and in your thinking of me remember that there is not a day of my life that I do not think "I love you" and my life made sweeter thereby.

Goodnight.

Devotedly yours,
Will

Letter 49

Fairhaven, Washington
Monday, October 13, 1890

My Darling Anna,

I send you today medicine for your throat. As I said yesterday this will be a venture until I know more about your special symptoms – in fact a prescription on general principles. I send two powders marked "No 2." Take one of these as soon as receiving it. Take the second one in three days. The other powder take three times a day and take four of the pellets every night before going to bed. You may also take the pellets whenever you have a cough worst at night of a spasmodic wheezing croupy character. While you are taking this medicine discontinue all others. When you give me a full account of your condition I will know more certainly what I will give though it may be that a change will not be necessary. Did not get a letter today though I rather expected it but think it will be here tomorrow all right. I think your idea of writing a long letter Sunday and any kind that you can in the middle of the week will work all right so I get the two a week.

Det Bird and Ed Robinson are out on a ranch (i.e. a farm) sacking and digging or rather digging and sacking potatoes. They are making a speculation in the succulent tuber, having bought up a large quantity for sale late in the season. I have not seen Clint Howard since I came back from Victoria.

I will not make much of a letter out of this as the powders will fill it pretty well, but will write again tomorrow. By the way I am going to enter politics – in a medical way. Either Fairhaven or Sehome will soon be made a sub-port of entry for U.S. Customs and among other things that will create the position of Port Physician. I believe the Collector of Customs at Port Townsend has the appointing power and I am going to make a try for it. It will be worth from $1500 to $2000 a year. I "laid pipe" while I was in Port Townsend and will have some of the physicians there working for me before the others here in town know that such a position will exist.

Well I must stop now. Goodbye dear.

With much love,

Yours Will

Letter 50

Fairhaven, Washington
Monday, Oct. 13, 1890

My Darling Sweetheart,

This is the continuation of the letter of this afternoon. I can't tell how long I will write. It may be only a page and it may be five or six. It is blowing and raining outside and owing to the increased draught – my stove is red hot inside so that I have to keep a window open. First a fiery blast from the stove catches me and then is followed by a cold breeze from outside comes in and congeals the marrow in my osseous tissue.

Added to this "I hab a code id by head," which I caught over in Victoria and brought over with me without having to pay any duty on it.

Notwithstanding all these little inconveniences I am feeling particularly and superlatively happy – for why? The afternoon mail brought a letter and in it was a picture of yourself. To say that I am pleased with the picture would be to draw it too mild altogether. It is much better than I expected from the proof, good as that was. I wish I could have a cabinet or even a larger picture made from that one. Everything about it just suits me – the position, expression – well, I said everything and that is just what I mean. It is the one good picture that you have had taken. Say Anna, you must have had some very pleasing thoughts when you sat for that, the expression is just simply lovely. It is what I have missed in the other pictures I have seen of you. The cabinet that I have, taken when you graduated is good, except that it has a rather severe expression, but this, this is a beautiful sweetness. I am going to have a large portrait made from this sometime because I am sure that I will never get another that will please me better, if in fact one that will please me as well. That would make a lovely picture in pastel Anna. Am I taking up a good deal of time talking about the picture? Not a line too much however. I want you to know how delighted I am with it. Perhaps I have made you understand a small portion of my pleasure at its excellence.

I was surprised to learn of Clara Cole's wedding but that was done just like Clara. Well now, I am envious again. When I was home in the spring they were going to wait some time, as he had his way to make, and it made me feel kind of satisfied to think that we were not the only ones who had to wait. But now they have decided to risk it at the start, and so I feel injured. Say, Anna that class of yours is getting pretty well thinned out isn't it? Wasn't Emma Day in your class? Likewise Georgia Pearce and May Weir, John Willits, Will Lee and I don't know how many others that have since committed matrimony. Suppose I should come home unexpectedly some day and want you to rush things that way! I wonder if you would do it. Well I envy Clara and her husband anyway. I think they have done a sensible thing. How people do change their minds, don't they? I didn't use to think that way. But increasing knowledge has brought a truer conception of women. They are loving and unselfish and not mercenary, as I used to try to make myself believe, through I just give myself the credit of not believing it very firmly.

Courtesy Iowa Wesleyan College Archives.

1890 Photo with inscription on back "Anna Kurtz." May Weir is front, second from left. Leigh Woolson is front, third from right.

The authors could not agree on who was Anna in the photo above. Griffin's choice is on left below, Nelson's choice is the right. Which one do you think is Anna?

Anna Kurtz

Say Anna, you have been giddy lately. If I didn't have the greatest faith in your love I would think that you didn't care much for me to be so gay and have such a good time when I am away, but as my faith is boundless, why I want you to enjoy yourself as much as you can. You shut yourself up too much last year.

Oh say, maybe you will rejoice to learn that I have actually discovered a school board that is worse than that of Mt. Pleasant, and a school system that is doing even more for the doctors than that of the "Athens of Iowa." It is that of Victoria. My fourteen year old cousin Nellie has just entered the high school and she has seven studies to recite in every day, four of which are mathematics and one Latin, together with English history and Physiology – why say, she has more than seven as there is also reading and spelling and dictation. The system of mathematics gets me. Arithmetic, algebra, geometry and a special work on numeration for a nervous fourteen year old girl! Nellie is very ambitious and works hard to keep up. Her nervous system is already so shattered that she walks in her sleep and talks and works nearly all the time that she is asleep. They make laws punishing a person stealing some article belonging to another person, but for the crime of stealing a child's health, there is no punishment! Oh, wise(?) and just (?) lawmakers! There are more shattered bodies and broken down constitutions especially among women today, as a result of the unnatural stuffing system at present prevalent in the schools, than the small increase of intellectual development will ever compensate for. It would seem as if they arrange it so that the heaviest work in the public schools should fall upon girls at just the time of life when they need all the energies for the sudden transition from girlhood to womanhood.

There, I am on my hobby again! But say, I do want to get on a school board sometime if only to ease my need of some ideas on the subject. I am very much in earnest on this subject because I know that many of the troubles that make women such good patients of the doctors had their foundations laid in too much work in school in girlhood. I would better "switch off" on this, however, or I will write a thesis on "The public schools as a factor in the nervous diseases of women." I am going to do it some time. Maybe you will think it strange that I write to you about this, but as I said before, I am very much in earnest on the subject and it makes me boil to see the idiotic ignorance of people in general and school boards in particular on a subject that is of such paramount importance.

I think I will stop and go to bed. While I think of it though, I will answer a question you asked in one of your recent letters in regard to where my office is. It is in the Mason Block.[43] *You can see the building in the photo I sent just opposite the large hotel. You will easily find them both as they are the most prominent in the picture off in the right hand side. To the left of the picture and in the distance is Whatcom. Sehome is hid around the point of land that you see. The wharf that you see in the foreground to the left is the ocean wharf of the Great Northern. If you get a mat of cardboard of about three inches around the pictures and a small oak frame, it will make a very pretty picture. Many people here have had them fixed that way.*

Well, I must stop now. I wish I could say "good night" in propria persona,

Whatcom Museum.

1890s photo showing the Fairhaven Hotel and, across Harris Avenue, the Mason Block.

instead of by the proxy of white paper and black ink but it cannot be for a long time yet, so I will have to be content with simply saying goodnight dear one.

Thursday – Well I didn't get at it again for a day or two. Had a letter this morning in which I found out that at the date of writing, you had just learned of my contemplated trip to Victoria and yet I have been back nearly a week. Verily it is a long distance to Mt. Pleasant.

The Fairhaven railroad company is having some fun at the expense of that suburb just at present.[44] The railroad runs on a trestle across the tide flat in front of Whatcom, and trains stop on the trestle for passengers from Whatcom. They call the station when they stop "North Fairhaven" and then add in advertising it, "Whatcom is easily reached from North Fairhaven by wagon or carriage." Some way the Whatcom people don't like it. Not withstanding all this however, just at present Whatcom and Sehome are lovelier looking and better looking towns – or rather a better looking town – than Fairhaven. Being right together thus bringing the eight thousand people into one community makes more of an appearance than Fairhaven can

Whatcom Museum.

North Fairhaven Station.

present. Besides owing to this greater age they present a more finished appearance. But another year will tell a different story.

My practice this month will not loom up as it has. The fever has nearly abated so the real struggle of working up is to come yet. Nevertheless, I don't fear that it will go so very hard. This epidemic coming just at the start has pulled me through a period that would otherwise have been rather trying, but now I think I can make it all right. The worst struggle for a while will be to add necessary books to my library, which at present is rather limited. But one at a time I think I can squeeze through on that.

Of course I was surprised to learn of Clara Cole's wedding. Your ideas in regard to Dr. Carothers coincide with my impression of him exactly. He struck me as being if not inferior, at least very mediocre. In marrying him, too, I think Clara has come down from the very high standard that she set up with regard to personal habits. The young gentleman uses tobacco in all its forms and while I don't think he is what would be called a drinking man, still he is not at all adverse to a social glass. Now I am not bigot enough to condemn him on this account but from Clara's standpoint in regard to this, I must say she has come down considerably. During the holidays when he was there visiting he was smoking on the street – when he was with Clara and she smiled on it sweetly – I suppose because it was "Robert" – But had some of her Mt. Pleasant acquaintances dared to do the same – whew! There would have been trouble in the camp. I don't doubt though that they will be happy. Clara is very loyal and is undoubtedly very much in love, so I think they will be happy. But I wish myself that it was some one else.

We are beginning to have a good deal of wet weather, and I expect the rainy season is most here. Do not find it particularly disagreeable however. I send you this time the pansies that I intended to send before I went over to Victoria – grown in Mrs. Templin's garden. Will stop now and peruse some Materia Medica – did you ever hear of that before?[45]

Say, Mt. Pleasant must have been quite gay for the past week or so. Wonder why I never happened to strike it, when it has a streak of hilarity. Am glad you are taking part in it. Hope you will continue to do so whenever opportunity offers.

Say Anna, when I get back "next Fall" you will have to take me in training for about a week before it will be safe to trust me in company.

Goodbye dear.
Lovingly, Will

Letter 51

Fairhaven, Washington
Sunday, Oct. 19, 1890

My Darling Anna,

The days are passing – some would say rapidly – though they seem to me to be going slowly enough. I would like to have the time pass more quickly. It grows very weary out here waiting for home, for wife, for practice – in fact for about everything that is desirable.

The past week has been very dull, and it would not surprise me at all if there would be two months of rather dull season. By the end of that time we will have connection with Seattle by rail, and also with British Columbia. The latter extension of the railroad seems to be delayed somewhat by the failure of some needed iron to arrive. The ship is overdue in which it is to come and has undoubtedly met with rough weather.

Practice has not been good for the past week. I am afraid that this month is going to fall off badly from last if it even comes up to the first. Of course there will be eight days out of this month – the time that I spent in Victoria. However, I get along, pay my current expenses and meet my old debts as they come due. Tomorrow clears off another fifty dollars, as well as some minor accounts. So I suppose that I ought to consider myself as doing very well. But I get rather impatient when I see my totals for a week foot up less than they have weeks previous. But we'll "get there" yet. Just give us time.

I wish sometimes in moments of despondency that I had not come out here – that I had gone south. There are cities in Alabama, Tennessee, Virginia and Georgia that are booming as much as the towns out here are and are nearer to centers of civilization besides. Birmingham, Alabama has a population of 50,000 and only two homeopaths – and other large towns of 20,000 and 30,000 have none at all. I saw this just a few days ago in the medical journal and for a few minutes I wished that I had known it before I came out here.

I have no doubt that we are going to have a fine city here, but I must confess that I get tired of the everlasting "boom – boom!" "We are the greatest" – etc. etc.

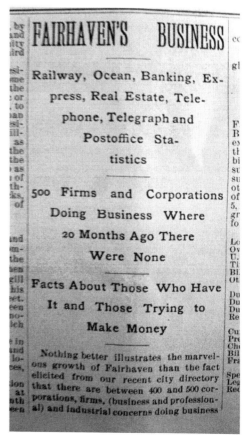

FAIRHAVEN'S BUSINESS

Railway, Ocean, Banking, Express, Real Estate, Telephone, Telegraph and Postoffice Statistics

500 Firms and Corporations Doing Business Where 20 Months Ago There Were None

Facts About Those Who Have It and Those Trying to Make Money

Nothing better illustrates the marvelous growth of Fairhaven than the fact elicited from our recent city directory that there are between 400 and 500 corporations, firms, (business and professional) and industrial concerns doing business

Fairhaven Herald, December 29, 1890. CPNWS.

and then the restaurants – ugh! And I can't afford to go to that boarding house that I spoke of for a while at least. The truth is I don't feel much like writing today, so I think I will stop.

I am sorry that no letters will go out today. There is a fierce storm blowing and outside of the harbor the waters are rising high. The mail boat is a flat bottomed affair like the Mississippi steamers, only intended to ply on the Sound. They are very fast in quiet weather, but can not ride in a wind, and so have to stay in the harbor until it blows over. The white crested waves are very beautiful, even if they are very dangerous. Goodbye dear.

Monday – *The wind is still blowing so that the "down the Sound" mail boat was about six hours late. It brought a letter from you, which made me feel very conscience stricken and also renewed my regrets at coming so far. I thought my Victoria letter would reach you about the usual time, but did not take into consideration the increased distance. I am very sorry dear that you had a moment's worry. And I want to say right here that you need never worry about any danger to me for I promise you that if there is ever anything really the matter with me that I will let you know of it at once, because I think that that is much better than suspense, so in my case always consider "no news good news." But I ought to have remembered that this is a hard time of year for you dear and so have sent my letters more frequently. I have reproached myself more than once for coming so far, but I thought it all for the best, but I can assure you that if we are not married next summer or fall I shall leave here and go where I can be near you. You need not have any fears on my account that when we are married that I will find it hard work to get away from you. I shall even make the effort but will try to take you every place that I go. Keep right on with the doilies because I will not be separated from you another year.*

Today is the 20th of October. Either we will be married before this time next year, or I will be where I can see you quite frequently. Just remember that I see things clearer now than I did. I know that love is the one good thing and that it is a mistake for two people to be separated for pecuniary reasons solely. I have no reason to complain of my success here and yet if I were to do over again I would not do as I have done.

I hope you had a very pleasant birthday and that my little remembrance and letter arrived on time. I would like to know what has been happening to you now. I am not going to worry because it is past and you are safe but it seems to me that you are having more than your share of disasters just at present. But say now, Anna, don't you think it just a little mean to intentionally keep me in suspense in regard to your latest adventure in revenge for my unintentional delay in writing? Never mind however, I forgive you.

Was called up to Mr. Hamilton's again this morning to see his little boy. When I arrived on the scene the boy had gone to school. The house was right near the schoolhouse so the boy was sent for and was found to be all right. Mr. Hamilton is one of those kinds of men that want to have things all right and be on the safe side regardless. I had quite a little chat with Mrs. Hamilton. Their house looks very nice inside. The floors are of yellow fir, oiled and polished with rugs thrown around promiscuously. One thing took my eye as illustrating very prettily your idea of a yellow and white room. It was a wicker rocking chair painted white and gilded on the edges. It had a yellow embroidered bag hanging to one side of it and taking it all around was very pretty.

By the way I ran across some very pretty china silk painted doilies in the Chinese quarter at Victoria. Thought once of getting some of those instead of the handkerchiefs but concluded that you would rather work your own doilies. Several little four room cottages are going up here now and very pretty little affairs they are going to be too. Every time I see one of them I wish that I could put up one about like it.

You spoke in one of your letters of seeing in the Post Intelligencer that the population of Fairhaven was 4,031 when the census was taken. Allow me to state that that is the Seattle estimate. The official census figures give Fairhaven 4,316. Seattle has not yet learned that Bellingham is a part of Fairhaven. Read the Post Intelligencer and you will notice how studiously that paper refrains from mentioning Fairhaven except to say something ill-natured about it. Some years ago a member of the Seattle Chamber of Commerce said in one of these meetings, "We must prevent at all hazards the growth of a future rival to Seattle on Bellingham Bay." That was when Fairhaven had not been dreamed of and Whatcom and Sehome were mere villages. Yet even thus, they feared the natural advantages of this point. They are following out that idea and do everything in their power to injure the Bellingham Bay towns. The population of Fairhaven today is 5,000 and in three years the rival of Seattle will be grown, right here on the Bay as that town will know her commercial sorrow. It may be thought that Fairhaven and the other towns are too sanguine, but when lumber merchants of San Francisco for their own protection establish a boycott on Bellingham Bay lumber and yet allow that of Seattle and Tacoma to enter their markets, it looks as if even that city feared the future of the Bay Cities.

Well, I will stop now and write soon again. It seems as if I don't feel like writing at a regular time anymore but would rather put my letters in when I feel like it: Sometimes I feel as if I would like to write every day.

Will probably write again tomorrow.

So good bye dear.
With much love.

Yours,

Will

Letter 52

Fairhaven, Washington
Wednesday, Oct. 22, 1890

My Darling Anna,

   The last few days have been about as dismal as they very well can be. Wind and rain have been trying to see which could do the most, but I think the rain finally got the best of it. For two days and two nights there was not five minutes of the time that some water was not coming down. I never saw such a steady rain. The "oldest inhabitants" say that it has been one of the worst storms they have ever known out here. How much of that statement may be attributed to "boom" remains to be seen. There are times, you know, when "boom" is synonymous with "lie." For your satisfaction however, I will state that I have not heard a moment of thunder or seen a flash of lightning this side of the mountains. Whether they have any in the winter or not, I can't say.

   Well, either a few of the doctors here must starve to death or leave town or the city must grow very rapidly. Three more have come here. That makes fifteen I believe and no country to depend on at all. Whether I will be one of those to starve I can't say, but I certainly won't leave town. I don't know whether this month is going to come up to the first month or not, but I am afraid not. That's "tuff" beg pardon – "Tuff," with a big T. Another patient has "skipped." I think about one more experience of that kind and I will begin to come down hard and will make everybody pay up just the moment I am through with them – but I do hate the business part of it. Don't believe I have much business ability anyway. There's where my colleague, Dr. Heacock gets away with me. I know from what he tells me that he does a goodly amount of boasting and actual "working" of people for practice. I can't do that, if I never get any – or rather I suppose I could, but I won't. If I have to flatter and fawn and "blow my own trumpet" to get practice I will go without. I don't intend to descend to any cheap John trick to acquire patronage. But I get very tired of sitting around in my office waiting for patients.

   One reason why my practice has fallen off I think is because my sign as been taken down. The lessor of the building wants to put on metropolitan airs, so he will allow no signs to be hung out at the entrance to the stairway and about a month ago took my sign down. All the other physicians have front rooms and have their windows lettered. My rooms being back, I cannot do that. Hence I have no sign out. About all the patients I have had the past month were directed to me by former patients. I want to be on the lookout for the first good brick building that goes up and secure good front rooms where I can have a prominent location.

   Monday night was out to tea at Mr. Hamilton's. Was called up there again just about tea time to see the little boy and they urged me to stay to tea and truth to tell, I didn't need much urging. And since then the restaurant has seemed worse than ever. The waiter in the restaurant rushes up to a person and shouts out, a la tough, "Well what do you want?" or "Well, whatyougointoeat?"! If I'm not feeling in very

Whatcom Museum.

Intersection of 10th Street and Harris Avenue before grading. Terminal Building upper left.

good humor I say: "Soup!!" with the latter part of it snapped off short as if it came out of a steel trap.

Don't believe I like being a pioneer very well. But it will be all right when we get our three or four rooms. I think I will be content anywhere then.

It is too wearing on the nervous system, you know, to be constantly worried about something, fearing that something has happened or may happen. I will try and worry through this year but that is the last. Either I will have you with me, or I will go where you are. This year of separation is enough to last me a lifetime. I know when I have enough and it has already been a great deal more than enough.

I wonder if you have been indulging in any more parties lately or if Mt. Pleasant has gotten over its little social flurry and will settle down to most monotonous dullness for the rest of the year.

And how is that throat of yours getting along? You know I am a little interested in that throat. In fact I feel a little personal interest as well as professional. Are you not surprised?

I will have to stop now and make a couple of calls. The only cases I have on hand. Remember me to all of the family. That will occupy you for some time. Especially remember me to Aunt May and Cousin Mary.

Good bye dear.

Lovingly, Will

Letter 53

Fairhaven, Washington
Saturday, October 25, 1890

My Darling Sweetheart,

What a wonderful difference a few sheets of paper traced with a few black lines will make with a person under certain conditions of mind. This morning I confidently expected a letter but it came not. As it is a rare occurrence for a letter from the East to come on the afternoon boat I had tried to reconcile myself to not having one until Monday. But from force of habit I went to the post office when the afternoon boat came in (it usually only carries mail from around the Sound) and behold the letter materialized when I have no letters.

I feel more tired and lonesome than usual, even, and I am sure that nothing on earth would seem quite as pleasant to me tonight as to spend the evening with you in Mt. Pleasant. It's all such a blank without you dear. The fact is, Anna, life isn't worth living without you. I just yearn for you all the time. I am not half filled for my work. I feel so miserable and lonely all the time. Say Anna, why can't we be married in June? Say yes and I know that I can make it. Maybe this is selfish to ask it as I can not give you as nice a home as you are in, but I feel that this living separated so far is awful. If anything should happen to either of us we might be dead before the other could travel half the distance. It almost sets me wild sometimes. I have often thought that a man ought not to ask a woman to marry him until he is quite well to do, but I believe that where they love each other they are stronger together. I know I need you Anna. I am not half a man away from you. Say the word Anna and I will make a home for you and we will end the heartache of separation next June. I never thought when I decided to come out here that it would be so hard. I think that I did not estimate the strength of my love and what a long separation meant.

I will try so hard to make you happy dear. Don't you think we can fight the battle of our life a great deal easier than we can this constant longing for each other? I am assuming that you love me as I do you. Say that you will marry me in June, dear and we will commence to plan in earnest. We are both of us uneasy and unhappy as we are. It can be done as easily in June as in October and I don't think it right to put off later than that. Besides I want you to get the benefit of the summer climate and become acclimated before the rainy season sets in. I am very serious, very much in earnest about this dear. I wonder at my own boldness because I cannot offer you luxury but we can make a home on my practice, small as it is and we will hope that it will be larger.

And while at a moment like this I do not want to dwell on the practical side very long, let me say dear that any increased expense that may be incurred when a physician marries is fully covered by the increase in practice. I know positively of practice amounting to fully one-third of what I have done that I would have had, if I were a married man. And heaven helping me, Anna, I know that I am man enough to provide for both of us comfortably by the middle of next June. If you say yes, I know that it will give me elation enough to last until the time, and energy to accomplish wonders.

There is one thing Anna, very sure, I will never go home and come back without you and I am going home next year. Either you come out with me or I stay where I can be near you. I will be near those who are dear to me, and you will never know how dear you are to me until your life and mine have blended into one loving whole. Anna, my darling, say that you will change it from sweetheart to wife when the June roses are in blossoms and you will always find me true and faithful. I will love you all the days of my life, Anna. I know that I am asking a great deal, but my love and my loneliness make me bold. Let us end the yearning and longing. If we set the time for June we will both be occupied in preparation and the time will pass, if not quickly, at least tolerably. I am going to quit for tonight, but am very likely to resume the subject tomorrow. After what I have said this evening, in closing need I say that I love you darling? Good night dear.

Sunday afternoon *– Here we are again. The photograph is of Fairhaven and Bellingham Bay. Fairhaven lying to the right along the heights and in front. Sehome and Whatcom lie beyond the point of the hill. Off beyond the hazy part of the water you will see the Hotel Fairhaven in the right hand section of the picture, with the scaffolding still up on the tower. Right across the street you will see another large block – that is the Mason Block where I have my office. The picture was taken in the early part of August. One taken now would present a much different appearance on account of new buildings and especially on account of new streets graded and planked.*

Whatcom and Sehome are to vote on consolidation soon again. This time it will doubtless be carried and there will be but two towns on the bay instead of four as there was a year ago. So it will be narrowed down to a rivalry between Fairhaven and Whatcom. I must say that just at present they are making improvements over there faster than they are here – that is substantial improvements. They are going to get ahead of Fairhaven in the matter of an opera house. Whatcom is to build a house to be completed in sixty days which will give that place the benefit of first-class entertainments. But as there will very likely be a street railway in operation in both towns, by the time the house is completed we will all have the benefit.

Today's paper contains a page article on Fairhaven's resources. It is the best one that I have seen. I will send you a copy tomorrow. I must close now, but don't fail to give close, serious thought to my last night's theme and let us work to something definite – in the immediate future and we won't talk any more about years but reduce it to months. I want to have you dear, wherever our love will not have to be diffused across four thousand miles of space.

Good bye dear.
Lovingly, Will

Letter 54

Fairhaven, Washington
Monday, Oct. 27, 1890

My Darling Anna,

The day has been a beautiful one, though presenting different phases. In the early morning there was a pearly translucent mist through which everything looked phantom like. Later on the sun shone through this mist like a great crimson globe. The water looks like glass with a rose tint on it, looking through the mist like a great opal with wondrous depths of color. The boats looked like dreams, every cord and rope and spar a mere suggestion. In the afternoon the mists cleared away, the sky was azure blue and sun shone brightly, a gentle breeze sprung up and the waters rippled and danced in the sunlight as if happy that the morning mist had lifted the burden from off their breast and given the freedom to sport at their will. Instead of phantom-like vagueness of the morning everything now appears with almost startling distinctiveness.

Whatcom appears only half the usual distance away. Mt. Baker, cold and white and beautiful seems but a few minute's walk away. Northward the distant peaks of the Selkirk range over in British Columbia show their hoary heads, irregular and jagged. The "Sisters" towering above their humbler relatives. Westward the Souf Mountains[46] are over on her Majesty's island of Vancouver, of historic fame. To the south and west the majestic Olympics rear their heads as if they would "o'ertop old Pelion." Nearer in the view are the dark green islands of the Sound, the whole completing a picture that will present kaleidoscopic changes of scene with every day in the year. The falling or rising of the wind, the changing of the atmosphere, the rising or the setting of the sun will cause a new picture to present itself. Always the same, in fact. Yet an endless variety suited to every varying mood of the human soul.

Come out! Ye dwellers of the plains when nothing greets your eyes save the monotonous stretch of prairies and see nature in her grandeur where she weeps with the sad and laughs with the gay. "Lift up your voices oh ye everlasting hills" and tell the multitudes of weary wayfarers in the drought stricken east that there is an empire in the Pacific Northwest, where nature has lavished her choicest blessings satisfying every desire of the human heart, where the beautiful and the sublime are blended with utility and productiveness, where the aesthetic goes hand in hand with the useful. Come out! And be content to dwell forever where the breath of the salt water will be unto you like a draught of the elixir of life, and when ye have come and tasted of its joys, ye will say with the mariners in "The Lotus Eaters." "We will return no more, we will no longer roam." "Oh, rest ye weary mariners, we will not wander more."

This is about all I want to say tonight but it was on my mind and it had to be said. Don't allow the little outburst to have any injurious effect on your health. Say Anna, how would that look in print? Do you know I have tried several times to write a letter to the "Journal" but some way it never seems to go. Suppose you do try your hand at compiling or editing a letter – joint authorship you know, on the

Howard Buswell Collection #Bus0508. Center for Pacific Northwest Studies, WWU.

Mt. Baker. Note Chuckanut Bay and the Chuckanut Sandstone Quarry center, and "Lord" Newton's cannery on right.

collaboration plan that the novelists sometimes pursue. By the way if you could get an engraving made of my drawing (?) of the crab and flounder it would look pretty well I think.

Say if you should fix up a letter, please exercise your prerogative as a school teacher and fix any glaring errors in construction. My syntax is sometimes fearfully and wonderfully made.

Well, I must say good night for the very good reason that Morpheus has camped on my eyelids with the effect of rending them a trifle heavy and to shake him off might offend him so seriously that he would not deign to return for several hours. A consummation that is not devoutly to be wished. So Goodnight dear.

Tuesday afternoon – Another letter came this morning and I was correspondingly delighted but I still missed the account of your narrow escape.

Say, Mt. Pleasant must be quite gay this fall with all the parties and teas. What's struck it all at once? Wish I could be there to enjoy some of it. I am becoming very rusty socially. Don't know what I will do about it unless I make some changes soon. I am like Clint Howard in regard to boarding at Mrs. Sherman's. I would like to do so very much but feel that at present I cannot afford it. About Clint and Ed Robinson having a restaurant, that is a mistake but they do run a lodging house I don't think they want it known so keep mum about it.[47] They made the instrument in some way last fall. Dave Kenworthy, who used to keep the Brazelton Hotel

Mount Pleasant town square with P.E.O. Memorial Fountain. Brazelton Hotel in center background. Hervey Crane's jewelry store was in the building with awning on left.

at one time, is managing it for them and they are not known to be connected with it by but a few people here. Say Anna, if you have started to study German I must commence to brush up what little I know of it. It may be useful sometime when we take our trip to Germany, for instance.

Wednesday – I stopped right there chiefly because I did not have anything more to say. This morning the "State of Washington" the mail boat and one of the fastest on the Sound ran on the rocks in the fog. Just below here in Chuckanut Bay and is a total wreck. She had just been in dry-dock for five weeks and been entirely refitted.

Have been spending a good deal of my time the last two days doing miscellaneous reading in "The Arena" and Scribner's. I like The Arena very much, better I think than the "North American Review" or the "Forum." Have you read Dr. Materialismus in the November Scribner's? It is a study in speculative physics. Those kinds of stories never fail to have a peculiar interest for me in some way. I was very much interested in an article in the "Arena" entitled "a glance at the "Good Old Days." It was an argument to show that the so called "good old days" were not such good old days after all. It was a good argument and it was beautifully written besides. I never read well a written story or article or essay that I didn't wish that I could write something as good. The old desire to write something lingers with me, but I feel impressed (or oppressed) more and more of my inability to do so. I wonder if all men feel as restless as I do and if it lasts all their lives. Always yearning to have something that I have not or do something that I can't do. Well I suppose that time will answer that problem and nothing else will. My reading does me little good here. There is no one to discuss it with after it is done so that it doesn't make much impression.

Well, I must stop now. My thoughts don't run easily today, so I would but disfigure the paper to continue.

Goodbye dear.
Lovingly,
Will

Letter 55

Fairhaven, Washington
Friday, Oct. 31, 1890

My Darling Anna,

For the past three days the Puget Sound fog has hung so heavy over the land that except at intervals where a bank of it rolls away for a few minutes it is impossible to see more than a hundred feet. Many of the boats running to this point have met with disaster.

The "Eastern Oregon" passenger steamer ran onto a rock at Port Townsend. The "Premier" passenger steamer collided with a ship at anchor at the same place and had one side wrecked. A freight steamer while trying to make a landing at the wharf ran into it and destroyed about two hundred feet of it. There have been several minor disasters. I should think if this fog were cut into blocks and stored up it could be shipped to Eastern Washington and Northern Dakota to considerable advantage.

Well today closes the third month of practice. With two calls to be made this afternoon, it foots up $110, a considerable falling off from last month but better than the first month, as there are eight days out of it. The time spent at Victoria. I am in hopes that next month will show a material increase. The real struggle will come in the next four or five months as all physicians say that the rainy season is

Galen Biery Collection (#1694). Center for Pacific Northwest Studies, WWU.

Fog settling in over the Puget Sound.

the most healthful time of year on the coast. I think however that I will get along all right but I will have to work for my practice. There are now seventeen doctors in Fairhaven, and some of them will have to starve out. If I have any "staying" powers at all, I don't intend that it shall be me, though doubtless, ere long there will be some hurt feelings and some animosities stirred up somewhere.

This is to be just a note to go out tonight. No mail goes out Saturday nights and it would make it quite a while to wait until Sunday. If I can just get enough money ahead to do so I am going to try and get around a little socially this winter – in the interest of business. Next Thursday night the Methodist Episcopal Church commences a series of ten star lectures and concerts by first class people. Joseph Cook is the first. The Swedish Quartet, Geo. R. Wendling, H. Miner Griswald, the Texas Siftings' man, Frank Beard in "Chalk Talk," The Buster Ideal Concert Co., Nella Brown Elocutionist, are in the course. So you see if we are in the furthest Northwest corner of Uncle Sam's dominions we are not quite cut off from everything. By the way, read the article "Nature and Man in America" in the November Scribner's. The author thinks that the Oregonian country in which he includes Oregon and Washington – the western part – will be the greatest in America. Well, I must stop now.

Goodbye dear.

With much love,
Yours, Will

Letter 56

Fairhaven
Sunday, November 2, 1890

My Darling Sweetheart,

Have just had another letter from you, and things are looking quite bright again. The fog has disappeared and today is as beautiful as anyone could wish. The bay is bright, the mountains are all in sight and the whole scene is altogether grand and lovely. I never get tired of the water and the mountains. It looks today very much like an autumn day in Iowa with that same lazy appearance in the distance. It has been a long time since I gave the post office a raking, hasn't it? Well this is a good opportunity. I wrote to mother the same day that I wrote your birthday letter and the next day I sent the letter to you with the medicine and directions and the box of pellets at the same time. It seems that from today's letter that the pellets had just arrived and mother's letter not at all. The post master here is of the "genus mossbackinus" and his clerks partake very much of the same characteristics. I think they make up the mails just about as they choose and send them out when it suits their convenience. But then, what can you expect in a town that grows out of its clothes as fast as this one does?

Say Anna, you ought to see me now. I have a beard that is so big and bushy it would be the envy of a German socialist. I don't know what it will be by this time next year. Probably I shall be able to part it and tie it at the back of my neck.

Just at that point was called out to see a sick baby. Poor little mortal. I am afraid its chances in this life are rather slim. In fact I have little hope that it will recover. Case of infantile summer complaint of ten weeks standing and it is so emaciated that the skin on its neck hangs in folds, so weak that it can not hold its head up and its blood so impoverished and thinned it collects in spots under the skin. It is going to take close study on my part to do what little that can be done. I will have to cut this short to study up so as to be prepared for any emergency.

I want to assure you now that if I smiled at all when you said that you were thinking of our future home when you had your picture taken, it was a smile of pleasure not of amusement.

I have been feeling for the last two or three days as if I ought to start for home. Tuesday is Election Day and I ought to be "going home to vote," as I have for the past two years. However next fall, (or summer?) I will be going home to vote. When there will only be two electors and the vote will be unanimous—it will be a vote for the protection of home industries.

Goodbye dear. Will write again tomorrow.

Lovingly, Will

Letter 57

Fairhaven, Wash
Monday, November 3, 1890

My Darling Sweetheart,

 The Sunday has passed by without my going to church. For why? I have a "Job's Comforter" that occupies a large area of territory on the back of my neck and lo-comotion is not rendered especially easy and comfortable thereby. Last night the house and myself sat up together, or at least I thought I would not be so disrespect-ful to the passing hours as to sleep in their presence, so Morpheus passed me by on the other side of the street. Once or twice he deigned to call for a few minutes at a time but brought with him a horde of unpleasant visions that tormented me as much sleeping as the "furunculous" did waking. I had one very tormenting dream. "Methought" I was in Mt. Pleasant and was going down to see you. I had just ar-rived at the top of the steps when I realized that on account of the pain in the back of my neck I had not cleaned the mud off my feet, and that my clothes were decided-ly dirty. I stood a moment pondering whether you had heard me. Then I decided to go up town and have my shoes bleached and my clothes brushed. So I proceeded to act upon that decision, and then – well, then I awoke, before I got back to the house and the result was I did not see you. I wonder if you can imagine how disappointed I felt? I tried hard to go to sleep again so as to finish the dream; but it was no go. I tossed and tumbled the rest of the night.

 Well today ends another month. Business on the books for the month $177.50. That is better than last month though it is far short of the second month. I hardly think that I will run as closely again for money as I was some time ago. I have forty dollars in my pocket now, and will make collections for the past month tomorrow. I am going to make an effort – now to put by something every month as a "wedding fund." About the house. I will try to tell you as near as I can, but they are all occu-pied now and likely to be.

 I don't know about the size of the rooms but they are small. The little business at the back is a kind of shed kitchen of rough boards. However, I think that the best thing to do will be to get some owner of a lot to put up a building a month or so before we are married and have it ready by the time we get out here. Or, we

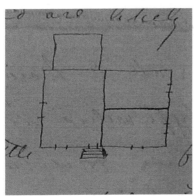

Illustration by W.R. Gray.

can get rooms in someone's house. I think that the coming spring there will be a great amount of residence building. At present buildings are hardly to be had for love or money. Dr. Van Winter, the dentist – has been looking for a house for some time. He and his wife want to get about three rooms for fifteen dollars a month, but have not yet been successful. But there will be a change here in six months. Many who are now holding lots will build so as to get an income from them.

About Frank Crane I hardly know what to say. Positions as type writers are hard to obtain except in larger cities. Here they would want a man who, besides being able to work a typewriter would understand general business principles and of course Frank has not yet had training in that line. That requires experience and the question arises, could he make enough to pay his expenses while acquiring that experience of some one business? I have not yet answered Frank's letter, but will on the same mail with this. I have not known what to say because I wondered whether his parents knew of or approved of his desire to come out here. I want to be assured of that. Of course you understand that I am very willing to do anything that I can, but want to be in harmony with the views of his parents, and for Frank's own best interests.

I fully agree with you that Frank's salvation lies in his having something to do, and a sense of responsibility. I think his father must desire something definite very soon, for his cherished desire of having Frank to go to college and make a scholar will never be fulfilled. Unless a boy has a very strong tendency towards a studious life, I have about come to the conclusion that Mt. Pleasant is about the worst place I know of for him to be in. If he means business, I will do all in my power for him because I have thought for a long time that he will be ruined if he stays in Mt. Pleasant and that he will be better off anywhere outside of it. So you may rest assured that I will do all I can, both for your sake and for his own.

I am on the lookout for a place for Ed Richmond too. There is no hope for him in Dakota. He has had considerable experience however in loans, real estate, insurance, general clerical work and book keeping, also in dry goods and moreover, has lived so long in a small frontier town that he knows about how to get along in a new country. That is something Frank has yet to learn. To a certain extent thus far he has "fed on the roses and lain in the lilies of life" though doubtless he doesn't realize it. I know it would be pleasant for you to have Frank out here. I have thought that perhaps you would get lonely without someone of the family and it has worried me a little. I know that it is hard for one person to suddenly take the place of a number of life long companions and it would be a very conceited man that would expect to, even if he does expect and hope to make a certain person happy.

Well you can't imagine how much I enjoy your letters when you talk about your plans for the future. It makes it seem delightfully near – and then I wish for more practice. I don't know how I am going to come out, but I feel that I must go after you in June. Life is too dreary without you dear. I associate you with every thing in the future and feel all the time that everything is just a mere temporary arrangement until we are married. Well, think I will see if I can't get some sleep tonight. Don't believe I will however. Good night sweetheart.

Lovingly,
Will

Letter 58

Fairhaven, Wash
Tuesday, November 4, 1890

My Darling Anna,

Today is Election Day and everything is very quiet under the Australian ballot system. Yesterday I had to sign my first death certificate – the child I spoke of in my last letter. It was dead before I arrived yesterday morning. Nothing could have been done. The poor little thing was almost a skeleton, it was so wasted by long continued sickness – a victim to long continued unintentional but ignorant neglect. It might have been stopped six weeks ago and the child's life saved, but as it was it was beyond any power to prolong its life. It is an experience that will come from time to time in the future, but I hope they will be far apart.

Practice does not improve much. Tomorrow will probably see the last of my fever cases off my hands. As they constituted seventy-five per cent of all cases last month, I don't know what the outlook of this month will be. Rather slim, I think.

Am going out to hear Joseph Cook tomorrow night – if nothing intervenes. There hasn't been anyone in to my office in the evening for the past two weeks but it would be just my luck to have some one come in tomorrow night and want me to go somewhere where I would be detained for two or three hours. Ah, yes, I have had someone in the evening, too. Last night, a man who had been imbibing too much election "redeye" and had a case of the "horrors" and wanted me to straighten him up. That's one kind of patients that we meet. Did I tell you the same man came in one evening and stayed until twelve o'clock and told me about everything he ever knew, but dwelling particularly on the fact that he wanted to end his miserable existence. He is a perfect slave to whiskey. This is the fourth time now that I have had to treat him for the incipient case of delirium tremors. But this is a digression, as the novelists say. The subject of the lecture is to be "Does Death End All?" I have committed the unwarrantable extravagance of purchasing a season ticket for the course of lectures and concerts – $5.00 for the ten.

You must tell me how the medicine I sent succeeds with your throat. I don't expect so very much from it inasmuch as it was prescribed too much on general principles and not enough on a definite condition.

I am looking very anxiously for all your letters now, in answer to my questions of a short time back. Perhaps you can imagine how anxiously in view of what the question was. I must stop now, but will write soon again, and hope that I can write a letter with some spirit in it. I can't do it now. Goodbye dear. With much love.

Yours, Will

Letter 59

Fairhaven, Wash
Wednesday, November 5, 1890

My Darling Sweetheart,

I have just finished reading for the third time your last letter wherein you scold me – yes, that's right – for being blue and it has commenced to occur to me that my letters recently must have had quite an indigo hue. Of course my practice does not begin to keep me busy. In fact it takes up but a small part of my time. Then I do some studying, but of course that cannot take up all the time. It is all so monotonous. Just imagine yourself spending all your time in one room, except an occasional visit to some shack day after day, with no one that you know ever or very rarely coming in – no one except an occasional patient, taking meals at a poor restaurant, and with no social advantages.

From the social side, I am as much unacquainted as when I came here. Nearly all my patients have been among working people, living in temporary shanties. Mr. Hamilton's being the only nice family that I have. I do not say all this by way of complaint, but simply to let you see that it is almost impossible for me to avoid being – well, we'll call it blue, for want of a better name.

There were eight or ten days last week and the week before when during all that time there was not a soul in my office – except when Det Bird and Ed Robinson dropped in for a few minutes once or twice. I had two fever cases on hand during that time, so that I was doing five dollars a day business, and hence did not feel bad on that account. But this being alone all the time is awful. In my former life I had at least the change of scene from the office to my room or boarding house, thereby presenting two phases of life daily, but here it is the one. I have no doubt that my business will get along very well, but it is the personal element that makes it hard. Then when I am sitting in my office hour after hour I get to thinking of you, and I think what a boon it would be if I could put on my coat and hat and strike out for East Washington Street and then – well, then is the time that I don't care for anything else.

I try as much as I can to keep cheerful but sometimes it is an impossibility and I expect that it tinges my letters sometimes, but I had no idea to such an extent as I begin to see from your letters has been the case – I will endeavor to avoid it in the future as much as possible. I have dwelt on this too long, though but I wanted you to know that my business is responsible for but a very small portion of my "despondency" but just simply too much of my own company. But we won't say anything more about this now and I will continue this later. Good night dear.

Friday *– Well, the election is over and it looks as if there had been a great rattling of dry bones and the Republicans so to speak "are not in it" though they do seem to be floundering in the Puree. But through all, Fairhaven rejoices because she cast nearly as many votes as Whatcom and Sehome combined and that is what she was most interested in. In ten days more there will be railroad connection with Seattle and Tacoma and in a few days more the northern branch to the Canadian*

Pacific will put on trains. There are only about two miles of road to complete.

Last night I went to hear Rev. Joseph Cook lecture on the subject "Does Death End All" in which he undertook to show without any reference to revelation at all that it does not. It was a logical and eloquent lecture all through. He held the audience almost spellbound for nearly two hours and the universal comment was that it was a great lecture. In his preliminary remarks Dr. Cook said that a section of Fairhaven ought to be taken to the World's Fair as an evidence of western growth and enterprise. The next entertainment in the course will be the Swedish Quartette, Nov. 26.

Yesterday morning Fairhaven had her good name for orderliness somewhat rudely damaged by a murder[48] – committed in a saloon – of course. The papers in

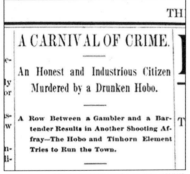

Weekly World, November 8, 1890. CPNWS.

the villages at the north end of the bay make it an opportunity to make an onslaught on Fairhaven calling it the resort of thugs, thieves, hobos, etc, and that notwithstanding, that they have been full of robberies committed in Whatcom and Sehome, lately, while Fairhaven has been free from anything of the kind.

I am wondering how you are getting along by this time. Was very sorry to learn than you have another of those villainous colds that seem to come to you every year. Hope that long ere this reaches you, that it is over with, and that you will not have any such siege as you had last year. Unpleasant experiences seem to be coming to you a little oftener than your share, but you seem to come through them all right.

I was accosted today on the street by a young man whose face looked very familiar, asking if my name was not Gray. Upon my answering in the affirmative, he introduced himself as a former student of the S.U.I. in the engineering department. He said he remembered me when I made my foolish little attempt in the oratorical contest and afterward in the medical department. I then remembered where I had seen his face. I did not know him when there.

Well, I must stop now and go out and make some calls – not regular visits, but two of my recent fever cases that are convalescent. I want to be sure that they are getting along all right, even if it does not count as a professional visit. This week has not been so bad – $37.75. I – it has just occurred to me that if this letter should be put into type, a requisition would have to be sent into the type foundry for an extra supply of capital 'I's. I'll promise not to afflict you that way again very soon.

Good bye sweetheart,
Lovingly, Will

Letter 60

Fairhaven, Washington
Sunday, Nov. 9, 1890

My Darling Sweetheart,

If you should undertake to imagine how hilariously happy your letter that came today has made me you would utterly fail reaching the true state of affairs. The letter was like you, and do you know, much what I expected. You are wiser than I dear, and I know that my fate will always be safe with you to counsel and restrain.

So make your preparations for June as well as you can. If we should think it wise to delay three months longer why then you can just add that much to your preparations for it must not be longer than fall anyway. I have felt that we ought to get our home started for some time. Even if we started with considerable money, a home is a growth – it takes time to build it – it takes time for all the little associations and experiences that cluster around it. And you need not fear Anna, that I will not be willing to start very humbly indeed if I can only be assured and feel that you will be content. You have been accustomed to a nice house and you may miss it more than you think, but I can assure you that I shall be content with very little to begin with. I am anxious for the beginning.

Do you know, I picture to myself sometimes what pleasure and pride we will take in every little thing that we may be able to add to our little household either for use or ornament. Right there though, I want to make a protest, and that is that the idea should ever occur to you that I might ever think of or regret what I might have if I were not married. Why, even if by remaining single I were able to obtain many luxuries, do you suppose they would bring me any pleasure or happiness by myself? Would I not rust out and grow lonely and melancholy and be a burden to myself and everybody else? Most certainly I should.

My darling the great trouble with you is that you are entirely too modest. You either do not see or will not admit to yourself that you can never be anything to me but a help. You have expressed the fear a number of times that you will keep me back and hinder my cases. That is a mistake. A true and loving wife and that I know you will be, can never be a hindrance but is always a help to a man, no matter what his circumstances may be. I should be nothing without you. With you, I feel that there is nothing that I will not be able to accomplish. So I shall work hard for practice so that I can tell you that I am ready as soon as possible.

About the white dress, of course I want you to wear a white dress but if white dress should mean delay, why I would say dispense with it. I want you more than the white dress. You say that I was feeling lonesome and wanted you when I wrote my letter. Yes, my dear, I was feeling lonesome and wanted you very badly, and I am not going to get over it – until I have you too. As to my being frightened when I look at it calmly and collectively, having your promise that you'll come with me when I am ready. I shall not be frightened. I do realize however that it is a large undertaking. It will be well indeed for us to look on the practical side of things. The practical side will present itself often enough after we are married, so we might as well discuss it practically with reference to our wedding.

The trip of course is expensive but it will have to be paid sometime. To commence the practical side at once I will give the probable cost of the trip. The fare from here to St. Paul would be thirty-five dollars – about – that would be on the "tourist" tickets. St. Paul to Mt. Pleasant - $10.50. Returning for two, the regular first class fare is about fifty-five dollars – I think can be secured from Burlington for that. Tourist tickets from the same place can be had for about thirty-eight dollars. Where the great expense came in when I came out here was on account of the various places I visited, and the payment of local rates. A Pullman would be two dollars a night, or for five days, twenty dollars. The Canadian Pacific however which would be the best route out here, run what they call tourist sleepers, which are scarcely inferior to that regular Pullman, for three dollars for the round trip. "You pays your money and you takes your choice." Then there would be meals on the way out. As you say, however, that you would be more economical than I will. You might want to bring a lunch basket and I – why I should consent. Now, tell me please what greater evidence could I give than that I would submit to any scheme that you might propose for economy.

I will say that my debts are the greatest obstacle in the way, but I hope to have them pretty nearly cleared out of the way at any rate. By next June I think that four room homes can be had for twenty dollars a month, – very likely nice little three room houses for fifteen. Three room houses can be had for that now, but they are uglier than a mud fence. However, I could stand it if you could. And I want you to believe that my dear that it is not from selfish motives that I should prefer bringing you out here in the early summer, rather than waiting until fall.

I am a little afraid of the transition from Iowa's dry fall climate to the moist one out here. It would be better for you to become acclimated during the summer and to accomplish that it will be necessary to be married in June or wait another year and I can't do that. I'll live any way you want to and count it infinite bliss. If you think that you will be willing to live more plainly than I, why I just give you the privilege of making all arrangements – that is, choosing them and I'll do the work.

Well consider it settled, then, my darling that we shall be united within the next year and next June if it can possibly be done. Your way of putting your answer is eminently satisfactory and you are a regular darling. You know what my friends who know about our engagement think of you – that you will be a help to me in my profession – that opinion is unanimous. I will close with much love and hope.

Good bye sweetheart.

Yours, Will

Letter 61

Fairhaven, Wash.
Monday, Nov. 10, 1890

My Darling Sweetheart,

I just sent off a letter yesterday but I feel impelled to write a few lines tonight, even if I do not finish a letter or send it away for two or three days. Everything has seemed so pleasant and cheerful within since your letter came giving me so much of hope for the not so very far distant future, that I feel that it was not half expressed in yesterday's letter.

Without today the weather has been on a strike – wind, rain, mud, fog, – one of the worst of the season and yet it has not oppressed me as other days have done. See what effect a word from one sweet little woman can have. By the way do you like that word "woman" – I do. It is a favorite of mine. Always seems to me to stand for so much more than any other word referring to the other sex – more than girl or lady. When I speak of a "lovely woman" it always means more than anything else. It is a proper companion for that other good old word "man." But I digress. I want to assure you that the blues are gone, notwithstanding that this is the poorest day for a month – only one dollar today – and that on the books and for a family that I have never had a cent from yet, though I have given them more treatment for various things than any one family in town. I ought not to have the blues, though it is hard to refrain when I sit around all day. It's all right when I have a few cases on my hands to keep me busy looking them up. I want to say right here that I am delighted to know that the medicine I sent helped you.

Did I understand you to say that you were out of the powders? I will assume that you are and send you some more anyway. It gives me a great deal of satisfaction because coughs and chronic sore throats are very obstinate and discouraging things to treat, in general. Had a little success in that line last night. Was up to Ross Sullivan's spending the evening and learned that Zetta, their little girl, was troubled with a cough that came on only at night – and in paroxysms lasting so long and so severe as to cause vomiting at the end. Mr. Sullivan has a small case of homeopathic medicine and I asked him if he had tried giving her Ipecac. He said, no. I told him to try it – the next time Zetta had a coughing spell. Well, I had not been gone but a few minutes when she was taken with a severe one. They gave her one dose – ten drops in half a glass of water, one teaspoon at a dose – the coughing was stopped almost instantly and in a few minutes she dropped off to sleep. You may use that if you should happen to be troubled that way – but it will not be of much benefit unless accompanying the coughing there is that tendency to nausea and vomiting.

This evening about supper time Sullivan dropped into the office and said that if I wanted a good supper to go up to his house with him. I went – had just returned when I commenced this letter. I don't know of anyone that enjoys his home as much as Ross Sullivan. Zetta is a lovely child – a regular little woman – not particularly pretty – but with a nice expression and very lovable disposition. I always enjoy going up there very much, they seem to be such a happy family. Templins live right across the street from them.

Thursday *– I stopped right there. Det Bird and Ed Robinson coming in. They drop up every once in a while. Clint Howard I hardly ever see although we have our offices in the same building. Clint has never been in my office but twice since I have*

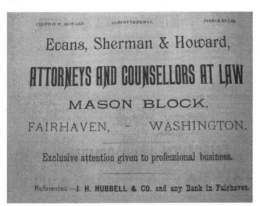

1890 Polk Directory. Washington State Archives: Northwest Region.
Clint Howard's law firm.

been here – once to see if I was the possessor of a hatchet, and another time to borrow my Bible for a quotation in a speech in the court room.

Mother's letter came this morning, containing news of Clara Carothers misfortune. It seems almost incredible to me that Dr. Carothers should not have known the regulations with regard to the hospital. Resident hospital physicians and assistant physicians are always chosen from among single men, in order that they may always be right on hand at a moments' notice. I am sorry for them for I can imagine how it would upset their plans. But they will come out all right. Clara has a great many resources and will devise some means.

I must tell you of my good luck. That is I call it good luck, and I will leave it to you to judge whether it is or not – that is whether I am not lucky enough to getalong. Last Saturday I started out with about $100 in bills, and was able to collect four (4) dollars. That afternoon some little bills came in and at night I was reduced to 75 cents. Sunday morning I had a fifteen cent breakfast, paid a nickel for a paper, leaving a nickel out of the quarter. That nickel I put in the basket at church – balance 50 cents. I then wondered whether I should go without supper or breakfast Monday morning, for it had to be one or the other. While I was pondering, I was invited to dinner – at a restaurant – by a young doctor – allopathic by the way. Well, that enabled me to have both supper Sunday night and breakfast Monday morning – then, I was "broke." But that forenoon Charlie Woods came in on his way with a surveying party up the Skagit Valley, and he was looking for a sleeping outfit to take with him. I was the lucky possessor of an extra pillow, which I sold to him for a dollar. Then that afternoon Ross Sullivan dropped in and invited me up to supper with him – needless to say, I went. So the dollar lasted until Wednesday (yesterday) morning, then I was down to "hard pan" once more – so my "face" had to serve me at the restaurant for breakfast, for dinner. In the afternoon a patron dropped in and paid me ten dollars. This afternoon, just a few minutes ago, he came in again and paid me the balance of his bill – twenty dollars ($20.00), so I am once more on top. And such is life in the great West. And now, judge, is my luck not all right?

Now I want to tell you of a scheme that has occurred to me. Whatcom and Sehome have one homeopathic physician. I am going to try and induce Dr. Baker – my old roommate to come out here and go into partnership with me – under the firm name of Drs. Gray and Baker – him to open an office in Whatcom under the firm name, I to do the same here. In that way we get both our names before the people of all the towns. Then when consolidation takes place, we will be known all over the city. Besides which, when we have cases when two are needed, surgical for instance, we can help each other and keep all the profits in the firm. Moreover, if should happen that one town should decline and the other go ahead, it would not be new ground entirely to move from one town to the other – what do you think of the scheme? You may be sure my dear, that if I can possibly hold on that I am not going to be the one to leave the place. Did you not say once that I had considerable persistence? I believe I can particularly hang on as long as the next man – when I get very blue I never have any idea of giving up.

Dr. Heacock goes to Kansas Monday to be gone a month and I will get some of his practice at least. Oh, we'll come out all right yet. You say you suppose that when you are not teaching school any longer that you will become very much uninterested in the profession. That's exactly what I want you to do. I hope to see you a very enthusiastic doctor's wife yet. Why Dr. Heacock's wife goes and visits the Dr.'s mild cases when the Dr. is out of town, and prescribes for them. How is that for looking after the Dr.'s interests?

Business continues fair. I shall be satisfied if it does as well for the next three months, as the rainy season is decidedly healthy. Allow me to say that the fog does not keep up all the time, but is somewhat of an extra. Today has been beautiful. Well, I must stop now and go and see a patient.

I keep right on longing to see you. That never stops. You can't imagine though how much more spring there has been in my step and how much more cheerful I have been since your letter promising to be ready when I am. My love keeps gathering force all the time, and by the time that I go after you, you may expect it to be a perfect torrent. Good bye sweetheart.

Lovingly,

Will

Letter 62

Fairhaven, Washington
Thursday, Nov. 13, 1890

My Darling Anna,

Again I have just sent off a letter today, but want to commence another to-night, if only for the sake of having the opportunity of writing "My Darling Anna." I wonder sometimes if you derive as much pleasure and satisfaction from reading it as I do from writing it. If so it is a great deal. I have nothing particular to say to-night but would like to talk. How I would like to drop in and see you tonight. This is Thursday and you would doubtless be tired and I should like to do my best to make it easy for you.

I received a copy of the Iowa Wesleyan today and I notice in the alumnal department notice of the marriage of Chris and Ed Havighorst and John R. Foulks – all three Phi's. It reminded me of a speech that Phil Winter made at a Phi meeting once when he was visiting Mt. Pleasant. He was called on for the speech and made it in the nature of personal reminiscences of various members while he was in college and after telling something about the particular characteristics of each one, he would end the biography by saying "he is now married and doing well." It was just shortly before Ed Kauffman's wedding and he warmed his remarks about Ed by saying "he will soon be married and doing well." It got to be pretty funny before he finished and for quite awhile the boys used to have that for a funny saying. By the way, wasn't Ed Havighorst a member of your class? Well, I remember that the inference that was drawn from Phil Winter's remarks was that if a man were married, as a matter of course he was doing well. I believe if I could enjoy the privilege of being with you tonight that I would be in a mood for reminiscences. We haven't indulged in any for quite awhile have we? We have been looking into the future instead of the past. But I think of the past quite often notwithstanding, and always very gratefully. And especially do I think very kindly of my resolution made near the close of the spring time of the year you graduated that I would cultivate the acquaintance of Miss Kurtz on my return from St. Paul in the fall.

But I have thought since what made me make that resolution. The germ that was to bear such a rich fruitage of love must already have been planted in favorable soil. But after all why talk of the past as rich as it is in recollections of so much that is sweet and happy, when there is a great future before us, in which to add so much more to all that has gone before. I feel that I must be a very happy man to be blessed with the priceless gift of your love. If I can only make you one half as happy as I know I shall be we will be as happy a couple as were ever united in holy wedlock. I am going to stop in a moment for the night, but before I do so I want to renew my love for you sweetheart and say that my one endeavor is for your happiness and thereby attaining my own. Good night my best beloved.

Friday 4:55 p.m. *– Well, I just thought I'd drop in for a few minutes – can't stay long. This is Friday afternoon isn't it? Tired? Of course you are – what a foolish question to ask. Wish I could come around this evening – it's the regular time,*

Whatcom Museum.

"State of Washington" stern-wheel steamer moored at Fairhaven.

but I suppose that it would be too far to walk and might be rather late by the time I get around. Well, we'll count this an extra one.

Today has been another of the beautiful ones, the rainy season notwithstanding. The steamer "State of Washington," reported smashed on the rocks, after two weeks spent in dry dock came in this morning with all flags flying, with a great deal of new timber and fresh paint about her hull.

I was walking past a residence today and in the yard noticed a rose bush in full bloom – large crimson roses. How is that for the middle of November? And yet up in the mountains winter set in a month and a half ago. On clear days, like today, when the ranges can be seen, the mountains are visible, covered with snow. It is said that the "Bastere" silver mine up in the Cascades has two hundred feet of snow on it – an avalanche having come down in it.

Well really, I would like to stay longer, but must be going. Collected two dollars and a half today and have the promise of fifteen more in a few days that I never expected to get. Let the good work go on. It brings me so much nearer to you. Who says that absence kills affection? I know better, mine only grows the stronger, the longer I remain away.

Good bye sweetheart.

Devotedly,

Will

Letter 63

Fairhaven, Wash.
Sunday, Nov. 16, 1890

My Darling Sweetheart,

What a jewel of a girl you are! I had another letter from you today and a very nice one too – how could it be otherwise? Had had a letter on Sunday for the last three or four weeks. It must come in on Saturday but they do not get the mail distributed until Sunday.

Three rooms "goes" if you will be content and want it so. And I expect that at the start we will have to take rooms in someone else's house whether we want to or not, simply because the houses will be scarce. The three room cottages that are to be had at present would rather disturb your artistic sense. There is a row of nine three room cottages that look very much like Mr. Jackson's house in Mt. Pleasant but they stand right along the street with no fence around them and are painted the most dingy color I ever saw. They can be had for fifteen dollars a month. They could be made very cozy inside, but I think by next June they will be superseded by something better.

Det Bird and Ed Robinson own a couple of lots in a very nice locality and I think I could get them to put up such a building as we would want – unless they should take a notion to do so before next June. I feel more and more that we must be married at that time. You know that I want you as the first and foremost consideration so I believe that you will understand me if I present a very practical side of the question.

I know whereof I speak when I say a young married doctor gains by increase of practice more than the increase of expenses incurred by the establishment and running expenses of a household. I was talking with one of the young married doctors here a day or so ago, a man younger than myself, and he told me of cases last month that he obtained simply because he was married aggregating over two hundred dollars over and above his ordinary practice. Another thing the married doctor gets a much better class of patients than the single man for the simple reason that he gets acquainted with a much better class of society. He is looked upon as a fixture if he is married. He is employed as a family physician, whereas before he must depend upon transient patronage. Now I'm not putting this at all too strong. I see it every day around me. There was a young physician just recently came here, a very nice looking young fellow, with a young wife. Numbers of the ladies of the town have called upon his wife, he has become acquainted with the families and he is already getting a nice practice – and he hasn't been here long enough to be known on his own merits as a physician – that is something that takes time. The wife has done the business.

Well, you want to know something about my patients. I wrote you that the baby died. The woman who changed doctors is alright, but she was down for over four weeks so I expect she doesn't think now that the six days that I attended her was such a very long time after all. Was called to see another fever case today. A boy

Homeopathic medication vials in boxed case.

about sixteen – he has been down a little over a week and for two days previously. Dr. Heacock was attending him, but the Dr. leaves this evening for Kansas, to be gone a month and the case has been turned over to me. I have no hopes whatever of his recovery. It is a very violent case – complicated I think with consumption.

I expect I would better tell you what the medicine is that I sent and then you can get it whenever you need it. The powders were "Hepar Sulphur 3x" and the pellets "Spongia tosta" 6x. Get them from the homeopathic physicians – they can't be had in the drugstores. Get the hepar sulph in trituration and the spongia in pellets. I am delighted to know that my prescription on general principles hit the case so well, only I wish you could describe the symptoms.

Well, I must stop now and go and visit the woman with the fever. Those two cases are the only ones I have on hand at present. Will write again soon. You needn't fear that I shall go to Mt. Pleasant and not bring you back with me. I am determined that I will bring you out here either next June or next September.

Well goodbye sweetheart and keep right on dreaming about that home of ours. We will have it in reality the first thing we know.

Devotedly,

Will

Letter 64

Fairhaven, Wash.
Wednesday, November 19, 1890

My Darling Anna,

Once more the facile (?) pen adorns my grasp. (I can't say quite as much for the ink as you may perceive.) I believe I mentioned in my last letter some enterprise under way here. I omitted from my list a twenty-five thousand dollar school building – the second. Since then another brick business block is under way and things are moving along very nicely. Yesterday was my largest day's business since I have been here – seventeen and a half dollars. It commenced at the very beginning of the day – 12 o'clock Monday night, or rather to be accurate – Tuesday morning.

I wrote you about the case of typhoid that I considered almost hopeless. Tuesday morning about half-past twelve I was summoned out there again and found that the boy's oldest brother had suddenly been stricken down by a convulsion which was the commencement of an attack of pneumonia, which is already commencing to take on malignant typhoid symptoms. It seems to be a peculiar characteristic of the family to be taken suddenly and to have the disease run a very brief and violent course, terminating in death. The two children that they lost formerly only lasted eleven days. This is the eleventh day of the younger boy's illness, and I have little hope of his lasting through the night. If he dies and the other one is conscious of it, it will likely carry him off too. There is just one other boy in the family and he has recovered not long since from a broken leg and is very nervous and excitable, so that he stands a good chance of taking the disease also.

This boy's attack is much more violent than was that of the doctor that died in the hospital in Iowa City, the first year I was there. The people are old settlers here, having been here seven years. They are well known and if it should happen that the boys recover it will be a great thing for me. It would bring me into prominence in a quarter of the city that contains a large population and would increase my practice greatly. On the other hand, the boy was not expected to live before I was called in so that it will not hurt me much in the event of his death. In fact, very likely none at all. It all goes to show how different cases are in actual practice from the books and lectures. I have three works on practice of medicine and in none of them do I find descriptions of either typhoid or pneumonia such as these two cases are. I haven't slept for the past two nights, thinking and pondering those cases. If they pull through, I will be about the most delighted man in Fairhaven.

Well, I expect that by the time you come out here that we will have so many conveniences and luxuries that it will not seem like a pioneer town. I don't think there is any doubt that in four months we will have an eighty thousand dollar opera house and public library. One of the wealthy men of the city proposes to put up such a building if he can find citizens willing to provide $20,000 having that much interest in the project. Already ten of the twenty thousand has been pledged, and there is to be a meeting tonight to raise the balance. The scheme will very likely go through because the manager of the Portland, Tacoma and Seattle theatres was here day before yesterday and said that if a first class house was built here he would bring all the attractions that appear in San Francisco and the other cities of the coast here and that he would take them to the town on Bellingham Bay that first constructed a suitable house. Now, I am certain that Fairhaven will not let Whatcom get ahead on this matter. The building will probably have some office rooms and store rooms in it, and if so I am going to look out for the best rooms in the building, if it costs me sixty dollars a month rent, as it pays to have prominent rooms in a good building.

The latest indication that Seattle fears the future commercial supremacy of Bellingham Bay is that her merchants threaten to boycott a large San Francisco steamship if it touches at this port before going to Seattle. The captain says this is the most direct route for him to come and hence will come here first. The steamship is the largest that has yet commenced to make regular trips to this port.

Well, this letter has been pretty full of my practice and Fairhaven, so I think I'd better ask you a question or two about how you are getting along. First, as to your health. How is that cold of yours? I regret to hear that you have been unwell every Saturday since school commenced. One more reason why I am determined that you shall come out here next summer. The dust of the schoolroom, chalk and coal dust together with the nervous strain is too much for you and it must be changed. I have written to mother that I am expecting to come for you either next June or September – the first if possible. I debated particularly on the practical side of the question. The ideal side is between ourselves for the present. I must stop now and go out and see my patients.

Good bye dear,
Lovingly,
Will

Letter 65

Fairhaven, Wash.
Sunday, Nov. 23, 1890

My Darling Sweetheart,

Ed Robinson has just dropped in and is reading a magazine while I write. Well, last Wednesday night I had an experience that I don't care to repeat for a very long time. I will simply say to start with that both my patients in the family I spoke of died on Wednesday night. The one who was taken last grew worse very rapidly and it became apparent Wednesday morning that his case too was a hopeless one. Wednesday afternoon I was summoned out there with the news that the younger one was dying. I went out and did what little could be done but was obliged to tell them that he could not last through the night. I was there about four hours or until half past seven in the evening. I then returned and made two calls that I had to make, had my supper and had just returned to my office when they came for me again, saying that Karl (the younger) was dead and that the other was very bad and to go right out. They also took out two other doctors who gave an unfavorable prognosis. I remained during the night. The second brother died about five o'clock in the morning. It was a remarkable case. He lasted barely fifty-two hours after he was first taken, being the most virulent case of typho-pneumonia that has occurred here. Practice continues about the same – possibly there is some improvement.

Ruth Crane Looker
Collection.

Helen Crane.

I was sorry to learn of Helen's trouble with her eyes. It must be a sure trial to her as she is so fond of reading – in fact it is very probable that she has been too fond of it in the past and the present trouble is the outcome of it.

So Mrs. Williams thinks she has a joke on me on account of Dr. Cowperthwaite using hypodermic injections of morphia on his father does she? But she is mistaken. Old Mr. Cowperthwaite has a very painful incurable disease that will soon take him off. Under such circumstances it would be cruelty to deprive him of the relief the morphia affords since he cannot live to suffer from the after-effects of it. If he had a curable affliction and many years to live it would be a different matter.

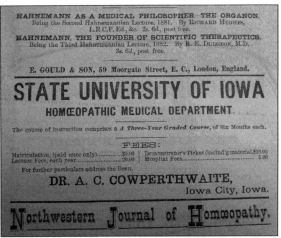

Medicine: Homeopathic: General, University of Iowa Archives, Iowa City, Iowa.
Dr. Cowperthwaite was one of Will's professors at State University of Iowa Homeopatic Medical Department.

Fairhaven continues to go ahead. We are all in hope that it is not true that Jay Gould has secured control of all the railroads east of Chicago and of all the Pacific roads except the Canadian. If he has it might make Jim Hill change his mind about building the Great Northern. In such case, Fairhaven would be, so to speak, precipitated into the consommé.

Well, I suppose that ere this reaches you Thanksgiving will have come and gone and the turkeys can take a recess until Christmas. Speaking of Christmas this will be the first one that I have not spent at home for several years. However we will spend Christmas at home next year, and a merry Christmas it will be. I saw a house a few days ago that would suit me splendidly, but it is a little costly – about sixteen hundred dollars. It had five rooms with large pantry, bathroom and numerous large closets.

Monday *– Was called out just at that time and didn't get back until too late for mail time, and this afternoon a patient came in (one of the voluble, talkative kind) and now I have but a moment before going out to make a call or two. That's the penalty you have to pay for being a doctor's sweetheart.*

Your letter came this morning and I just want to say that you're a triumph. I have stepped around quicker all day. I walked out past the houses I spoke of this morning purposely to have a look at them. Haven't time to tell what I thought then. Will write tonight at length if nothing interferes, but must stop now.

Goodbye dear.

Lovingly,

Will

Letter 66

Fairhaven, Wash.
Monday, November 24, 1890

My Darling Sweetheart:

Here I am once more, but it is late, so I may only write a few minutes. I say, may because it might happen that I will feel like writing on indefinitely. Whenever letters come like the one today I always feel as if there were a hundred and one things that I want to say, but when it comes to writing, it never seems satisfactory.

Right here, while I think of it, don't let me hear of your doing such an unsanitary thing as eating a lunch of crackers and pickles, even if it was on account of a letter of mine. Just reflect on that a moment my dear – the future wife of a doctor eating a lunch of crackers and pickles! Don't you think yourself that looks rather bad? Methinks I hear you say "crank" at that, or call me an "old granny." Well that's all right, if I could only be around to hear you say it. I tell you my dear, I am hungry for a sight of your dear face and no mistake. You may be sure that all I said in former letters about my being satisfied and content in a very small house

and a very small start I will still maintain provided you are satisfied and happy. And as you tell me not to fear taking you from your present home to a much smaller and humble one, I will not say anything more on that scene. Those three room houses I spoke of are ugly and no mistake. They were put up to rent – early in the history of Fairhaven and are stuck along the side of a sandy hill with nothing around them – not a tree or shrub or blade of grass. The inside plan is about like this (see drawing).

Illustration by W.R. Gray.

There is a kind of rough summer kitchen at the back as shown in the cut (?). But I think that by the time we want a house there will be something nicer for the same money. I can get someone to build. You ask me about the school. Are you really in earnest about that school? Of course you know that I am still of the opinion that I expressed about it before. That is that if you want to have the school, it is all right. I have not done anything with regard to it as I thought it a little premature to say anything about it yet, but I will commence to work it up if you really want the school. But say, my dear, could you have a school in three rooms? It would take a more pretentious house than the one I have been describing to attract a desirable class of pupils.

While I think of it, I have at last seen the skate. This morning I was down at the wharf and there was one swimming around close in to the piling of the wharf. It was about four and a half feet in length. Three feet in width, and didn't look to be more than a half an inch in thickness. I should judge that out of the water it would be a very ugly looking animal, but it made up in gracefulness for its want of beauty.

The way it glided through the water was beautiful to behold. Well I think I will close for tonight and finish this tomorrow. Good night sweet heart.

Tuesday – *Today the first train arrives over the line to Seattle so that we now have connection by rail with the cities in the south – Tacoma and Seattle, and it will only be a few days now before we have connection on the water with the Canadian Pacific. Hence we continue to grow. Business continues pretty fair – encouragingly so. It has been a little dull today so far, and only one call to make this afternoon, but there is no telling what may turn up before the end of the day.*

Tell you what Anna, it won't do for us to wait any longer than next June. Everybody seems to be getting ahead of us and now comes Harry with intent to commit matrimony Christmas Eve. That is rather rushing affairs. I wish we could have the Christmas holidays at least to talk over our affairs.

Say Anna, what kind of wedding are you going to have? I want you to arrange all that and let me know. I want you to have things exactly as you want them and instruct me as to what I am to do. You know my ignorance is dense when it comes to such details. I expect, however if you take me carefully in hand that you can have me trained properly between now and June.

I think I told you in a former letter that I had written to mother with reference to our hopes and expectations. I don't think she will have much opposition to make against it. I put the practical side to her pretty well, I think, and will drop a line with reference to it from time to time. I think you were wise to consult your Aunt May about your arrangements as she will be able to give you many valuable suggestions, even if you don't always agree as to details.

Speaking of a mud house, it would be an easy matter to get enough mud just at present to build a whole town, but it would be exceedingly hard to dry it after it was built, so will abandon the mud house. But what a gay time we will have together anyway on our trip and planning after we get here! We will have just about as much fun as two people can crowd into a transcontinental journey and into one small house.

The Swedish Quartette sings here tomorrow night; and it will be quite a treat. I will be there if possible.

Well I must stop now and make that one lone call. Will write again soon.

With much love,

Yours devotedly, Will

Letter 67

Fairhaven, Wash.
Thursday, November 27
Thanksgiving 1890

My Darling Sweetheart,

Your Thanksgiving letter came yesterday but it was just as good as if it came to-day. You see I had a chance to read it yesterday and then read it again today. So it was better than had it not arrived until today.

The day has been a beautiful one, bright and warm. I am writing without any fire in my room and with the window open, permitting the fresh air and the ever increasing rumble of the streets to come in. Well I was not fortunate enough to be invited out to dinner today but we had turkey at the restaurant – in fact a pretty good dinner. Ed Robinson and I were together and we had quite a gay time.

Before I go any further I want to disclose some news that perhaps will give you some idea of the future prospects of Fairhaven. The franchise for the construction of an electric street railway has passed into the hands of a company composed of ex-Senator Platt of New York, Senator Hiscock of the same state and Samuel Hill, son-in-law of James J. Hill, of the Great Northern Railroad, and president of the Minneapolis Trust Co. These are men who do not put their money where they are not sure of making large returns.

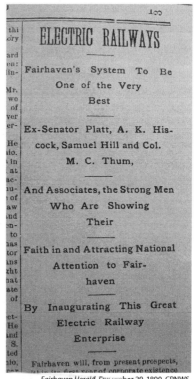

Fairhaven Herald, December 29, 1890 CPNWS.

I understand that a report had reached Mt. Pleasant that Fairhaven had flattened out. That report emanated from Seattle, and the "wish was father to the thought." But Fairhaven's boom has not flattened out, by a large majority. There are more buildings under construction at the present time than at any time since I have been here, and a better class of buildings at that. Just as sure as that Puget Sound is going to be the great shipping center of the Pacific Coast, just so sure is it that Fairhaven will be one of the largest if not the largest city on the Sound. I have written to Dr. Baker in Iowa, of my little scheme with regard to partnership. It will probably take him some little time to decide but I hope he will decide to come soon. There is no chance for him beyond a little country practice where he is.

Last night I went to hear the Swedish Quartette. They are very fine, and I enjoyed the entertainment very much. Miss Lura Borden, an elocutionist accompanying them, also a Swede, is one of the most natural readers I ever heard. "The house was large and enthusiastic."

But what has all this to do with your lovely Thanksgiving letter? Yes, it has something to do with it because it is about the prospects of our future home. I think of that home all the time and while I realize that there is much to be done, still it seems to be nearer and nearer all the time. Unless something unforeseen should happen we will have our next Thanksgiving in our own home. I look back on the past with a great deal of pleasure, even if there is a sadness mingled with it that it is the past and then I want to work all the harder for the future. I have not had an attack of the blues for some time. Of course I know that they will come back sometimes and I feel lonely all the time, but not as I did a few weeks back. I am lonely enough to be a very sober individual most of the time. You know a man can't be jolly without some congenial spirits to be jolly with, and those I lack. Never mind, I will be jolly again when you are with me. I could see your picture of the parlor and the grate fire and the soft rosy light – and I longed to be there to be in the picture.

You ask if we will not be other than altogether prosaic and practical. Well, I should hope so. There will be so much of the prosaic and practical that will force itself upon us, that we will not be required to see that side of life, but it is the ideal, the poetic, the sentimental, if you will, and the living side that makes life worth having, after all. The practical, unnecessary as it is, is the material and in the present age is set up on too high a pinnacle.

I say now, as I have said before, that I expect to be a lover all my life, as well as a husband, and you will always be my little sweetheart, as well as wife. We will have all the romance in our home life that we can get into it and I believe that will be considerable. We will have a very happy home and we have waited nearly long enough for it. We must commence to build it soon. The wait will not be such a very long one now compared with that which has gone before, and I know that I could not bear to think of as long a one as has passed.

I will write again in the next mail.

Good bye sweetheart,

Lovingly, Will

Letter 68

Fairhaven, Washington
Thursday, December 4, 1890

My Darling Sweetheart,

Here I am nearly out of paper – only these two scraps left. But they will be enough as this letter will have to be cut short, owing to the simple fact that I am busy. Yesterday and today have been the busiest days I have had. There have been days when my receipts run as high, but not that took up so much time. Either the fever is breaking out again or my practice is increasing.

Yesterday there was a call before I was up. When I got back from that call there were two men waiting in the office wanting me to make calls in their families. Not less than fifteen miles were covered by me yesterday and by night I was about tired out. I have one patient that I think I shall fall in love with. A young lady about eleven years sold. She is as pretty and bright as she can be. The only really interesting case, from a personal standpoint, that I have had for some time.

I wish you could be here today. It is the most perfect day we have had for a long time. Not a cloud in the sky – nice and warm. The mountains are becoming more beautiful every day now. They …

Just at that point I was interrupted by a patient who kept me some time so that this will be very short now. That makes seventeen dollars on the books – business today and the evening still to commence. That is including two calls that I have yet to make. By the way one of them is to one of the proprietors – or rather proprietress of my restaurant – a case of fever. That insures my board for sometime to come at any rate.

But to resume, in regard to the mountains, it is winter in the mountains while the roses bloom in the valleys, and they are now covered completely with snow and under the sunlight are brilliantly white with a rosy tinge here and there.

I will have to stop now, but will resume tonight. So au revoir until this evening. As ever,

Lovingly,
Will

Letter 69

Fairhaven, Wash.
Friday, December 5, 1890

My Darling Sweetheart:

Here I am once more, and again it seems as if there were only a few minutes in which to write before mail time. It seems that my few calls seem to take a great amount of time. The town is scattered and so are my patients and I have not yet learned the art of rushing away in a few minutes to "see another very critical and important case." However that will come in time.

Well, I caught another call last night, so that the day's business was nineteen dollars – my best day thus far. It would look as if my practice was increasing but the end of the month will tell a truer tale with regard to that.

Had a letter from you this morning and am consequently all right and wish I had more time at my disposal to answer it. But I will get in a long one next time – generally "try" to write one long epistle each week for which you have my sympathy. It strikes me that for a sleepy little Iowa town Mt. Pleasant has been altogether too gay this fall. What is the reason for it? Wonder if it was because my lugubrious countenance has been removed thence. They never had such a gay time when I was there.

So "Jeff" spent his Thanksgiving in the metropolis of Henry County – lucky fellow, how I would like to have been there and had such a time as we had the day before I left town. However we will repeat that when we have that return ride on the Pacific Coast. By the way I must write to "Jeff" – I feel ashamed of myself. How I would like to have been with you Thanksgiving! I duly ate the microscopic turkey and the sour cranberry sauce at the restaurant and thought of the very generous dinner proved ideal by the boarding house in Iowa City last year and concluded that that boarding house was not so bad after all.

But next Thanksgiving I will enjoy myself – wherefore because it will be under our own vine and fig tree – at fifteen dollars per month or thereabouts, even if the "Turk" does cost twenty five cents per pound and it will be cooked by the best cook in the whole "blooming" universe and the table will not be covered with oil cloth, the cups will not be an inch thick, and we will not have to sit on a stool. I think I will be able to purchase two cheap chairs. If I can't what's the matter with a nail keg? Now, that's a gastronomical outburst isn't it? "Say" this is provoking. I'd like to talk for awhile and my time is up but I'll finish tonight sure in good shape.

So good bye dear
Lovingly,
Will

Letter 70

Fairhaven, Wash.
Sunday, Dec. 7, 1890

My Darling Sweetheart,

Well, I didn't get to write the other evening as I expected to do. Ed Robinson and Det Bird came up and spent the evening. In fact they are coming quite frequently of late. I like Ed first rate – much better than I did in Mt. Pleasant – in fact I did not know him very well there. He and Det seem to like to come up to the office frequently. It makes things a little pleasanter to have them come occasionally.

Christmas time will go hard with me this year and will seem doubly lonesome after spending my Christmas at home for the last few years and especially the last two years. I hope however that you will not have to spend your Christmas as you did last year – in bed. There is one flattering emotion that I lay to myself when these anniversaries come round and that is that it is the last one we will have to spend apart and I wonder if you can imagine how much sweet satisfaction I derive from that thought.

There is one thing that I know you can't imagine and that is the consuming envy that possesses my soul against Fred Stone and Mr. Glover and Mr. Pierce and Mr. Kopp. To think that I should ever envy the festive Kopp![49] But you see, we never know what strange things may happen. I wonder if the above mentioned parties realized to the fullest extent what a privilege it was their fortune to possess and that there is one person on this green football that would very joyfully have changed places with them. There is another wonder. Think of me wanting to change places with Kopp again. And yet such are the indubitable facts in the case.

And so you have deposited fifteen dollars towards a wedding outfit? That settles it! I go out tomorrow and some of my creditors will have to give up enough cash to enable me to cover that deposit. I can't have you getting ahead of me in that way.

Just at that point I have had a call to go and see one of my patients who doesn't seem to be getting along as well as the parents wish and they feel a little worried. I expect you will begin to think from the number of times that I say I have a call in my letters that my business must be pretty extensive. It does seem as if it happens that most of my calls come just when I sit down to write to you. But it seems that way anyway. Perhaps if I should write oftener my practice would increase. I believe you are a mascot, Anna. Well, I must stop now.

Good bye dear,

Lovingly,
Will

Letter 71

Fairhaven, Wash.
Wednesday, Dec. 10, 1890

My Darling Sweetheart,

It seems to me that when I look back on the letters that have emanated from my goose quill lately that they have not been exactly satisfactory. The fact is at this time of year it is hard to be content with writing letters. I feel as if in a few days I ought to be on my way home to talk instead of write. It seems as if it must be so. At this season of the year it will seem especially lonesome out in this corner of the earth. However I will not say much about that until Christmas is actually here.

Practice seems to improve to some extent. At least the first ten days of this month is considerably in excess of the corresponding time for last month. At the same time collections have been as good as they were the first month. The general business depression is being felt here in many ways but I think in a couple of months when the spring immigration commences things will be a little better. Another homeopath will locate soon in Whatcom. That will make four on the Bay. There is one more at Lynden, a small town north of here. We will soon have enough for a county society which will be of great benefit to all of us. The newcomer is an old man, so I will remain the only young man in my school on the Bay.

By the way had a little experience a few days ago with Dr. Lawrance of Sehome. I was called to see a fourteen month old baby. It was a very sick baby and its symptoms were so complicated that I was at a loss what to call the trouble. There was fever and some convulsive movements, as if it might have convulsions. Breathing was very quick. One side of the chest and under the left arm considerably swollen and tender to the touch. I thought it had pneumonia and also said that possibly there would be an abscess where the swelling appeared. I left some medicine and said I would come around in the afternoon.

When I called in the afternoon the child seemed to be a little better, but the parents had got an idea that I had not seemed to understand the case very well in the morning and the mother remarked that I was a rather young man to know much about babies anyway. I admitted the soft impeachment but said it was not my fault that I was no older. I saw that they were not satisfied, though they thought themselves that the baby was improving. So I said that perhaps as they were not satisfied, they would better have some older man see the case, and suggested Dr. Lawrance of Sehome. They said they would like to have him. So I went after him and brought him over. He examined the case and thought that there was possibly a little pneumonia present, and that the swelling was just a little muscular soreness, assured the parents that there was nothing the matter that I could not handle, that there was no abscess, recommended one of the remedies that I was giving but advised the change of another, pocketed his consultation fee and departed.

The next day the swelling commenced to get very red and I feared erysipelas.

Next day a white spot appeared in the middle of the redness. I inserted an exploring needle, found there was pus present – got out my lancet and made an incision and found an abscess as large as my hand, and you know that is not a small one. Yesterday I had to make another incision lower down and the baby is now doing well, and the parents are convinced that I know more about the case than the "old doctor" after all. Of course I can't tell how it will finally come out, as it is a very extensive abscess for so young a child and the discharge may exhaust him, but I have every reason at present to expect a favorable result.

The remedy that Dr. Lawrance advised me to change was the proper one under the circumstances, so I felt that I was doing things about right, even if I wasn't certain of the condition present at the first. It was one of those cases where the symptoms seemed to obscure the real trouble.

Well, that's a pretty long dissertation on professional topics. I collected forty dollars the day after I had your letter saying that you had laid up fifteen dollars, but it will most of it have to go in the payment of debts. Those horrible debts! But then, if I didn't have them I would be foundering along in school another year, and miss the year's experience so I would be no better off than I am. Never mind. I will soon be working for ourselves.

Well, I must stop now. Will write soon again. Goodbye dear.

Lovingly,

Will

Letter 72

Fairhaven, Wash.
Sunday, Dec. 14, 1890

My Darling Sweetheart,

Today has been a miserable day all round – windy, rainy, gloomy, cold – in the fact, the most disagreeable day that I have seen since I have been here. There were a few flakes of snow. Added to all this I have felt lonely – unutterably lonely. You know that a rainy day nearly always used to take me around to see you and I always especially enjoyed my visits – at such times – it was so cheerful inside compared to the outside. So when these kinds of days come, I always want to see you even more than usual. I wanted to see you more than usual too after reading your last letter, which came yesterday. It was a lovely letter and made me particularly desirous of seeing the writer.

The holidays this year will not bring me much pleasure. I have about concluded that I can't afford to go over to Victoria at Christmas time.

Monday p.m. *– Was called out at that point to see my little sick girl. A complication that bid fair to be quite alarming had set in, but this morning she seems better and I now have good hopes of her doing well. Am sorry the interruption occurred just when it did as it prevented me getting this in yesterday's mail and it will make quite a little time between letters. I had a letter from mother a few days ago in which she said that my erstwhile preceptor Dr. Drake was going to leave Mt. Pleasant the first of January. I think if I had known that Drs. Boynton, Drake and Pitcher would all leave Mt. Pleasant inside of a year, that I would have settled right there for a time at least. I know I could have caught some of the business from three of them. The wind is howling again today. The bay looks grand with the great white caps rolling in.*

I told you in a letter some time about the manner in which my debts are distributed did I not? If I did, I didn't want to repeat it. If not, I want you to know my debt will be paid in part – at least before next summer, if the boom doesn't flatten out in this country. It is very dull now all over, but we think it will brighten up in a month or so when the next year's immigration commences.

Oh, I must tell you while I think of it of a little hard luck I had today. I was sailing down the principal street when a gust of wind caught my hat, carried it in the air, bumped it against a telegraph pole, and then carried it over the tops of the buildings. I made a search around the block but the "chapeau" was not to be found so I was forced to purchase a new one – two great big round hard dollars literally "blown in." And you can't imagine how I freeze to the good hard dollar in these days. It breaks my heart every time I have to pay one out – no matter what the necessity.

Last night Ed Robinson and myself called on the Templins and Sullivans. Had a very pleasant call. This week the Odd Fellows and Knights of Pythias combined to present the great and thrilling emotional drama "Damon and Pythias." I am happy to state that I am "not in it." Last Thursday night the humorist Griswold of the "Texas Siftings" lectured here, subject a "Tour Around the World." It was illustrated by pictures by a large and very fine stereopticon. Every other picture was of some point of interest on the tour. While the ones between were comic pictures drawn by the artist of "Siftings" to which the lecturer furbished the story. He kept the audience alternately convulsed and interested for an hour and three quarters. The views in foreign countries were very fine. And yet there was nothing that equaled the scenery of the west of the United States. The next entertainment will be Miss Nella F. Brown, elocutionist.

I will see that mother is remembered at Christmas all right, and you may be sure that you will not be forgotten. I am going to commence my Christmas letter to-night. It may reach you a day ahead of time as I want to make sure that it is not behind time.

On the practical side of things as you say in regard to the school, we will need a larger house if you carry out that project. Last night while talking with Mrs. Sullivan about the children going to school I asked if she thought a private school would not do well here. She thought it would. As Ed was there I said nothing specifically in regard to it, so she supposed I presume that there was nothing more than passing interest in my question.

Well, I will stop now and this evening my Christmas letter will be commenced. I promise you a "fat" one. I suppose that before this you know the result of last month's business and consider it satisfactory. I do, if I can collect a goodly portion of it. My next letter will be free from business. I will assure you and very probably will not be altogether "practical."

Goodbye dear,

Lovingly,
Will

Letter 73

Fairhaven, Washington
Monday, Dec. 15, 1890

My Darling Sweetheart,

This is a new tablet secured especially for the purpose of transcribing thereon your Christmas letter. How do you like the paper? It struck me as being rather neat, and just the thing in which to write the good "fat" letter promised in my last, finished and mailed this afternoon.

Well, this is to be a Christmas letter. First I must tell you about your Christmas present. A few days ago Ed Robinson went over to Sehome where there is a Japanese store hoping to find some novelties there. There is little that is nice in the stores here. I had remarked a day or two before that I must be on the lookout for some Christmas presents. Ed suggested that we go over and buy something together. I agreed. After making the young lady that waited on us, get down nearly everything in the establishment we decided to purchase a cabinet such as I send you. We bought two almost identically alike, except for a little detail. Ed didn't say who his was for, not did I tell where mine was going, but we each have an idea, I think. At least it was a perfectly well understood fact that they were both going to Mt. Pleasant. So if you have curiosity enough you can find out whether Lulu Satterthwaite has a Japanese cabinet – like yours for a Christmas present. I would be willing to wager that she has.

Also you might find out whether Lulu is studying German. Ed has taken a sudden notion to furbish up his German. A few days ago he came up to the office and wanted to know if I had any German books here. I was fortunately able to answer in the affirmative, since which time Ed has been coming up here to study "Deutsch." I am expecting him now as he said that he was coming up this evening to take his German lesson. Well – I hardly expected him so soon, but here he is, just came in as I was writing that last sentence.

But to return to the Christmas present. We had considerable fun over at the store. Ed was purchasing a present also for a cousin down in West Virginia. He was indiscreet enough to say so, whereas the young lady clerk looked very incredulous and Ed saw that he had put his foot in it. As I am starting the letter a few days ahead of time for sending it, my present is reposing here in the room. I contemplate filling the drawers with some little articles, but don't know what they will be. Will report on them later on in this epistle.

I want to say that this is not what I wanted to send you this Christmas. While I was over in Victoria I had my eye on an ivory card case, beautifully carved, that was in one of the Chinese stores. I had intended having Aunt Jennie get that for me and send it to me but the duty would have been fifty percent, the cost of the article there being ten dollars. It was a sore temptation for I would like to send you the finest that could be procured. Then I thought of the coming year and what we hope it will bring forth, and decided to wait until we are in better circumstances and then perhaps I can get what I want to for you. I don't tell you this in apology for what I send because I am going to assume that in this I may judge you by myself and that you will value it for the sake of the giver, at the same time I want to let you know that there was one special thing that I wanted to send you. I know that I will value whatever you send for your own sweet sake, whatever it may be – you see, like you, I don't intend to be forgotten. Well, as I intend this to be written at different times, I am going to stop for a little while and will continue later.

Tuesday – Ed stayed until quite late last night, hence the thread of my narrative (?) was somewhat broken. The wind still howls and the bay is still worked up into foam. The wind is not cold however. If it continues very long it will spoil the doctors' business as it is very rapidly drying everything up and carrying off the foul vapors that have accumulated. But this is talking business isn't it and I promised to refrain from anything very practical in this, didn't I? So the practical must be banished for the time being.

Say Anna, you served me a regular Yankee's trick in your last letter. I asked you a question and you answered it by asking another. I asked what kind of wedding you wanted and you refer it back to me. Well, I take what might be called the man's view of it, I suppose and say that I am not particular as to the kind or manner of it, so that it takes place that is the great fact that I am interested in and I want the method and detail to be exactly as you wish. However, I will say that the less fuss and style there is about it, the better it will suit me. I would like a plain quiet wedding, without a great crowd, just relatives and a few intimate friends. Of course in a quiet way I would like things nice and "about right." See? That's about all the idea that I have of it at present, but as you say, we can talk that over soon.

I agree with you in thinking that Harry Grahn and Miss Clark are going to be a little too commonplace. There ought to be some romance about such an affair and something that makes it stand out from the background of all the other events of life – something that will mark a change of conditions. To go from a boarding house back to a boarding house would be pretty hard for me. And it seems to me that if they wait a year for their trip it may be a long time before they accomplish it and besides it will have lost its chief charm – the freshness. In this connection I remember that the first night – the ever memorable 21st of August, you stipulated that we should not board – you agreed even to two rooms, but drew the line at the boarding house. Say Anna, we'll have a good long trip at any rate, won't we?

Only nine days until Christmas – and what a lovely one it will be. I know that I shall spend the most of my time thinking of last year. It was a pleasant Christmas afternoon to me, and one fact almost compensated for your being sick, and that was the pleasure it was to me to be able to do something for you. I wonder if you know what a delightful thought it is to me to be able to do something to add to the fullness of your life. How vividly the picture of that last Christmas afternoon is impressed on my mind! And I know that the most vivid part of it is how lovely and loving and lovable you looked as you lay there with your hair down and tossing

Whatcom Museum.

Deception Pass before the bridge from Whidbey Island to Fidalgo Island was built in 1935.

about. There is considerable love in that last sentence, but not half as much as there is in my heart. This will indeed be a lonely Christmas, but I will console myself by thinking that it will be our last one apart, and also that through distance may come between us, it can't crowd out love. I shall spend the day with you in my thoughts if not in person, and expect to get some comfort of that fact.

Well, Ed has come up again and though he is reading still I want to be alone to write freely on this occasion, so I will write later tonight, no matter how late it may be.

Later – Everything is quiet now except the howling of the wind. Off south, in view from my windows, a forest fire is raging, the red forked flames leaping up and casting a lurid color over everything. A large portion of the townsite is being cleared in this manner. As one gentleman remarked this evening, the "suburbs" of Fairhaven are in ruins. Well it is decidedly dismal and lonely anyway even if the sight is a grand one.

I have been wondering if my letters lately have not been late. It has been so stormy on the Sound that the steamers have been laid up part of the time. There is a narrow pass between here and Tacoma known as "Deception Pass." That is almost impassable in bad weather. This letter will be sent a day or two ahead of the usual time to circumvent the storms on the Sound and the snow blockades on the railroads.

So I will wish you all kinds of pleasant thoughts and many kindly remembrances, and all the happiness that can come to one person. My own Christmas will be a lonely one, and yet I will have with me all the day a consciousness of possessing the richest gift that a man can have – a sweet woman's love, and that woman – you.

My Christmas will not be lonely after all when I think of that and the promise for the future and I want you to think of me as holding you in memory all the day. It seems to me that each year but adds to my love and makes it more and more a part of myself. I can scarcely conceive now that it could ever have been otherwise. I am going to make this letter a kind of continuous one during the holidays and write at least every other day and for a day or two every day. Permit me to "formally" wish you a very Merry Christmas and Happy New Year and also extend the same to all the family including Anna and Lollie and Jessie. In closing, I want to renew our vows of affection, and say once more, I love you my darling. And now good bye sweetheart.

Yours devotedly,

Will

Letter 75

Fairhaven, Washington
Friday, Dec. 19, 1890

My Darling Sweetheart,

Have just mailed a short note and will now start another letter at least, though it cannot go out until Sunday night. We keep writing letters and great comforts they are too. But there are times when a letter is an utter failure in its ability to express the thoughts and feelings that come surging up into the mind. There, that is a statement that we have both made a dozen times at least in its various forms and yet it continues to hold the same truth or why should it now be updated? Wonder what kind of a scheme it would be to get phonographs and exchange cylinders. But no, even though the voice were there in its natural cadences, the features, the glance of the eye would be missing and that's what I am yearning for now.

Do you know that sometimes I feel as if I could give up the prospects for the future to be able to enjoy the present with you, if only for a short time. And at such times I feel inclined to call myself hard names for coming so far away for an uncertainty and thereby cut myself off from the happiness of looking into your eyes and beholding there what I would give up everything to see now. I am most starved for a sight of you, Anna and yet I must sit down and try and write cheerful letters when my heart is far from cheerful – sometimes it is not in nature to do it – and this is one of the times I am not "blue." Don't imagine that at least not morbidly blue or from lack of expected success. I have all of the latter than I can reasonably hope for. But I am just love hungry. Do you take in the full meaning of that expression? I think that expresses it, only I am afraid it is not quite strong enough.

What a fool I was to think that a little financial success would compensate me until such time as we could be united! I know more now. The only thought that makes it at all tolerant out here is that I am working for your future comfort. That is a very consoling thought too, at most times, but at other times it fails. Then nothing but your own warm loving flesh and blood presence with sweetness on your lips and love in your eyes is worth the living for. I am not a demonstrative fellow, Anna. I never tell the half of what I feel and so I wonder sometimes if you really know the depth, the strength, the torrent of my passion, if you really have a full conception and then again I think that with your woman's intuition you do know and feel how it is with me. And loving you thus it is strange that I oftentimes think I did a foolish thing in coming so far away to establish myself? A man of energy can succeed eventually anywhere – if he has the elements of success in him at all, but what is it worth if all that he holds dear are thousands of miles away, beyond the reach of his voice, the touch of his hand, the gleam of his eye.

Life is too short, my darling, to make it worthwhile to thrust Love aside and tell him to wait until wealth or fame or home is secured. I know that perhaps I ought not to disturb your content and peace by this breaking out – in rebellion, for such it is, especially since it was my own act that bought me out here, but sometimes a man must tell all that is in him. Blindly (manlike), I would not see that you did not want me to come out here because the proud woman's heart would not say so, but I know that you did not want it. And that is the way men are always unconsciously causing sorrow to those who love them. And so I, like the rest of mankind, brought sorrow to both of us when I might have done just as well nearer home.

Yes, this is a love letter, I know, and I intend it to be that and nothing else. I intend that for once I will pour out my soul to you as I think of you. Who dare tell me I am cold now? Why I am all fire. Were I with you tonight you would not say that I was silent. The heart would give the tongue words faster than it could utter them, and what was lacking in words would be eked out in action. Oh my darling you will know sometime how completely you have wrapped and entwined yourself about my heart and become life of my life. It is wonderful how it has happened. It never had a beginning that can ever be definitely fixed, but it grew gradually until now, I have no existence away from your side. To be with you, to provide for you, to comfort you, to give you pleasure and joy and contentment has become my highest happiness. And this is never changing. When my letters are coolest and freest from expressions of endearment, my heart is just as full of you as at other times, but it has seemed to me tonight that I must give it voice, or I would have the blues, with a vengeance. And what a blessed thing it is to know that I have your love! What would life be without it! It would be a blank as it was before I possessed it. Who was the prevaricator who said that absence brought forgetfulness? It only adds to memory, not takes anything from it.

You should see me with your letters now, I rush from the post office and open them with the same feverish haste that I did the first one I ever received from you – the one written from Bluff Park three years ago, or nearly three years. I am going to stop now and say good night – and as you read this I want you to go and stand by the parlor door and imagine "you and I and the hat" on the scene, and hear me whisper "Good night darling."

Saturday Night *– Again the wind is howling outside and the rain is beating against the windows. This storm has lasted for ten days now, and the waters of the Sound have been churned into suds by the wind. No small craft venture out at all, but remain tied up at the wharves, where there is shelter. But with a cheerful fire inside, it is endurable. I hope however that it will not be my lot to have to go out tonight. But there, that touches a little on business doesn't it? And I have determined to keep "Shop" surely out of this letter.*

Well, I think I will leave you again for this evening. Will cut my stay short as I came late and so must leave the owner. Oh, my dear, if I cannot have you either in June or September, I don't know what I will do. I feel as if it would be a difficult task to wait until then. But I must say good night.

Good bye, dear.
Lovingly, Will

The Letters of 1891

WILL'S ACUTE LONELINESS during the 1890 Christmas season seemed to cause a change in his spirit and his determination to make a go of it in Fairhaven. His longing for Anna and the familiar sights of Mount Pleasant and the declining state of his medical practice and the Fairhaven economy became more and more prominent in his letters. His increasing "blue" moods became more in evidence in his writing. In his December 24th letter he tells Anna that "if I feel as lonely and miserable tomorrow as I do today it will be a very gloomy Christmas." He wrote again on the 27th reporting that he had felt too lonely to write on Christmas day. "It was the loneliest day I ever put in"

Most of his letters after that dark day reflect his growing discontent and his realization that his Fairhaven medical practice was failing. On December 29th he reported gloomily that there were now fifteen doctors in Fairhaven, that he had not had a patient in his office in almost two weeks and that collections were terrible. Early in January he reported that he had billed $200.00 for the month of December but had only received $11.50 in cash and that he had $400.00 in patient fees outstanding.

Will Gray's woes were compounded by a national money crisis which was drying up the availability of credit throughout the country. Fairhaven had entered a very slow economic period which was to gradually worsen and eventually destroy the Fairhaven Boom and its dreams of grandeur.

The letters increasingly portray the growing possibility that Will's western adventure was not going to be successful and a realization that he might need to give up and return to Iowa. While his correspondence with Anna focuses on his difficulties, they also include many interesting passages of life in 1891. We have printed excerpts from those letters arranged in chronological order.

Friday, January 2, 1891

Tomorrow night the railroad will be completed to the connection with the Canadian Pacific and Monday morning work will be commenced on our $100,000 opera house.[50] *New Year's Eve, the raising of the necessary bonus of $20,000 was completed and work will be commenced at once. It will be the finest house on the Pacific coast – not excluding San Francisco, and that in a town where in Sept. 1889 there were only one hundred and fifty inhabitants. The opera house is to be completed in time for the next season, so that next fall Fairhaven will have the fine attractions that appear in the large cities of the country. I told you, didn't I that Whatcom and Sehome have consolidated under the name of New Whatcom? That reduces it to two towns right together. Another year and it will be one.*

Northwestern Lumberman.

The proposed Opera House was to be built at the northeast corner of Harris Avenue and 13th Street. In January 1891, E.L. Cowgill's home, pictured center, was still located on this corner. It would be moved a few months later up the hill, two blocks east of Wardner's Castle, seen high on the hill in this photo.

Saturday, January 3, 1891

I have been feeling a little discouraged lately. Collections are so hard. And this month business is very light. I haven't had a new case for four weeks, except the boy with the broken leg. I am a little afraid that he will not pull through. I found out to-day for the first time how the accident happened, though the boy still denies it. He was riding a pony which fell down with him underneath. This happened a week before I was called in. Then he had been hobbling around on that broken limb for a week, setting up a constant irritation and the result is that besides the broken bone I have a case of blood poisoning on my hands, which is always a very uncertain condition and proves fatal in the majority of cases.

I had a letter from Cousin Ed Richmond a day or two ago, stating that he would start for this country the 7th of this month – day after tomorrow. Also had an announcement of Harry Grahn's marriage – another source of envy. Oh! Those debts of mine. If I ever get out of debt I'll never get in again. I know that very well.

Our post office is in a horrible condition, however. The powers that be at Washington are unable to realize how Fairhaven has grown. At the time the postmaster was appointed, Fairhaven's population was 150. Hence we have a little fourth or fifth class post office with the business of a second class post office and sufficient cancellations to give us a free delivery. So mail is piled up, as there is not help enough in the office to handle it. I expect if they should delve down among the packages they have piled up in the office, the candy would be unearthed.

Dr. Van Winter and I are figuring on going into an office together to save rent. There are two rooms on a good corner that we think we can get for twenty-five, though they ask thirty per month. Of course it will not give us quite as much room but it will be cheaper – saving in rent, fuel and lights. Besides which we could help each other. I would have the best of the bargain, as I would have my personal consultation room and would use a part of the other room as reception room. Twenty dollars a month for rent eats quite a hole – besides what I could save in this would go to some length in paying house rent, and you know I am looking forward to that.

Thursday, January 8, 1891

Everything here is most fearfully dull and everyone is complaining of the tightness of the money market. It made me scratch to pay my rent this month, but I made it all right. Practice is also very dull. All the doctors tell the same story of little or nothing to do. However, we will pull through some way I think.

I suppose that by this time you are back in the school, instilling some facts into the noodles of Mt. Pleasant's frisky kids. I should say useful facts. By the way Mt. Pleasant is resting in the matter of matrimonial affairs is it not? Whenever I see the Press or the Journal, the ubiquitous obituary never fails to be on hand, but I miss my Aunt Alice's gorgeous "write-ups" of the weddings that she never attends. I suppose though that the stringency in the money market and the McKinley Bill are at the bottom of the deficiency.

I have heard that there have been dry times back in Iowa. Wish we could lend them a little of our surplus moisture. We would very readily spare a little of it and yet, after all we don't have so much rain, but it just stays misty and cloudy. The past two days have been beautiful and bright, however, except that this afternoon there has been some fog. The fog is rather pretty though with the sun shining through it. Speaking of fog—down in Oregon (of course such a thing couldn't happen in Washington) the fog was so thick that when a man was shingling the roof of his house he shingled out four feet on the fog before he discovered that he had got out past the roof, and it wasn't a very foggy day either.

Well, I must stop now, but just allow me to state that I want to see you, not a new want at all, but I just wanted to mention it again, for fear that the little fact might slip your memory. I agree with your belief in the inefficiency of pen and ink to express certain thoughts.

Say Anna, what an outpouring we will have some time, won't we? When our words will have neither time nor space to traverse and where words are lacking there will still remain looks and actions and it can't come too soon.

Sunday, January 11, 1891

The past week we have been having some of the most beautiful weather that I have experienced since coming to this country. The days are bright and sunshining and there is a frost at night. The mountains have never looked as beautiful as they do now with the deep snow on them. Just a little while ago Ed Robinson and myself were out taking a walk and went out on a high point that runs into the bay[51] where we have a view of the cities of Fairhaven, Whatcom and Sehome and the mountain ranges on three sides of us and Puget Sound on the fourth, and we both agreed that we would never want to live in a flat country again. This is the place if we can only hold on and don't get frozen out. It is very dull now though the real estate men say that things have been picking up a little for the past few days.

Our post office has at last secured the attention of the post office department and been raised to an office of the third class and the p.m.'s salary raised to $1,600 from $600. As the newspapers say "this marks another step in the onward march of our vigorous young city."

Tell you what Anna, even if I should not stay in this country I am gaining experience that will serve me in good stead in the next place I may go to. If this case were in a family of any means it would bring in a good fee, but as usual with my patients they are as poor as Job's traditional turkey, so I will probably get little or nothing but the experience out of it. However, that is worth something. I have to go and visit the case every six or eight hours to see how he is getting along and will have to go now.

Thursday, January 15, 1891

It seems as if everybody that I know is doing better, getting along faster – in the world than I am. Clint Howard was yesterday appointed attorney for the City of Fairhaven by the new council.

My old roommate Dr. Baker marries. Harry Grahn, ditto. Ed Robinson and Det Bird own considerable real estate. Walt Bartlett has an established business of his own and even Elbert Smith – little Elbert, the kid, is in business. Harry Ambler is county attorney of Henry County in the commonwealth of Iowa and so on ad infinitum. This all sounds envious, doesn't it? Well it is, and I can't help it.

Some time ago Mrs. Sullivan said that they were trying to get Mattie Stearns to come out here and would get her a position in the schools. They could probably do so as Mr. Sullivan is bookkeeper for the Fairhaven Electric Light and Water Company which is largely composed of the members of the Fairhaven Land Company, and so could bring powerful influence to her and "inflooence" is largely what controls things here.

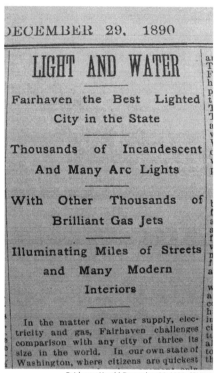

DECEMBER 29, 1890

LIGHT AND WATER

Fairhaven the Best Lighted City in the State

Thousands of Incandescent And Many Arc Lights

With Other Thousands of Brilliant Gas Jets

Illuminating Miles of Streets and Many Modern Interiors

In the matter of water supply, electricity and gas, Fairhaven challenges comparison with any city of thrice its size in the world. In our own state of Washington, where citizens are quickest

Fairhaven Herald, December 29, 1890. CPNWS.

Besides this, there have been one or two teachers hired every three weeks since school opened last fall. At that time the number of school children (in the schools) was about 400. Now it is 700 and still increasing. Every three or four weeks the school directors rent another storeroom somewhere and start another room. If she gets a position in the public schools, of course, that can't affect your scheme for a private school.

Wednesday, January 21, 1891

You will doubtless think from the appearance of this paper that things are getting down pretty fine in which surmise you would be eminently correct. These fugitive leaves are extracted from an old note book used at Iowa City. You will begin to think after awhile that I do not use loverlike care in selecting fine paper on which to engross my affections. I wonder how many makeshifts I have resorted to. The worst one I think was when I used the brown wrapping paper to write a note or the time I sent you my Phi pin when I was returning to Iowa City. This represents the best I can get however, as I am out of paper and out of money. Think of it! "Broke" once more.

The first of February the Fairhaven railroad will be turned over to the Great Northern and payment made. That may relieve the tightness of money a little and

cause a revival of business. If not, the town stands a good chance to be at a standstill for a year or so in which case I will be frozen out. Dr. Heacock has recently returned from a two months trip east and says that the tide of immigration is setting toward Texas for the present, and that but little of it is coming this way. That looks bad for this community as it is not yet supporting and is dependent upon eastern muscle and capital. But I suppose we must look at it as bravely as possible and try and weather the storm.

Am thinking a little of going into an amateur dramatic performance here, not for the benefit of a library club, but for the benefit of the individual members of the cast. Do not know yet whether I will nor not. I might be able to make enough out of it to pay a month's rent which would be very desirable.

Sunday, January 25, 1891

My boy with the broken leg is coming along very well. The ankle joint will be all right, in fact with the exception of a small lump or two on the side of the bone he will be all right. That one case is about all I have had this month so you can imagine it will run small.

I have just been wondering what it is that decides people to get a certain doctor when they don't know who it is they want. This reflection was occasioned by a little incident that happened a day or two ago. There are four doctors' offices in this building on the same floor. Two in front and two at the back with a kind of court between the front and back rooms. A day or two ago as I was going down the stairs a man came up. I know from the general uncertain air that he carried with him that he was looking for a doctor and also that he had no idea who he wanted and stopped to see where he would go, thinking possibly he might go in at my door. He stood and stared at the sign on the first door for a moment – looked perplexed and then went on to the next door. Then he turned around and looked at my door. My cardiac organ thumped up against my soft palate – but no! It was not to be. He turned and looked at the sign that directed to Dr. Teel's door,[52] came back and looked at the first one he came to and then passed down the hall to the office of Dr. Teel, the latest comer to the town. Now what passed in his mind and what took him down there? Is the conundrum I asked of myself, but no satisfactory answer was forthcoming. Doubtless I have caught some in the same way, but it is all very funny. So you see how much I have to occupy my mind.

Today we have had about the wettest rain that has prevailed since I have been in this country and yet it was not a hard pour such as we see in Iowa. It seemed as if the cloud just settled quietly down on the earth and made everything wet.

Am going to Sullivan's tonight to supper and to see the baby which is sick. Allow me to remark parenthetically that I don't like baby cases. That is where experience is needed more than in any other class of cases. Well, there is one consolation – the experience will come after awhile.

⚬

Broke Again

BY JANUARY 21ST WILL WAS REPORTING that he was "out of paper and out of money" and "Broke once more." He was so broke that he had to resort to writing letters to Anna on scraps of paper torn from an old college notebook and yet ten days later the irrepressible and perhaps impractical doctor was in Victoria, B.C. traveling with his cousin Ed. Richmond.

The descriptions of his adventures in Victoria on this trip and a subsequent return trip in June are some of the most charming passages in his letters. His descriptions of "Chinatown" and the "Regatta in the Gorge" are shown with remarkable photographs of these very locations and events provided by the Royal British Columbia Museum in Victoria and the City of Victoria Archives.

These jaunts to British Columbia were happy escapes from an increasingly somber reality.

Saturday, January 31, 1891

As you will see from this I am again in Victoria. Cousin Ed Richmond arrived in Fairhaven this week and was anxious to have me come over with him. I had nothing to do with no prospect for some time and so concluded to come for a day or two. You know it is only a run of about sixty miles by boat. This is but a note, but I will write a letter tomorrow. My cousin Jennie is waiting for me now to go up town with her to get a pair of shoes and mail this letter. So I will say good bye for the present.

Friday, February 6, 1891

Here I am back from Victoria. Returned yesterday morning having had a very pleasant visit. The only thing in connection with the trip that might prove of interest was an hour spent at the Chinese theatre. My far famed powers of description would prove entirely inadequate to give any intelligible account of that curious place of amusement. I understand that the play that was on hand commenced about three months ago and that it would take a month longer before it reached the end of the last act. The performance commenced at a quarter of seven and continues until one or two each night.

The audience room was much like an ordinary theatre with raised seats and gallery. Where the stage is usually was a platform at the back of which sat the orchestra – and that orchestra. They kept up an incessant blather on gongs, tom-toms, Chinese fiddles and banjos. The play was half opera (?) that is partly spoken with ordinary tone and modulation and partly like the recitation in Italian opera. Two doors hung with curtains on which were Chinese hieroglyphics, one at either

Courtesy City of Victoria Archives (M00422).

Entrance to Victoria, B.C., Chinatown 1882.

end of the platform admitted the performers and also the spectators who passed across the stage while the performance was in progress. The "supes" came in and placed chairs and properties in positions or removed them while the actors were on. To the imaginative Chinese mind little things like that make no difference. As one Chinaman said, "No suppose see anything but play." Likewise he doesn't need any scenery. Imagination furnishes that also. The costumes were quite gorgeous.

The orchestra smoked cigarettes so did the audience. So did the actors. The atmosphere grew hazy. It was likewise permeated with an odor that was not that of roses or new mown hay, to put it mildly. I should have said at the beginning that the theatre was down a long narrow alley where a man has a feeling that he wants to keep his hand on his revolver. When we felt that we couldn't stand it any longer and were in condition to be treated for asphyxias, we left. It was almost as bad as the man that blows out the gas.

We had planned a trip to Esquimault where the navy yard is and where John Bull keeps his big gunboats[53] to guard the sealers in Bering Sea, but it rained and spoiled the trip. On the way back there was quite a heavy sea on and the boat tossed up and down and rolled from side to side in a manner to strike terror to the hearts of the timid ones. It likewise sadly deranged the digestion of some of the people on board. I escaped being sick on board but all day yesterday after landing I could feel the motion of the steamer.

Canadian Hydrographic Office Marine Chart.

Esquimalt and Victoria harbours, circa 1920. Note the Gorge Waterway extending from the city centre 5 miles northwesterly to Portage Inlet. The circle denotes the actual narrow gorge, site of the annual regattas of days gone by.

My trip to Victoria this time was a valuable one in that it opened my eyes to a little fact that I had not before suspected and that is that my esteemed colleague here is doing what he can to injure me and that in a very unprofessional way. When I went over to Victoria I left my case of fractured leg, giving a full history of the case from the beginning. He promised to look after it. I had been dressing the leg every day as the amount of discharge from the wound it had been necessary to make rendered it imperative.

Dr. Heacock went down and practically did nothing. The only reason I can assign for it is that he thought from the looks of the premises and family that he might get little or nothing for it. He told the family that if he had had the case he would have set the leg and left it without any more attention, that I did wrong to open the leg and finally said that he didn't think the leg was broken at all. The family assured him that Dr. Gray said the leg was broken. "Well" he said that Dr. Gray was a young man just out of college and had no practical experience in such matters. He made these statements in the face of the fact that he did not even remove the bandage and examine to see whether the leg was broken or not. I think he wanted to make the people believe that he was such a great physician that he did not need to examine but could tell by feeling the pulse or looking at the tongue whether the leg was broken or not. But he over shot himself. The evidence in favor of the limb being actually fractured was so plain even to the eyes of these people and it was so certain that it was positively necessary to save the boy's leg that it had to be opened, even to the family that I only stand the firmer with them and Dr. Heacock injured himself.

This instance is sufficient to make me believe it is not the first time that Dr. Heacock has endeavored to injure me. It is the more surprising as an old physician usually aids a younger one when he can instead of making his youth a fact against him. It is an especially small trick in this man inasmuch as he is wealthy and is only here for speculation purposes, his practice being a mere side issue. He does not even expect to remain in the city but a few months longer. Well the longer we live the more we find out and the knowledge doesn't tend to increase our faith in human nature. Dr. Heacock by the way is a prominent member of the Methodist Church, the members of which help to increase his practice.

Monday, February 9, 1891

At present everything is so very discouraging that it just seems as if the bottom has dropped out of everything. Not that this country and this particular spot has not a glorious future before it but things have been so inflated and over done that it will take a long time for the development of the outside country to be commensurate with the growth of the cities.

Here in Fairhaven we are living off of each other. We produce nothing and consume a great deal and have about reached the end of the string. Those who can hold on and weather the dull times, will reap a glorious harvest, but the question is whether some of us can hold on long enough. I worry over the matter all the time. I had hoped to accomplish so much this year, and now that things are at such a standstill, the outlook seems very gloomy. I try my best to be cheerful and not get discouraged, but I can't disguise the fact that I have been grievously disappointed in my hopes here. Not so much on account of practice – that has been as good as I could reasonably hope for. But the town stands on such a hollow financial basis, that it is almost impossible to collect two percent of what money is due. People have practically quit paying – the money isn't in the country to pay with.

Sunday, February 15, 1891

This has been a very different letter from what I wanted to write, it has been so disconnected. I feel as if I were five years older this week. I have had three desperate cases and they have given me constant anxiety. I have hardly slept at all and have not had more than eight meals since last Monday and some of them were hasty lunches. Last one, case of a little child, sixteen months old – by pneumonia. The child had been teething so the parents were not at all alarmed and did not call for medical aid until the case was hopeless. It was in a state of stupor from suffocation when I first saw it, from which it never aroused, dying in about fourteen hours. I have another desperate case of pneumonia and one of fever, the latter a very peculiar and critical case. Whooping cough is getting a good start here now and there are a good many cases. I find the practice of medicine one constant anxiety.

Dr. Heacock left town yesterday morning going back to his old home in Kansas. I have heard rumors to the effect that he failed to pass the examination before the state board, but can't vouch for the truth of the matter. This leaves the field free for me unless some one else should come in. If so I shall try to associate them with me in partnership, so that we will not be working against each other.

Had the greatest treat last Wednesday night that I have had in years. The Emma Juch Grand Opera Company rendered "Carmen" here. Inasmuch as this company is the successor to the "American" Company and is the finest operatic organization in America today, it was a great thing for Fairhaven to secure them. They were secured by subscription seats in the lower part of the house being five dollars and the upstairs two dollars. I paid the two dollars and felt compensated for all the meals I lost this week. The music was better than the meals I missed. In fact it put more life and energy there a good time.

Howard Buswell Collection #508, Center for Pacific Northwest Studies, WWU.
The Silver Spike celebration connecting the Fairhaven & Northern with the Canadian Pacific at Blaine.

Yesterday was a great day in Fairhaven.[54] *The silver spike was driven at the international boundary on the line connecting us with the Canadian Pacific R.R. The British Columbia parliament adjourned and attended the exercises, as did also the mayors and city councils of Victoria, Vancouver, New Westminster and Fairhaven. The road was formally turned over to the Great Northern and the Fairhaven and Southern RR ceased to exist. As the papers would say this "marks another step in the forward march of Fairhaven toward the growth of her greatness."*

Thistle Block 1905. Located at 11th Street & Mill Avenue, today an empty lot used for parking.

Friday, February 20, 1891

Dr. Van Winter and I are going to office together.[55] *We have secured three rooms in a good location – all three nice light rooms. We are to pay $25 per month until the first of May and $35 after that. As I pay $20 by myself now and Dr. Van Winter pays $25 it will be considerable savings for both of us, especially when we take fuel into consideration. We will have a reception room in common and each have our own operating room. With the furniture that both of us have the rooms will be better furnished than if we are separate. The rooms are something after this plan. Another advantage the rooms will have is in the fact that at present, the only hall or opera house that Fairhaven possesses is in the same building, the entrance to the same being directly opposite our doors, which little fact will be of some benefit from the advertising it will give us. So taking it all in all I think the move will be very advantageous.*

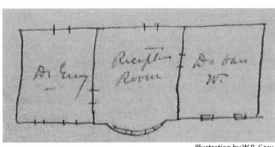

Illustration by W.R. Gray.

While I have been writing this there have been just the faintest murmurs of thunder. The first, I believe that I have heard since coming to this country.

I think I wrote you in my last that I had a bad case of pneumonia on hand. Wednesday I had to discharge myself as the boy was getting well. My boy with the broken leg I am about through with as he is on the high road to recovery and with those people I am the greatest doctor on earth. That is the family that Dr. Heacock told that I was just out of college. They say that whether I am just out of college or not they will put me up against any of them. Now just listen to that will you for a piece of professional vanity. Here is another. The worst case that I have had. I will not enter into any details but will simply say it was the case of a young mother. Two other physicians were called in consultation with me and gave an unfavorable prognosis. I also detailed the symptoms at the worst stage to Dr. Lawrance of Sehome – an old man – he simply said in so many words "that woman will die." Of course all this was very discouraging to me. I had just lost the baby with pneumonia, as I told you in last letter and while that case was hopeless, yet a death always hurts a doctor in that immediate neighborhood and I felt that if I had another so soon I would be pretty nearly ready to give up. However I went ahead and did my best. There was over a week that I hardly slept or ate – in fact there were five days out of the week that I only took one meal out of the twenty-four hours. But this morning she seems to be progressing towards convalescence although even yet an unfavorable turn may occur, but at present the outlook is very hopeful. If she gets well it will do me a great amount of good though they are poor people who have just recently come here and are comparatively unknown. I don't know whether I will get a cent out of the case or not, but I have worked just as hard.

Friday, February 23, 1891

Am glad you liked "Fairhaven Illustrated." Of course it is "boom" literature but at the same time nearly all the illustrations were taken from photographs and are quite accurate.

I agree with you that your Aunt May and Mother must be getting quite "chummy." Mother would be quite jolly if she didn't have to work quite so hard. If times improve so that I can collect any money this summer I am going to try and induce her to come out here and we will keep house. It will not be so much more expensive than it is with me now, living around and she would not have to work hard. I am afraid she would have a hard time climbing Fairhaven hills however.

It was news to me to hear that Stirfoater was married (if it is a fact) though it was nothing more than might be expected from him. He was ruled by passion and caprice. But it seems a mystery to me how people can toy with the most sacred relations on earth. As for Leigh Woolson he ought to be horsewhipped for his treatment of Anna Crane. I can well believe that her outward gaiety is but the mask that conceals the sorrow for hers is not a light nature to rally quickly when she is injured in her affections.

I am going to close this for tonight and continue tomorrow. I hope that all I have written will be understood, though it seems so incomplete. It seems to me as if I could write a volume, but I will not inflict that on you, though perhaps you would *know more of what is in my mind. But good night my darling. I will continue this tomorrow. I would give anything to look into your dear face. I think if I could hold you by the hands and look down into your eyes, that it would not be necessary to speak the feelings of my heart. You could read them in my eyes. Good night dear.*

Whatcom Museum.

Cover of 1890 *Fairhaven Illustrated*, produced and distributed by the Fairhaven Land Company. A rare copy can be found at the Whatcom Museum Photo Archives.

Thursday, February 26, 1891

The past week we have been having some snow. It is such a rarity that everybody and his wife have been out coasting every hill in the city, and they are not few. They have been crowded with people, on pleasure bent – old and young. And you ought to see the rigs. Of course there was not a regular sleigh or cutter in the country and so all kinds of makeshifts were resorted to. The most numerous kind was a species of bob-sled with barrel staves for runners and they made pretty good sleds too. For the cutters, the wheels were taken from buggies and runners made of bent gas pipe were attached to the axles. There were several accidents but I was not fortunate to catch any.

Monday, March 9, 1891

I have learned several things since coming out here, and were it not for pride I think I would have been back before this. And it is not because of failure or lack of success either. I know that in ten years residence in this country I will be better off than in the same time back home. But these other considerations that have a great deal of weight, so that time after time the thought comes to me, shall I stay or not?

This is a beautiful country and has a great future but what constantly keeps me restless and undecided is the problem whether it is worthwhile to be a pioneer all one's life. "Society" is composed of the speculators. Town lots, real estate and the almighty dollar are all that people think of. In the short time that I have been here I sometimes think that mentally I have degenerated. The only field for the intellect here – I mean in a general way of course, because there is always room for development along professional lines – is in trying to overreach someone else. The man who can do that is a "smart fellow." And again and again the thought comes to me, is not life too short to spend it in such an atmosphere.

I am beginning to long for some of the things that people take an interest in back home. Art, literature, morals, all these things are at a very low ebb out here, and I frequently long to be nearer the great centers of thought in this country and believe that the same energy that is necessary to succeed out here, if applied back there would succeed equally well. I am giving you these impressions not because I feel like giving up here, but simply because I think it well to look at these things fairly and discuss them at least. I am of the opinion that you are, that I have been fairly successful and would think so myself were it not that I am anxious to be married. The hard times came making collections hard, and that casts a dusky hue over things. But I have had as much practice as I ought to have and do justice to my patients.

New buildings are springing up in every direction. Nevertheless, I don't feel that I want to weather another such winter of hard times as we have had this past winter. I suppose though that if I should return it would be better to wait for the return of fever that will inevitably come again with the advent of warm weather. People here have not learned their lesson, notwithstanding that last year there were deaths all around them, and so they go on persistently living under unsanitary conditions that could be remembered to some extent.

Sunday, March 22, 1891

Was up to Ross Sullivan's last night and had quite a time with their baby, aged three. She was sleepy and wanted to be rocked and for that purpose clambered up into my lap and nestled down and wouldn't go to any one else. It was a new experience and a very pleasant one. I think after awhile I will get on with the children. Have a good deal of practice among them by virtue of my homoeopathy.

Friday, April 3, 1891

Yesterday I started out to collect, it being the first of the month and found that parties owing me in the aggregate eighty dollars had "skipped" and so it goes. And as I say, I have never felt so thoroughly disgusted since I came here. I think another month's experience of this kind and I will be about ready to seek a locality where the great mass of the people are leavened with a few honest ones. If some of this years crop of graduates should come along with more money than good sense, and should offer a few hundred dollars for me to get out, I would accept the offer so quick that the aforesaid graduate would suffer from an acute attack of vertigo.

Seriously, Spring is about here and yet the real business outlook is no better than it has been for the past four months. Few people are coming here or to the Sound for that matter and those who are here have no money. We are producing nothing so that we have consumed what every one brought here. A great many men are out of employment and altogether the outlook of the town for the next two years is gloomy in the extreme. In the meantime we close our jaws tightly on what there is here and hold on.

Sunday, April 5, 1891

Last Sunday was Easter. Ed Robinson and I went to Whatcom to attend the Episcopal services there,[56] having understood that the music would be very fine. We were late in arriving; the church was small and packed. We were just able to stand inside the door so after a short time we came away. All we gained was a ride in the new Whatcom street cars which commenced running on that day.[57] New York is going to build a monument to General Grant and Fairhaven is going to have a street car line, but which will be completed first is something that "no fellah" can find out.

Whatcom Museum.

Original St. Paul's Episcopal Church on Walnut Street.

Whatcom Museum.

Opening Day celebration of the Bellingham Bay Electric Street Railway on Easter Sunday, March 29, 1891.

Monday, April 6, 1891

We are having Spring days now – real soft, balmy, lazy days. I feel as if I had no ambition in life but to lie out under some big tree and listen to the birds and the insects. Two or three days ago I saw a big butterfly fluttering along seeming to enjoy himself exceedingly. The peach and plum trees are in bloom and vegetation is getting quite a start.

Fairhaven had one little favor shown her recently that looks encouraging. This place has been made a terminal point by the railroads. That is freight and passengers are sent from all eastern points at the same through rates as to San Francisco, Portland, Tacoma or Seattle. This means considerable to the town. We have recently put on another metropolitan air – we have a professional baseball team[58] *and a place in the Northwestern League consisting of Portland, Spokane, Tacoma, Seattle and Bellingham Bay.*

Was up to Ross Sullivan's yesterday and had supper with them. It was a great treat to have a nice clean meal once more, one that could really be enjoyed. I don't know whether I wrote

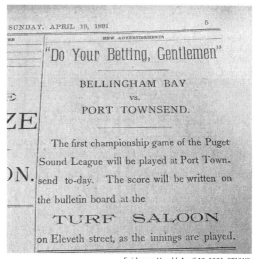

SUNDAY, APRIL 19, 1891   5

NEW ADVERTISEMENTS

"Do Your Betting, Gentlemen"

BELLINGHAM BAY
vs.
PORT TOWNSEND.

The first championship game of the Puget Sound League will be played at Port Townsend to-day. The score will be written on the bulletin board at the

TURF SALOON

on Eleventh street, as the innings are played.

Fairhaven Herald, April 19, 1891. CPNWS.

to you about the position he is going to take, but if I did not I will now. He is going to Mt. Vernon, the county seat of Skagit County, just south of here to take the superintendency of the new electric light and water company to be managed for the Mt. Vernon Land Company. He will go up there the 15th of this month and wants me to go and look at the town sometime after he gets started there, probably early in June. There is a population of 1,500 with quite a large farming population along the Skagit River. There is only one doctor in the place and he is spoken of as being full of good red liquor most of the time. Sullivan thinks that there is an excellent opportunity to make money for a year or two and that I would have an opportunity to "stand in" something that is very necessary and desirable in this country. I think I shall take a run up there in June, but will not think of changing locations unless I can see a sure thing. I go nowhere else in this country without knowing exactly what I am getting into and whether there will be anything in it of advantage to me.

Sunday, April 19, 1891

I am relieved to know that May Weir's baby is to be called Paul. When you wrote and told me that you had been informed of the arrival of Moses Weir Williams, I was disgusted. It would be a shame to handicap him with the name of Moses. Might as well call him Solomon Levi at once. Think of a boy being spoken of as "Mose."

When I arrived on this terrestrial sphere it was proposed to call me Nicodemus. Anna, do you think you could ever have love a man named Nicodemus. Think of you sweetly speaking of me as "Nick"!! That would be worse than "Crank." I suppose you have read of how Mark Twain walked in on the family conclave when they were discussing that all important question of name and said "Father, I will not be named Samuel."

Tuesday, April 21, 1891

It begins to look more and more as if it would be a case of necessity for me either to return to Iowa in the Fall or go elsewhere. Things do not improve at all. These statements by the way are between you and me, as I would not wish to send out any reports from here that would help to injure the town. A scheme is afoot now by which it is hoped to hold up the town until the Great Northern road is completed. An election will be held the 2nd of May to settle the question of bonding the city for the purpose of putting in sewers and making other improvements. It is a desperate remedy, but it is a necessity. There is no money left to carry on street improvements and when the street work stops, it means that about one thousand laborers will be thrown out of employment and Fairhaven will lose that many in population. This will wreck all branches of industry and business. By bonding the city for the purpose of carrying on these improvements, it is hoped to prop up the city until it is a little more able to stand alone. All over town businessmen say "If the bonding proposition fails to pass, I can't get out of Fairhaven too quick." That is the general sentiment. If it fails, Fairhaven will be flat on its back for the next two years. Then it will come up again for nothing can ultimately prevent its advancement, but two months more of such times as we had during the winter would freeze me out. So it behooves me to be ready to move – that is one of the pleasures of being in a boom town. It is kind of hard to look such facts in the face, but it can't be helped.

Tuesday, April 28, 1891

I have just finished reading your answer to my letter stating my resolution with regarding to coming home. After I had finished, I think that if I could get away in any kind of shape at all I would take the first boat in the morning. It seems to me that every day that I am away from you seems harder to bear. I want to tell you how happy it made me to know positively how you feel about my coming home. I will not need to hesitate on that aspect of the question anymore. But what a time we are having to be sure. My resolution is as solid as ever. I don't suppose that it will be possible to find a purchaser for my practice by June but as I said before I will be home in the fall, unless I should be doing so well as to make it unwise to leave. If I go home I will have enough to get started in some kind of shape.

Of course I will take all my medicines, books and instruments with me. I have gone through the hardest times I will ever have in starting, I think, so will not have quite as much worry again wherever I may be. But be sure of one thing. If I come home in the fall it will be to stay in Iowa, unless you should go with me, wherever I may go. I feel that I have got around to our old view of the case, and that when I see you once more I will not have the strength to leave you again. If I go home in the fall, and come back to Washington, you will come with me.

Monday, May 4, 1891

Saturday the election for the purpose of bonding city for $250,000 was held. The vote was 771 in favor of and 27 against. Don't know whether this will make any great change or not very few people seem to be coming in at present and but this all an old story.

Friday, May 8, 1891

I had two children to take care of. Mr. and Mrs. Sullivan went to Mt. Vernon Thursday leaving Zetta and Willie with Mrs. Templin, intending to return Friday evening. Friday morning the whole Templin outfit boarded the boat for Orcas Island leaving the two Sullivan children alone to go to the restaurants for their meals. It happened that morning that I was down at the boat on business and so undertook to look after the children – took them to my boarding house and saw that they were provided for. They were at the office a good part of the day. Oh, I will get to be quite a domestic individual yet, before we are married. You know that is a quality that mother greatly deplores my lack of. As I write this a dancing school is in progress in the opera house just across the hall. In the light of your remarks on dancing some time ago, I am almost tempted to go in sometimes and take some lessons. However, I think I will resist the temptations.

The enclosed heliotrope was plucked from a plant belonging to Dr. Van Winter which he keeps in the office. Please consider all the sentiment that usually clusters around that particular species of blossom as accompanying this. Rainy weather still seems to hold the upper hand. The greater portion of the past week has been very dismal. We are all longing for the summer season.

*Yesterday Ed Robinson and I were strolling around to a considerable extent. I see more of Ed than any of the Mt. Pleasant folks. Clint Howard I hardly ever see. He has had his head turned to such an extent by his success in "standing in" with the land company that he scarcely knows his former acquaintances. He is carrying himself in a way to make himself extremely unpopular in the future with a great many people. I am afraid he has acquired **one incurable attack of hypertrophy cerebri – an enlarged cranium.** Ed Robinson has improved in many ways since coming out here. I have learned to have a very sincere respect for him. Det Bird is the same old Det he always was.*

Wednesday, May 13, 1891

Mr. Clark, Will Taylor's partner was here yesterday on a business trip. He tells me that there is more money in Iowa than any state in which they have dealings – that bills are paid more promptly there than elsewhere. He also says that he thinks there is a good opening at Oskaloosa. I have asked him to investigate it for me and he has promised to do so. I know that while you say that whatever I may decide will be all right, after all you would rather not come out here to live. I am certain of that. And as I am not particularly anxious to remain, why I might better go back to Iowa, or somewhere around in that vicinity. At least I will leave for home as soon as I can get away without making a sacrifice. I couldn't do it now. As soon as times become a little better. I feel pretty certain that I can get two or three hundred dollars for my practice, besides what I get out of my accounts.

Friday, May 22, 1891

Tomorrow I will take in the excursion to Victoria on the occasion of "Her Majesty's" 72nd birthday. Ed Robinson and Det Bird are going with me.

I had a letter from mother yesterday also, and she seems to think that as I am as well established as I am here, it would be unwise to leave. What do you think of that? It seems to me that all the people I used to know are getting married. Mother writes that Walt Bartlett is one of the immediate victims (?). Would I were a "victim."

Clint Howard enjoying life in Fairhaven's High Society. Clint is standing, 2nd from right. Julius Bloedel (back row seated with large mustache) co-founded Lake Whatcom Logging Company at Lake Whatcom in 1896. He donated land for the Bloedel Donovan Park in 1946. Other members of the party were Charles E. Taylor, Rita Christopher, Mr. and Mrs. Dudley Inslee, Elsie Wardner, M.C. Dickinson, Minnie Christopher Harvey, Thomas Newman, Charles Darling, Kathy Wardner, Polly Benson and Marion Canfield.

I invested in a light tweed coat and vest today – a saque coat – quite English you know. Have also joined the Fairhaven Lawn Tennis Club[59] composed of the people of the "Focal City." I don't expect to play much tennis but it may lead to something professionally and socially. So you may expect that I shall be quite giddy during this summer. Has the scheme your approval? You know that is a very important part of it.

I will close this now and write as soon as I get back from Victoria.

Will's Adventures at The Regatta

Courtesy of Royal B.C. Museum, B.C. Archives, Image A-02900.

The 1890 Regatta at the Gorge.

May 23, 1891

You mustn't infer that we did not have a good time on the voyage to Victoria because of mishaps. On the contrary we started out with the intention of having a good time and had it. There was a Dutchman on board who furnished plenty of amusement for the whole crowd. He went to the purser of the boat and changed his plans and his destinations half a dozen times at least before he finally decided to go to Victoria, so with him to act as jester and our own good spirits, we derived considerable sport from our misfortunes.

Well, when did we leave off? At the sports Monday morning? Returning to the house we had such a dinner as the three of us had not eaten since we left home. Then we started for the regatta – six of us – Aunt Jennie, Will and Jennie No. 2. The regatta was held up at what is known as the Gorge. It is an arm of the sea that runs up for a long distance through Victoria and out into the country back of it. It winds about like a river with here and there a little bay on either side with a boat house or two in every cove. To get up to where the excitement was we had to go on barges – flat scows fixed up with board seats and towed by small tugs. The water was covered with all kinds of boats – skiffs, canoes, sail boats, yachts, and steam launches – in fact every description of pleasure craft. They were all gaily decorated, and everyone was having a good time. Up at the starting point a string of naval flags was stretched across the water and here was the most animated part of the scene.

There could not have been less than a thousand boats along either side of the stream and dashing hither and thither. The scene was exactly as I had imagined the university races held on the Thames that we read about in "Tom Brown at Oxford." A description of the races is impossible but there was one that was more exciting than any of the others – one Indian canoe race. There were four huge canoes, each holding twelve dusky boatmen. When the signal was given to start, the whole forty-eight paddlers dipped the waters as if they were controlled by one man. They just drag the water, the paddles flashing in and out like flashes of lightning. At the finish two of three were almost abreast of each other. The winner only gaining by a few feet. It was the most exciting race of the day.

But the funniest thing of the day was right at the gorge. This is a place where the water is narrowed to about 30 feet in width by two masses of rock that project out and confine it in that narrow channel. When the tide is coming in the water rushes through at tremendous speed. Beyond the water expands into quite a lagoon and is quite still and calm. Parties in row boats would drift through the pass with the tide and later rowing about in the quiet water for a time would undertake to row back. They would make it all right until a certain point was reached and the boat would stand still and all efforts were in vain to send it forward an inch. The banks on ether side were lined with spectators watching the fun. When this particular point was reached several wags on the banks would shout "Pull now!" There was one party of four in a boat, consisting of two ladies and two gentlemen, one of the latter who was with one of the ladies was rowing and wore one single eye glass. When they reached the sticking point, the wag shouted "Pull now Cholly" and then the crowd yelled and "Cholly" pulled but in vain. Then the wag yelled "Take off the eye glass Cholly and you'll make it" and Cholly got red, looked mad and pulled harder, but they couldn't make it and dropped back into the still water and then the crowd would cheer and yell and wait for the next boat. This scene was repeated over and over and seemed to get funnier every time.

In the evening we went back to the park to listen to the music and see the fireworks. And here another beautiful scene was presented to view. Across the artificial lake, were festoons of Chinese lanterns radiating from the fountain in the center to trees around the banks. There was just a little breeze, so that the lanterns danced on the lines and the water was rippled on the surface, making the reflection of the lanterns in the wake very pretty. Around the edge of the lake were water lilies and it seemed as if there were millions of frogs in the water and every individual frog was

"Cholly's Challenge" at the section of the Victoria Gorge that boat owners call "The Can Opener."

chirping and croaking. This with the lights on the water, the moving crowds on the banks and the sound of the music coming through the trees made a veritable fairy land out of it. After returning to the house for a little while we went down to the boat, not expecting at that time to stay over another day.

It Is Settled!

UPON WILL'S RETURN FROM VICTORIA, his letters begin to exhibit the inevitability of his leaving Fairhaven. The economic depression deepened, the exodus from Fairhaven began and Will could no longer collect his old accounts. The die was cast, the end was near.

Monday, June 22, 1891

I believe I am getting a genuine case of homesickness at last. Ed Robinson left Friday night for Mt. Pleasant. He will spend a few days in Salt Lake City, so this will probably reach home ahead of him. I miss him a great deal. With Ed and the Sullivan's gone, it makes things kind of lonely. I don't know how the Tennis Club will pan out. At present they are having an internecine warfare over the problem as to who was the originator of the club and considerable bitterness is being stirred up. As it developed just prior to the time that I joined, I am staying surely away from it until it is over. So I am deriving no benefit from the Tennis Club. I think there is little doubt that I will be home in the Fall. I hardly see how it is possible for any appreciable improvement to take place in the business of Fairhaven inside of one year. And that is too long for me to hang on.

Monday, June 22, 1891

I want to tell you that I think I can appreciate how you feel at the idea of your friends leaving one by one and especially at this season of the year. It made me feel more than usual that I want to be with you and help. We all need help at times. I have felt the need of it, in making up my mind about what to do about leaving. It has been a hard matter to decide. If I had any property here I would not leave, but as I have not it looks to me the wise thing to do and yet at times I have my doubts. There is one thing though, I don't anticipate – in fact I am certain that there is very little money to be made here by me this coming year. "They" say "hold on – things will boom here in a short time" but they don't boom and I can't see what is to make them boom for a year at least.

Well, I can't stand separation and hard times too. When things become honestly and decidedly prosperous in Fairhaven, or any other town on the Sound, why then I can bring you out here if you wish to come, but I don't intend that we shall be apart any more.

Tuesday, June 23, 1891

Yesterday Det Bird and I went over to New Whatcom to see them celebrate the arrival of the first through train over the Canadian Pacific. One can travel now from St. Paul to Bellingham Bay without change of cars. But Fairhaven will not reap much benefit from that for some time to come. The truth is that this year the other end of the Bay has the best of us. I have held on here hoping that times would improve all the time, but even some of the most sanguine of Fairhaven's business and real estate men admit that they have little hope of seeing a revival of business for the next year. Many people are leaving the city. Of course some others are coming to take their places to a certain extent. We won't say any more about this since it is settled that I go home some time within the next two months and a half.

*I had heard from Det of Grace Woolson's illness. He is waiting anxiously every day for news. He had a letter yesterday from **Mrs. Babb**[60] saying that she would write from day to day if Grace got worse. I sincerely hope she will come out all right.*

We will have that home of ours started before a great while and we won't be very far separated until it is either. Our year of absence has brought the truth home to me very positively that there is nothing to compensate for it. Do not fear that I shall do anything to injure my professional career. The truth is that it has been injured by being out here away from all that made me contented than it possibly could back home. Oh, I have learned a great many things since coming here.

Wednesday, July 1, 1891

Just at present Fairhaven is making preparations for the celebration of the great and glorious Fourth. We will have the ubiquitous, omnipresent – not to say infernal firecrackers in the hand of the numerous small boy. The anvil at sunrise will awaken a man just when repose is sweetest. Then we will have a novelty in the way of a street parade composed of the fire companies. The band, floats representing business houses and the time honored liberty car containing forty-five little girls dressed in red white and blue. Chiefly white, some looking very pretty and some not quite so pretty, and all looking very self conscious. This will be followed by literary (?) exercises composed of music (!!) by an improvised glee club and poem (?) and a spread eagle speech. Our illustrious fellow townsman Clint Howard will deliver the address of welcome. The great National game will be played. There will be a yacht race and various foot, sack, potato and wheelbarrow races. In the evening there will be a grand display of fireworks (6 or 7 pin wheels three roman candles and a rocket and possibly a paper balloon) and a grand ball. There will also be an amateur home talent, comic opera, "The Little Tycoon." Now there is one celebration in a nutshell in advance. I don't expect to get quite as much pleasure out of it as I did three years ago when we spent the forenoon in the park, the afternoon at a ball game and the evening in a general good time, if it did rain too much for the fireworks.

The Woods' families are here at present. Det Bird and I were out to call night before last. Hugh Templin's family and the Woods are living together and it makes

Whatcom Museum.

An 1890s 4th of July celebration at the intersection of 11th Street and Harris Avenue. Terminal Building with Henderson & Templin's office to the right.

a great household. Jessie has gone on a trip to Tacoma. I imagine she is trying to find something to do. It was a great piece of folly in Templin and Woods to move their stock of goods out here at this time. They don't know what they are going to do with them yet.

Tuesday, July 7, 1891

I have just finished reading your last letter – the one in which you tell of how you caught it from everybody in regard to my coming home. If I were a vain man, I think that I was a very important personage whose outgoings and incomings should be watched so closely. I told Det at one time that I hoped to get away the 15th of this month. But as you probably already know from my last letter it is very uncertain just when I can get away. So I will have no difficulty in following your instructions with regard to mystifying people as to the exact time. As to what my plans are they are rather indefinite – except as to the fact that I am going back. That fact is settled. I had a letter from mother tonight. She said she wanted me to be sure that I was doing the very best thing, but in her unselfish way she meant the best thing for myself. But she added that it suited her exactly, so you see I now have the wish of the two people dearest to me to have me go back. That ought to be sufficient for any man that was not harder than a rock. I shall seek a location in Iowa as near Mt. Pleasant as possible and will not lose very much time about it after I get back.

Monday, July 13, 1891

From a business point of view Fairhaven continues to get worse. It is estimated that fifteen hundred people have left town within the past three months and it is utterly impossible to get money for it is not in the plan. A few days ago a gentleman wished to use a hundred dollars. When he first came here he bought a piece of business property in the heart of the city, pay therefore $2,300. He was told at the bank where he went to make the loan that they couldn't give him fifty dollars on that security.

Word came last night that Mt. Vernon's business centre had been completely wiped out by fire. I am afraid that Ross Sullivan may have suffered some from the fire, as I think their residence (rented) was in the business portion of the town. No particulars have reached here as yet.

Saturday, July 18, 1891

Have been out trying to collect a bill and have taken a horse in payment, taking the chances of selling it. Will probably be able to get something out of it. Would get nothing had I not taken the horse. The situation in Fairhaven becomes worse all the time. Saturday last, thirteen families left town and six more followed Sunday morning. The collection of debt is almost impossible. There is a failure of some business house every few days. I will leave here about the forth or fifth of August, unless I should to decide to go over to Victoria for a few days. In any event I will be in Mt. Pleasant about the middle of the month. If I cannot dispose of my animal by next Monday I will take it over to the islands where I think it will be more likely to find a sale at a fair price.

Sunday, July 26, 1891

The people of Fairhaven just simply have no money and it is impossible to get what they do not possess. I never saw such a bankrupt community in my life. And yet, I realize that times are very hard everywhere and may not find it much better back home. I think I will pack my goods and ship them tomorrow, so that I will not have to wait so long for them on my arrival.

Monday morning –The last few days we have been having weather that will get me a little accustomed to Iowa summer weather again. In other words it has been hot. Tomorrow the historic San Juan Islands will find me perambulating over their surface and hailing each and every relative with the inquiry, "do you want to buy a horse?" And incidentally I may be able to find a few new varieties of flowers. Am also going to take my medicine case along and may find a patient or two while over there, hope so at any rate.

Letter 112

Saturday, August 1, 1891

My Darling Sweetheart,

    Have just returned from the islands where I succeeded in disposing of my horse, but at a ruinously low figure. Will start from here on Tuesday, so that I will arrive home about Monday of next week – August 10.

    I just write you a note now, as I must pack up today and it will be quite a task. The letter writing for a time anyway is about over, and we will have no "go betweens." I regret every minute now that keeps me away from you, and you may be sure that no boom country will ever lure me away again.

    Hoping to see your dear face again soon and hear the sound of your voice.

I remain,

Yours devotedly, Will

WITH HIS FINAL LETTER FROM FAIRHAVEN, Will acknowledges the end of his dream and his western adventure. The "boom" had "busted" and he joined the throng of people fleeing the economic emptiness that pervaded Fairhaven. "There is no money." "There is no business." His young practice had dwindled to almost nothing and it was impossible to collect for the services he had rendered. He was reduced to taking an unwanted horse in payment for medical services. People like Will who had no financial reserves had but one choice, they had to leave. He sold the horse at a "ruinous price" and headed for home. The decision by railroad czar J.J. Hill to terminate the Great Northern in Seattle, coupled with an international money crisis, had brought the "boomers" of "The Imperial City" to their financial knees.

Will boarded the Fairhaven & Northern train north to Blaine, where he connected with the Canadian Pacific R.R. for the long trip across the continent and the eagerly anticipated reunion with Anna, pledging that he would never again "be lured to a boom country." One must believe that mingled with his sense of defeat and failure, there must have been great joy and relief in his anticipation of holding "Darling Anna" in his arms once more. It had been almost fifteen long months since he had seen her. Nine days later he arrived at Mount Pleasant, from whence he had begun his adventure. He returned with little to show for his travails other than invaluable medical experience and a major experience in life. He was perhaps not aware of it on that August day, but he also returned with an abiding love for the beauty of Bellingham Bay and a latent desire to return one day.

"Committing Matrimony"

Mt. Pleasant Free Press, Thursday, August 13, 1891. Personal.
—Dr. W.R. Gray reached home Wednesday morning fresh from the Pacific coast. The Dr. is in good health and spirits and his many friends are delighted at his return.

WILL OPENED HIS NEW IOWA PRACTICE shortly after his return home to Mount Pleasant and to Anna. He rented offices in a new building built by the Henry Saving Bank on the Town Square. He apparently planned on permanently settling in Mount Pleasant, the home of not only his fiancée, but his mother, Aunt Alice and so many of his friends. He placed an advertisement in *The Iowa Wesleyan,* the university's monthly publication, which ran for a number of months. He agreed to become the Wesleyan's alumni editor and they happily announced his appointment in their September issue.

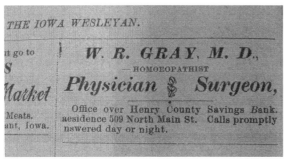

Courtesy Iowa Wesleyan College Archives.
W.R. Gray ad for his office in the Henry Building.

The Iowa Wesleyan, September 1891
"Our Alumni department is in charge of a new editor, Dr. W. R. Gray. Dr. Gray is a young physician of this city, an ex-ed. of the *Wesleyan.* He is well acquainted with our Alumni, also with the students and besides he is brimful of college spirit. We are confident that under his management this department will be not only interesting to the Alumni but also to the students themselves."

Just two months later *The Iowa Wesleyan* announced that Will was leaving Mount Pleasant for Le Mars, a town of 4,000 people located at the extreme western edge of Iowa about 60 miles north of Sioux City.

The Iowa Wesleyan, November 1891
"We very much regret the absence of our Alumni department this number. Dr. Gray, our editor has removed to Le Mars Iowa where he is practicing his profession. Let us assure you it is not abandoned entirely; it is only for this number."

Ironically, despite Will's pledge to stay away from "Boom Country," Le Mars was enjoying a bit of a boom of its own and its optimistic economic outlook is surely what lured Will to set up practice there. He established his new office in the Le Mars Opera Block building just as he had in the Thistle Opera Block at 10th & Mill back in Fairhaven. His deep and abiding interest in theater must have attracted him to such locations.

Will's fledgling practice must have begun well, for his oft stated insistence on building an adequate financial base before "Committing Matrimony" was apparently satisfied within the first ten months. Other factors pressing for a rapid completion of the wedding was surely the strain of the "Fairhaven" separation, the short stay in Mount Pleasant and their almost four year engagement. It is likely that they could simply wait no longer to experience conjugal bliss.

The marriage was planned in the yet-uncompleted new home of Uncle Hervey and Aunt May. The original stone house had been torn down in January 1892 to make way for a new home that Anna dubbed, "The House of Seven Gables."

> *"Uncle Hervey and I are trying to work a scheme. I remarked one day that I would rather be married over home than any place else, if it was in the kitchen or yard. That would seem more like home. Uncle Hervey said then, that if the roof was on, I could be married there, if I wanted to. Well, the roof is on, and they are plastering now, so if the plastering is dry, which it will probably be, why I can have the use of the house. Of course, the woodwork won't be commenced even, and things will be well, you can imagine how, but I don't care, it seems like home to me."*
>
> Letter from Anna Kurtz to Will Gray, May 2, 1892
>
> <small>From Victorian Period Home Architecture, Courtesy Mount Pleasant, Iowa, Public Library</small>

The long awaited wedding was held on June 14, 1892 and was nicely reported in the *Mt. Pleasant Free Press* on June 18, 1892. Will was thirty; Anna would soon be twenty-eight.

Another Wedding.
Kurtz-Gray

A very lively and particularly interesting wedding was that which took place at half past five, Tuesday evening June 14. A large circle of relatives and friends assembled in response to the cordial invitations issued by Mr. and Mrs. H. N Crane at their lovely new home, on East Washington street, to witness the ceremony that united their niece, Miss Anna Kurtz, to William Radford Gray, in the holy bonds of wedlock. A beautiful day, bright and balmy, in fact all nature seemed to be singing the praises of the young couple and was quite in harmony with the thoughts of the happy guests.

The parlor of Mr. and Mrs. Crane was a perfect paradise of beauty and had been transformed, as it were by the magic touch. Vines, roses and all flowers of the season were used most profusely in the delicate and tasteful decorations.

In his solemn, earnest manner Dr. J.T. McFarland, of Jacksonville, Ill., made them one with all the special marriage service of the Episcopal church. Never had the bride seemed more lovely to her friends, as attired in a very modest costume of white broad cloth, entrain, high corsage, without ornament, save the beautiful bride roses which she carried.

She is remembered as a high school scholar, a student of the IWU from which she graduated a very successful teacher in our public schools, a member of Pi Beta Phi, and of the history class. She will be greatly missed from these circles.

Dr. Gray, the most fortunate knight looked every bit the true man that he is. He must be content for once, to admit the supremacy of the feminine charms and graces.

We were almost envious of him in his capturing one of our fair and most popular young ladies and taking her from our midst. He is well known here as a very intelligent, worthy young man making very successful anything which he attempts. We well remember his fine productions during his college year at IWU and the active part he took in our library entertainments.

He is one of the most popular members of the Phi Delta fraternity. He is now practicing medicine at Le Mars, Iowa, having graduated with honors at the medical department at Iowa City.

The flower decorated tables presented a fairy like vision and all were served most gracefully by young friends. The time for the young couple's departure came only too soon, as they left on the 7:20 train and were spirited away while the guests were still enjoying the bountiful supper.

Never were the congratulations and best wishes more earnestly given, all felt that they deserved the happiness and joy that an ideal home can offer.

Quite a number of relatives and friends from abroad were present.

The newlyweds immediately moved to Le Mars. Anna quickly became pregnant and just ten months after the wedding delivered their first and only child.

Margaret Elizabeth Gray was born in Le Mars on April 16, 1893. She was born in her father's medical offices in the Le Mar's Opera House, a proper beginning for one with theatrical leanings.

Will sold his Le Mars practice in 1898 and the Grays moved back to Mount Pleasant. The 1900 census shows them living on North Main Street, just a few houses down from Gray Club. Will was listed as practicing medicine; Anna as a teacher, not working; and daughter Margaret as attending school. Ultimately Mount Pleasant failed to satisfy Will Gray and he determined to head West once more. This announcement in the *Mt. Pleasant Daily News* greeted his decision.

> *Mt. Pleasant Daily News,* July 3, 1901
> **Return to Fairhaven**
> "The many friends of Dr. Gray will regret to learn that he will in the near future move to Fairhaven, Washington. The Doctor has many friends here who will regret to see him go. There seems to be an excellent opening, however, for him."

Come Out, Come Out!

"Come out! Ye dwellers of the plains when nothing greets your eyes save the monotonous stretch of prairies and see nature in her grandeur where she weeps with the sad and laughs with the gay. Lift up your voices oh ye everlasting hills and tell the multitudes of weary wayfarers in the drought stricken east that there is an empire in the Pacific Northwest, where nature has lavished her choicest blessings satisfying every desire of the human heart, where the beautiful and the sublime are blended with utility and productiveness, where the aesthetic goes hand in hand with the useful. Come out! And be content to dwell forever where the breath of the salt water will be unto you like a draught of the elixir of life, and when ye have come and tasted of its joys, ye will say with the mariners in 'The Lotus Eaters' We will return no more, we will no longer roam. Oh, rest ye weary mariners, we will not wander more."

W.R. Gray, October 27, 1890

THE LURE OF THE PACIFIC NORTHWEST and the remembered beauties of its forests, waters and mountains were to bring Will Gray back to Fairhaven on Bellingham Bay. In late July 1901, he again boarded the train at the Mount Pleasant station, this time accompanied by Anna and their eight-year-old daughter Margaret.

By 1901, Fairhaven was showing signs of an economic recovery. The establishment of Pacific American Fisheries in 1898 and the purchase of the Eldridge and Bartlett Mill by E.K. Wood Co. were providing steady employment and a growing economy. Several other large saw mills fronted the bay and improvements in rail and sea transportation were making development in the far Northwest more feasible. The basic industries of logging, lumbering and salmon packing were in their growth period and Fairhaven's population was increasing. It would have been a propitious time to return and start a medical practice.

In a 1971 interview recorded with Galen Biery, Margaret said of her father's return, "He always wanted to go back out there," and she described their July 23, 1901 arrival at Fairhaven's Great Northern railroad station that had been built at the foot of Harris Avenue.

Now, for the first time, Will was to realize his dream of a warm family life in a house that he could call home. How different this life was to be from the loneliness of his prior time in Fairhaven. Instead of a cottage covered with roses, Will and Anna settled for the second floor of a store at 1617 McKenzie Avenue, squeezed in between the towering Germana Hall and the Hayden Grocery. Margaret was enrolled at the 14th Street School which had been built in 1890 at the height of the "boom."

Whatcom Museum.
The Congregational Church stairs lead to 12th Street. The home next door still exists. The top of 14th Street School can be seen in the background.

Will and Anna attended the Congregational Church at 12th Street and Gambier Avenue where they became regular parishioners. Margaret attended Sunday school there. Will worked at establishing his practice and the Grays quickly engaged themselves in the community, participating in the theatrical and cultural opportunities of their new city.

Dr. Gray first rented offices on the second floor of the Nelson Block. Two years later he moved to the upper floors of the Knights of Pythias Building. Both buildings still stand on 11th Street adding their dignity to the ambiance of the Fairhaven Historic District.

W.R. Gray was recognized as an important pioneer doctor, but the early 20th century would have been a difficult time for homeopathic practitioners. As medical knowledge slowly increased, the practice of medicine became more of a science and less of an art. Allopathic medicine, the term that homeopaths applied to traditional medicine, was gaining ground. Homeopathy was now clearly on the wane. Will Gray's homeopathic medical school at the State University of Iowa was closed in 1919.

Will was abundantly successful in other ways.

> *"But say, I do want to get on a school board sometime if only to ease my need of some ideas on the subject. ... I am going to do it some time. Maybe you will think it strange that I write to you about this, but as I said before, I am very much in earnest on the subject and it makes me boil to see the idiotic ignorance of people in general and school boards in particular on a subject that is of such paramount importance."*
>
> W.R. Gray, October 1890

Will made good on his 1890 promise. He stood for election to the Board of Education of the recently consolidated City of Bellingham. The election to select three persons to the Board was held on December 1, 1906. Ten candidates filed. Will Gray lead all candidates with 1288 votes. He had clearly made his mark upon the community and he had found an activity for which he had great passion and would achieve great success and recognition. Will Gray was to serve on the Board of Education for eleven consecutive years, ten of which he would be the Board President.

Washington State Archives, Northwest Region

Tally of votes, Board of Education minutes.

In 1907, the Gray family made the improbable move to "Wardner's Castle" the huge and imposing mansion located at the top of Knox Avenue. Built by millionaire Jim Wardner in 1889, it was the largest house in Fairhaven. Their residence here would last just one year.

The 1908 City Directory finds the Grays another block up the hill at 1026 16th Street, renting the home of lawyer Thomas Newman. Will and Anna rented that house for five years.

Their final move was surely downward in social stature as well as in altitude. The Grays rented an 1890-period hotel building, the former Davey House, at 1430 14th Street, down hill from the present location of Sacred Heart Church. They moved into its upper floor, above a boarded up basement and first floor that had been empty for years.

Margaret graduated from Fairhaven High School, then known as South Side High School, and was valedictorian of the class of 1911. Will continued as President of the Board of Education and was honored to preside at the opening of the new Silver Beach School in 1912 and to oversee the construction of Lowell School in 1914, which was built to replace the 14th Street School. As President of the School Board he surely would have had the great pleasure of presiding at the occasion of Margaret's graduation and valedictory address.

She was the highest ranking student graduate in Bellingham. The graduation ceremony was held in Beck's Theater on Cornwall Avenue.

In January 1918 Dr. William Gray resigned from the Bellingham Board of Education. His resignation after such long service engendered the following tribute from his fellow Board members on February 18, 1918, which was published in the Bellingham Herald the following day.

Fairhaven High School *Aurora* 1914

W.R. Gray, (center) Board of Education.

WHEREAS; Dr. W.R. Gray served this school district in the capacity of a member of the Board of Directors thereof, during several terms, covering in all a period of eleven years, and

WHEREAS; During ten of the eleven years service as a Board member, he served as President of the Board of Directors, and

WHEREAS; During the time Dr. Gray served as one of the Directors, the school department of Bellingham was almost completely transformed in character; old buildings were remodeled and made more sanitary, hygienic, and serviceable; new buildings and modern school buildings were built to take the place of old ones; The Course of Study for the schools were greatly enriched; the standards of the schools noticeably raised; the equipment largely increased; and the general efficiency of the department raised to a high state of perfectness; and

WHEREAS; The highly ethical service rendered by Dr. W. R. Gray as a public servant, has done much to lift the ideals of the department and to purify the professional atmosphere of the schools; and

WHEREAS; During all the years he served on the Board of Directors, the work of the Board was characterized by harmony, goodwill, and friendships, and

WHEREAS; The service rendered reflected the highly professional, honest, unselfish character of the man; Therefore

BE IT RESOLVED; That in the retirement of Dr. W.R. Gray from the Board of Directors of Bellingham School District No. 301, this District has lost the services of an honest, unselfish public official; and

BE IT RESOLVED; That in his retirement his colleagues have lost as an associate, a gentleman of high ideals, a courteous, just and generous presiding officer, and the teaching force has lost a trusted, just, and progressive school official; and

BE IT RESOLVED; That in testimony of the splendid service rendered as a director, in appreciation of the high respect in which Dr. Gray is held by those with whom he served officially, and as a token of just merit, that these resolutions be spread in full upon our records, that they be published in the local press of the city and a copy properly engrossed be sent to Dr. W. R. Gray.

Respectfully Submitted,
Committee: (signed) C.H. Hurlbut
Elmer L. Cave
William McCush

WILL GRAY HAD EARNED THE LOVE, RESPECT AND GRATITUDE of the community that he served and was a revered citizen. He would continue to honor his Mount Pleasant intellectual and cultural roots. He was a contributing member of the Hobby Club, a group of significant men, who monthly read papers that they had prepared on subjects that interested them. In the ensuing years, he continued to pursue his love of theater and in May 1922 was looking forward to his role in an upcoming play. On Sunday afternoon, May 7, 1922, it was likely that Will and Margaret were headed to a rehearsal of that play scheduled to open in two days.

Gordon Tweit Collection.

W.R. Gray, Board of Education.

On Monday, May 8, 1922, the *Bellingham Herald* reported –

DR. GRAY IS STRICKEN AT WHEEL OF HIS MACHINE

Pioneer Physician Loses Control of Auto and It Strikes Curb on Elk Street

Stricken with paralysis while driving with his daughter, Miss Margaret Gray, yesterday afternoon between 2 and 2:30 o'clock, Dr. W.R. Gray, one of this city's pioneer physicians and for eleven years a prominent member of the board of education, lost control of his automobile and the machine dashed down Eleventh street at the rate of thirty-five miles an hour constantly gaining momentum as it swept into Elk Street, was running forty-five miles an hour when Miss Gray seized the steering wheel.

Dr. Gray was taken to St. Joseph's hospital, where hopes are entertained for his recovery by his physicians, Dr. S. R. Boynton and Dr. E.F. Larkin. The paralysis seems to be confined to Dr. Gray's right arm.

Dr. Gray was still unconscious this morning. The stroke follows sickness, of which Dr. Gray complained Saturday, when he was ill all day. He also was tired when the stroke came. He had gone on the ride in the belief that the drive would help him.

Speed Increases

Dr. Gray and his daughter were driving to North Bellingham. As he is a very cautious driver, Miss Gray wondered at the increasing speed of the car as it neared Elk Street on Eleventh. At, or about Bennett and Eleventh she asked him to slow up. Instead the speed increased. Then realizing that something was wrong, Miss Gray, who sat beside her father, seized the steering wheel. The machine was then going forty-five miles per house, but she succeeded in bringing it to a stop a block and a half distant after throwing it into the curb.

Dr. Gray is one of the best known physicians in the Northwest. He is also known as a deep Shakespearean scholar. At the coronation of Miss Aletta Day as queen of tulip land last Friday night, Dr. Gray impersonated Father Time. He was to have taken a leading part in "The Rivals" which the Knights of Columbus were to stage Tuesday, but Dr. Gray's illness has necessitated its postponement. Miss Gray was to play the part of Mrs. Malaprop in the same play.

For eleven years, Dr. Gray was a member of the Bellingham Board of Education and for ten years he was its president.

DR. WILLIAM RADFORD GRAY died seven days later in St. Joseph's Hospital. The fateful day was May 15, 1922. He was only sixty years old.

The funeral was held on May 17, with many attending. Will's former Iowa Wesleyan classmate, C.E. Todd, helped to officiate the funeral.

A special street car was provided for the many students and faculty of Fairhaven High School to attend Dr. Gray's funeral.

ANNA WOULD LIVE ANOTHER 32 YEARS without her beloved Will. She refused to move out of their home, that former boom town hotel on 14th Street. Anna and Margaret shared the old home as it continued to deteriorate over the decades. Finally in 1948, Margaret could take no more. She purchased a home on 15th Street, across the street from Lowell School, and moved her mother there with her.

As President of the School Board, Will Gray had taken great interest in the building of Lowell School in 1914. In her 1971 interview with Galen Biery, Margaret mentioned that during its construction her father had been at the school morning, noon and night. "So I look out on that building and think, well that's my father's monument."

Anna died at the age of ninety on February 16, 1954, at O'Cain's Nursing Home at the top of Knox Avenue. She was buried beside Will at Bayview Cemetery in Bellingham, Washington.

The Legacy

SO ENDS THIS STORY OF A MAN AND WOMAN, a place, and a time in history. The letters of Will Gray tell eloquently of the love and aspirations of this idealistic and sensitive young man trying to make a future for himself and Anna in the turbulent economic times near the end of the nineteenth century. The letters tell of his love and loneliness, and his dreams of the idyllic life that they will share together. The letters also portray for us the gradual intrusion of reality into Will's idealism. Life has a way of doing that.

His Northwest adventure fails in the economic decline of 1891, perhaps accentuated by his aversion to collecting the bills owed him. We know little about his ten-year return to Iowa other than his marriage, the birth of daughter Margaret and his longing to return to Fairhaven.

His dream of marital bliss must have been tested by economic realities and life's usual abrasions. We are sure that Will Gray had some disappointments, but life when lived with passion also brings pleasant surprises and rich rewards. Will Gray was a passionate man, passionate about his Anna, his daughter, his community and the theater arts. His life reaped rich rewards. He was universally loved in his community, and he was an obvious success as a Board of Education member. He was clearly a carrier of culture from his prior home in Iowa to the rough planked streets of Fairhaven.

The final proof of the success of his life is found in the life of his daughter, Margaret, who brought Will's gifts and spirit to generations of her students in the schools of Bellingham. The legacy left by the Grays of Mount Pleasant lives today unrecognized for what it is by its beneficiaries. Their legacy is that tradition of excellence in dramatic musical productions still alive in the Bellingham School District and the interest in and appreciation of drama and literature still alive in the minds, memories and imaginations of thousands of Miss Gray's former students.

> *"Do you know Anna that in your letter this morning you touched me very closely. You said that my love for you has stimulated in you an ambition to do good and do some good in the world. I think that I too have been feeling that more since I have been out here."*
>
> **W.R. Gray, July 28, 1890**

Epilogue

Will Byford Taylor (1863 – 1953)
In 1899 Cousin Will Taylor and his friend, William Clark, bought the Halsey Brothers homeopathic drug business, moved to Chicago and changed the name to the Chicago Pharmacal Company in 1900. Will continued for over 50 years in the pharmaceutical business. After his retirement, Will and Golda enjoyed their travels to Europe and Hawaii. He died at age 90, survived by his wife and four children.

Harry Grahn (1862 – after 1930)
As Will feared, Cousin Harry should not have rushed into marriage with Lulu Clark. Divorced in the late 1890s, Harry married Carolyn Getner in 1900 and moved to Philadelphia. They had three children.

Aunt Rosie (1844 – after 1930)
In 1930, Rose Long Richmond was 86 and living in Minnewaukan, North Dakota, next to her son Ed and daughter-in-law Bessie. Her husband Jacob died in 1927.

Ed Richmond (1868 – 1942)
Cousin Ed Richmond married Irene Spencer from North Dakota in 1894 and had two children. He became a widower in 1897 and remarried in 1900. Ed remained in Minnewaukan living next door to his parents. He worked in Real Estate and by 1930 was Country Treasurer. Ed died in North Dakota at age 74.

May Weir Williams (1867 – 1897)
Soon after their marriage May and Carl Williams moved to Chicago, Illinois. The October 1891 *Iowa Wesleyan* sadly reported "Again death has claimed a victim among our alumni, this time the infant son Paul of Carl Williams '84 and May Weir Williams '87 whose little spirit went back whence it came early last week." May and Carl went on to have three more children. When May died in December 1897 she was only 29. Had she lived as long as best friend Anna Kurtz, she would have welcomed the arrival of 10 grandchildren and 14 great grandchildren.

Ed Robinson (1860 – after 1920)
Ed did not marry Lulu Satterthwaite. He returned to Mount Pleasant and took a course of Commercial study at Iowa Wesleyan in 1897. He became a pharmacist, married in 1899 and moved to Burlington, Iowa, just 23 miles from Mount Pleasant. He had five children. Ed owned the pharmacy in Burlington for over 20 years.

Clint Howard (1865 – 1937)

Clint became the City Attorney of Fairhaven, Washington, from 1891 to 1892, and then Assistant County Attorney for Whatcom County from 1892 to 1893. He was the first secretary of the Cascade Club of Fairhaven which occupied the 3rd floor of the Mason Block and was a charter member of the Fairhaven Lodge of Masons.

In 1893 Clinton W. Howard and Thomas G. Newman formed Newman & Howard, which was regarded as one of the strongest law firms in Western Washington. In 1912 the firm added Joseph Kindall and was renamed Newman, Howard & Kindall. From 1910-11 he served as president of the Washington State Bar Association.

In 1912, Clint Howard became Judge, U. S. District Court, Western District of Washington. He received a recess appointment from William H. Taft. His service was terminated on March 3, 1913, after nomination was not confirmed by the Senate. Clint lived in a beautiful home on prestigious Eldridge Avenue. He married Beth McCord in 1901. Beth died in March 1931 and by December of that year, Clint was engaged to Hildreth Willis, 37 years his junior. Clint died at the age of 73. In his will he had asked to be decently buried, with proper regard to his station and condition in life. Clint is buried at Bayview Cemetery next to his first wife, Beth. He was survived by his second wife, Hildreth Willis Howard, age 36.

I .C. Templin (1842 – 1901)

Isaac C. and Emma Templin remained in Fairhaven, but visited family in Iowa frequently. In 1901 he became ill and died while visiting family in Newton, Iowa. His obituary described him as a "kind, good man, a devoted husband and father, a genial friend, an upright, honorable citizen. His education at Iowa Wesleyan followed him through life as he was known for his well-storied, gifted mind, and to his good education was added the results of long, continued and intelligent reading."

Det Bird (1862 – 1907)

Leslie L. Bird returned to Iowa with considerably less money than when he arrived. The 1900 Census for Mount Pleasant shows Det, single, resident of a boarding house without an occupation. In 1902 he sold the Fairhaven property he owned at 15th and Gambier to Emma Templin, I.C. Templin's wife. Det died at the age of 45 due to complications from surgery to remove one of three bullets from his head "placed there by his own hand." He is buried next to his father, Wellington Bird, in Forest Home Cemetery.

Thomas Henderson (1837 – unknown)

Thomas became the City Treasurer of Fairhaven. On February 6, 1892, he left for Iowa with Ross Sullivan. As reported in the *Fairhaven Herald*: "City Treasurer Thomas Henderson started yesterday for a visit at his old home in Mt. Pleasant, Iowa, and also in Michigan, and will be absent several weeks. It is said that Mr. Henderson will not return alone. His many friends in this city will wish him joy."

Ross Sullivan (1855 – after 1930)

Ross and his wife, Anna, left Washington State. In 1900, they were living with daughters Zetta and Edna in Arkansas. By 1910 they returned to Washington State to live with daughter Edna (the baby that Will took care of in 1890). In 1920 he was living with his daughter Edna and her husband in Port Gamble. By 1930 the family was living in San Bernadino, California.

William R. Jeffrey (1862 – 1937)

After "Jeff" married Jessie, they moved to Ainsworth, Iowa, and he became the Superintendent of Public Schools. He later became a Methodist Minister and worked in several churches throughout Iowa and South Dakota before moving to Knoxville, Illinois. He and Jessie had five children. He died at age 75.

"Mother" (1841 – 1915)

Will was never able to convince Elizabeth Gray to move west. In 1895 she finally purchased the large home at 509 N. Main Street. On this site in 1927 was built the P.E.O. Memorial Library. In June of 1915, Will, Anna and Margaret returned to be at Elizabeth's bedside during the last days of her life. Cousin Will Taylor and his wife were also at the bedside of their beloved "Aunt Lizzie." Elizabeth died on June 17 at the age of 74 and is buried next to her sister Alice and mother Mary at Forest Home Cemetery in Mount Pleasant.

Anna Crane (1867 – 1959)

Will must have been thrilled in 1899 when his favorite "cousin" Anna wed Timothy Whiting, a prominent banker. The Whitings had two children, Ralph and Edith. Anna died at the age of 92; her daughter Edith lived to be 102. Anna's neice, Ruth Crane Looker, turned 98 in June 2009 in Mount Pleasant and provided the photos of Anna, Lollie and Helen Crane.

Mr. Woods (1837 - unknown)

John and his family returned to Mount Pleasant in November 1891 to reopen the Templin & Woods store at its original location.

James H. Heacock (1842 – 1917)

Dr. Heacock returned to Parsons, Kansas. He enjoyed a lucrative medical practice in addition to his position as president of the board of United States pension examiners. He died at the age of 75.

Hugh Templin (1839 – 1911)

After the unsuccessful venture in Fairhaven, the Templin family did not join the Woods family in their return to Mount Pleasant. They moved to Orcas Island, one of the San Juan Islands visable from Fairhaven. Hugh died at the age of 72 and is buried on Orcas Island, San Juan County, Washington, along with his wife Mary and five of his children.

Aunt Jennie (1848 – 1924)

Jennie Long McCulloch remained in Victoria the rest of her life and died at the age of 76. Her husband William died in 1906.

Aunt Alice (1842 – 1912)

Will Gray's wish for the widowed Alice Long Taylor to go live with her son was never realized. Aunt Alice lived with her sister Elizabeth on North Main Street for the rest of her life.

On June 27, 1892, not quite two weeks after Will and Anna's wedding, the town of Mount Pleasant was shocked to discover that Alice's husband was not deceased, but had been in an Illinois insane asylum since 1869 due to trauma suffered in the Civil War. A scandal over her use of his pension ensued, but was later resolved.

Alice's husband, Dr. John Scott Taylor, died in 1893. His obituary appeared in the Journal of the American Medical Association which noted, "He lingered 24 years in an insane asylum before his death, leaving an estimable widow and talented son to mourn with us his loss to the world." His funeral was held in the Gray home on North Main Street. Today, the simple "JLT," is barely readable on his headstone which also includes "Father."

Alice died in 1912. Her obituary noted, "She did more for the town to cultivate and maintain a high intellectual atmosphere than will ever be realized by the community." Scores of friends attended her funeral. The entire membership of the Ladies' Library Literary Association was in attendance. She is buried at Forest Home Cemetery with a simple "ALT" and "Mother" on her headstone next to her husband.

Hervey N. Crane (1841 – 1896)

Just a year after the wedding of Will and Anna, Uncle Hervey and Aunt May sold their newly constructed home to Judge Webb Withrow for $5,300 and moved to another home. The 1895 Iowa Census lists Hervey as insane and not living with his family. His tombstone bears an unusual inscription, "He gives his beloved, sleep." The years before his death must have been harrowing for everyone. He died at the age of 55.

Ella May Allen Crane (1849 – 1936)

After the deaths of husband Hervey in 1896 and son Leigh in 1897, Aunt May, along with her children, Frank, Lewis and Mary moved to Fairhaven, Washington. When Will and Anna arrived in Fairhaven in 1901 it would have been a wonderful reunion. In 1903 the wedding of cousin Mary took place at May's home on 14th Street in Fairhaven.

She continued to live with her son Frank for many years in Sedro-Woolley and by 1930 in Seattle. May died at the age of 86. Her ashes were returned to Mount Pleasant to be buried with her husband at Forest Home Cemetery. Son Frank's ashes were returned the following year.

Leigh Woolson (1866 – 1941)

Leigh married his "love at first sight" Lillian Mandeville in May 1891. They had one child, a son, in 1892. Lillian died in 1898 in Mount Pleasant, Iowa. Leigh was admitted to the Bar in Omaha, Nebraska, in 1900. Later he was a member of the Chicago Bar Association and Acting Counsel for International Estate Adjustment Company. Leigh married Viola May Holiday and had another son in 1902. Leigh moved to California to practiced law and died at the age of 75 in Toluca Lake, California.

Clara Cole (1866 – 1945)

Clara's husband, Dr. Carothers, became a successful doctor and surgeon in Cincinnati, Ohio. Clara and Robert had four children. A son William followed in his father's footsteps as a physician and surgeon. The couple lived in Cincinnati, Ohio. In 1925 Clara, age 58, took an around-the-world cruise. She died at the age of 79.

Lulu Satterthwaite (1867 – 1943)

Lulu taught school for six years in Mount Pleasant, married Hiram Nettleton, a furniture dealer, in 1898 and moved to Seattle, Washington. They had two children. She is buried next to her parents in Forest Home Cemetery in Mount Pleasant.

Alice Bird Babb (1850 – 1926)

When the original chapter of P.E.O. celebrated its 33rd anniversary in 1902, they presented Mrs. Babb a handsome star, the emblem of the sisterhood, richly studded with diamonds, in recognition of her great service. She moved with her husband to Aurora, Illinois, in 1906. Alice died in 1926 and is buried at Forest Home Cemetery in Mount Pleasant, Iowa.

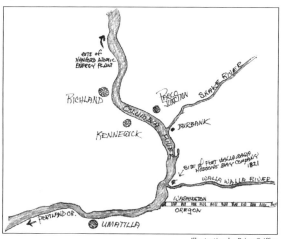

Endnotes

1   Nine hour movement (p. 28, Letter 2)
In 1890 most Americans worked a 12-14 hour day. Labor organizers had been pressing
for an 8-9 hour day for many years. It had been the central demand of the Chicago labor
movement since the end of the Civil War. Ugly riots resulting in police brutality, bomb-
ings, arrests and executions had occurred just four years previously in Chicago. The
A.F. of L. had set May 1, 1890, as the target date for the shortened work week in America, the beginning of "May Day" celebrations in the U.S. This event in St. Paul was potentially dangerous and something to be avoided. By 1905 the 8-hour day was installed
in the printing trade, but it was not until 1938 that the 8-hour day became federal law.

2   The car was handsomely carpeted in Brussels (p. 32, Letter 5)
"Brussels" was a machine-made carpet material fashionable in the 19th century. The
loops of the pile were uncut, a technique which originated in Brussels, Belgium.

3   About the first man I saw wore a big Phi pin (p. 32, Letter 5)
Refers to his college fraternity, Phi Delta Theta. This large national fraternity was organized in 1848 and is one of the first of the Greek letter
fraternities. It is a member of the "Miami Triad," three early fraternities founded at Miami University in Ohio. The fraternity was on the
campus of Iowa Wesleyan in 1871. The Phi Delta Theta pins of Will
Gray's day were twice the size of the modern pin shown.

4   Polonius says "Keep me a farm and carters." (p. 35, Letter 6)
Will was known as a serious Shakespearean scholar, and quoted from *Hamlet* throughout his letters.

5   The great Snake River runs by. (p. 40, Letter 8)
Our traveler was a little confused
as he peered at the great river
running by Umatilla. He was
in fact looking at the Columbia
River. The Snake River had
already entered the Columbia
35 miles upstream at Burbank.

Illustration by Brian Griffin.

6   I have made the acquaintance of Dr. P. P. Gray (p. 41, Letter 9)
No relation to Will Gray, Paschal P. Gray, a graduate of the Homeopathic Medical College of Chicago in 1880, was a close personal friend of cousin Will Taylor. Dr. Gray moved to Ellensburg in 1887 to open his medical practice, also serving a few terms as Mayor of the city in the late 1890s.

7   The great boom across the mountains along the Sound. (p. 41, Letter 9)
The "Sound" is short for Puget Sound, the inland marine waterways in the northwestern part of Washington State, named after Lieutenant Peter Puget, who accompanied George Vancouver on his expedition through the Northwest in 1792.

8   If the irrigation scheme goes through (p. 42, Letter 9)
The rich desert lands of Eastern Washington needed only water to grow abundant crops of grains, hay, fruits and vegetables. This arid country had little rainfall but a bountiful water resource in the rivers that flowed down from the huge snow packs in the Cascade Mountains to the West. Gravity irrigation systems were required to get the water to the farmland above the river bottoms in those days before motorized or electric pumps. Water flumes bringing water from higher up-rivers were the solution, and wooden or earthen flume systems were built, usually financed by taxes levied on the agricultural lands that would benefit. Wooden irrigation flumes were a common sight along the valley walls of most Eastern Washington watersheds and the ruins of the old flumes are still visible here and there.

9   It was almost wiped out by fire last year (p. 42, Letter 9)
Ellensburg, like so many of the towns of the early West built almost entirely of plentiful and cheap lumber, suffered great fires which virtually wiped out their central business districts. Ellensburg burned on July 4, 1889. The fire consumed 200 homes and ten business blocks. The present city, built largely of brick, rose quickly from the ashes.

10   A suspected case of consumption brought on by the "grip." (p. 42, Letter 9)
Tuberculosis has been called consumption, because it seemed to consume people from within, with a bloody cough, fever, pallor, and long relentless wasting. Grippe or La Grippe (pronounced grip) usually referred to influenza or the flu.

**11   If I was acquainted with Leigh Hunt I would go to Seattle and see if
I couldn't get on his paper, the *Post Intelligencer*.** (p. 51, Letter 11)
Will is talking about Leigh Smith John Hunt, the Superintendent of Mount Pleasant Schools from 1879 to 1882. Leigh, born in 1855, was in his early 20s at the time.

Leigh Hunt was destined for greater things; his life story seems to be out of a far-fetched movie script. Self-educated through correspondence courses, Leigh went on to become the third president of Iowa State College in 1886. By 1887, at the age of 32, he had moved to Washington State and quickly became owner of the influential *Seattle Post Intelligencer* newspaper. This was accomplished by what he would describe as the "mystery of investing," no doubt fueled by the crazy real estate boom in Seattle in the late 1880s. His properties, Yarrow Point and Hunt's Point, are today two of the most valuable real estate locations in the United States.

Photo taken by McAdams Bros., Courtesy Mount Pleasant, Iowa, Public Library.

Leigh Hunt and other important members of the Mount Pleasant School District circa 1880. (Top Row: A. Rommel, Belle Mansfield, James Faulkes. Front Row: N. Howe, Prof. Cocrane, Carrie Reed, Leigh Hunt, Alice Carpenter and E.E. Linn.)

Hunt, along with many other wealthy individuals, lost his fortune in the Panic of 1893. He went to Korea for gold mining opportunities which resulted in the Oriental Consolidated Mining Company, worth $5 million dollars in 1897 ($127 million today). One of his investors included William Randolph Hearst. Hearst would go on to own the *Seattle PI* decades later. In the early 1900s Hunt became an aide to President Theodore Roosevelt and a business partner with Booker T. Washington growing cotton in Sudan, Africa.

In 1923 Leigh Hunt moved to Las Vegas, Nevada; the land he purchased would later become known as the "Las Vegas Strip." His dreams of starting a resort there died with him in 1932. It is hard to imagine that a former superintendent of Mount Pleasant Schools was the largest landowner in Las Vegas until another entrepreneur, Howard Hughes, arrived to develop the Las Vegas Strip.

12 I caught a glimpse of an arctic bird, the great auk skimming over the deep,

(p. 54, Letter 13)

Will Gray was obviously not an expert ornithologist. The great auk was a large flightless bird endemic to the north Atlantic. It was hunted to extinction for its meat, eggs and down and last seen in 1848. Perhaps he was seeing the tufted puffin.

13 In a little real estate office I found Mr. I.C. Templin, Mr. Henderson,

(p. 54, Letter 13)

Iowa émigrés Isaac Clinton Templin and Thomas Henderson purchased dozens of lots in Fairhaven in 1889 and 1890, They joined forces as Henderson & Templin, a real estate firm at 1105 Harris Avenue. The building no longer remains, but its next-door neighbor, the Terminal Building (1888) is known as the oldest commercial building in Fairhaven and has been in continual use since that time.

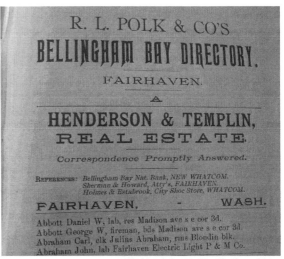

Washington State Archives: Northwest Region

1890 Bellingham Bay Directory.

A restaurant, located in the Terminal Building uses the former location of the real estate office for outside seating.

Described in the *Fairhaven Herald* on December 29, 1890:

> "The firm of Henderson & Templin was organized in September, 1889 and is composed of Mr. Thomas Henderson and I.C. Templin. Mr. Henderson came to this city in July, 1889 and in looking about for a location for a real estate office, decided upon the site now occupied by the firm on Harris street, but the price $1,000 he considered exorbitant and hesitated about purchasing it. A few days later he paid $2,250 for the lot and was glad to get it at that price, as he has been repeatedly offered $6,000 for it ever since. He also paid $1,800 for 50 x 100 feet in block seventeen and coming along there one day shortly afterward he heard some parties discussing the purchase, and heard one of them say "a darn fool from Montana had bought the property and would never get his money out of it." But all the same, Mr. Henderson sold the property three weeks later for $3,500. These incidents are given to show the increase in values in city property and Messrs. Henderson & Templin have been in a position to take advantage of those opportunities for themselves and their clients.
>
> "Mr. Templin came to Fairhaven in September 1889 from Mt. Pleasant Iowa where he was and is still conducting a prosperous dry good business, which he intends to bring to this city next spring. His first trip was made merely in the interest of sightseeing, but he was so favorably impressed with the prospects that he at once decided to send for his family and remain. Messrs. Henderson & Templin have a vast amount of real estate to handle and some of the most desirable property in the city. They do a great deal of business for non-residents and are thoroughly experienced and reliable."

Brian Griffin Collection

Stone lithograph presented by the Fairhaven Land Company, 1890.

14   They are just constructing a $75,000 hotel. (p. 54, Letter 13)

The grand Fairhaven Hotel was the centerpiece of the Fairhaven Land Company's promotion of Fairhaven. It became the icon of the city and was evidence to many of the future greatness of Fairhaven. Its actual construction cost was $150,000. It stood at the northeast corner of Harris Avenue and 12th Street until 1955 when a major fire resulted in its demolition. Much of its brick and stone were dumped along the waterfront to form what is now Boulevard Park.

15   Fine business blocks many of them as fine as those of St. Paul have been built since the fire. (p. 56, Letter 13)

A great holocaust consumed early Seattle in 1889. In June of that year a glue pot in a cabinet maker's shop boiled over and ignited. The resulting fire burned 29 city blocks, four of the city's wharves and its railroad terminal.

Author Griffin's grandfather, Arthur C. Miller, burned out in that fire. He was the first cigar maker in the Territory of Washington. He had just received a shipment of tobacco leaf via ship and the tobacco was still at the wharf. Miller hired a wagon and an armed guard, bought a tent and rescued his tobacco from the smoldering wharf. The men took the laden wagon to the small Prefontaine Park near Pioneer Square, set up the tent on the grass and while one man stood guard with a shotgun, the wagon driver and Miller threw buckets of water on the tent to prevent it catching fire. Miller's shop burned to the ground, but the tobacco was saved and he was back in business selling cigars the day after the fire.

16   Great Northern Railroad has purchased the Fairhaven & Southern

(p. 65, Letter 16)

The great Fairhaven boom was predicated on the belief that the Great Northern would terminate in Fairhaven. The railroad was being built across the continent in the late 1880s and Nelson Bennett, a former railroad man and friend of James J. Hill, President of the Great Northern, was confident that Hill would end his rail at Fairhaven.

Bennett and Larrabee formed the Fairhaven & Southern Railroad to connect Fairhaven with Sedro-Wooley where there was a large coal mine. Their other purpose was to provide a connection with the Great Northern, then being built across the plains of the Dakotas. They expected the Great Northern to cross the Cascades at the Skagit River watershed. Shortly after they completed the southern route they extended their line to the north to Blaine, connecting with the Canadian Pacific. That line was called the Fairhaven & Northern. The Great Northern purchased the Fairhaven & Southern in 1890, creating a frenzy of excitement among Fairhaven boosters.

17   Pasco Junction (p. 68, Letter 18)

Pasco was in 1890, and remains to this day, a critical railroad junction where trains from the east stop and re-organize their cargos to either go down the Columbia River Gorge to Portland and points south, or north and west across the Cascade Mountains to Tacoma, Seattle and Vancouver, Canada. It was also the place where the transcontinental trains would stop and re-route passengers and freight to the small lines going to places like Walla Walla, Pendleton, Omak, etc.

18   "There have been boarders enough at our house for the last six to eight years to last a lifetime." (p. 69, Letter 18)

In 1880, Elizabeth was living in a large rented home at 509 North Main Street, just south of the Iowa Wesleyan campus. The was also home to her son, Will Gray, her mother, Mary Long, sister Alice Taylor and nephew Will Taylor. To make ends meet, Elizabeth took in boarders and the house came to be called Gray Club. Eventually it housed Will's fraternity, Phi Delta Theta.

Gray Club was located between Iowa Wesleyan and the train tracks. Its proximity to a busy train route would have made it a very noisy place to live for the family and the young male students. The Roper home next door housed its second fraternity, Beta Theta Pi. By 1926, the Gray and Roper properties were purchased by Iowa Wesleyan to become the location for the new P.E.O. Memorial Library in 1927.

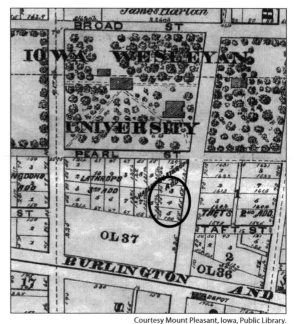

Courtesy Mount Pleasant, Iowa, Public Library.

Location of Gray Club (circled).

19 It would even be a relief, I think, sometimes if Bluff Park could be talked about once in awhile. (p. 78, Letter 21) In the 1890s, Bluff Park was a popular vacation resort for people from the surrounding areas of Iowa, Illinois and Missouri. It was located on the Mississippi River in the far southeast portion of Iowa near Montrose, Iowa. In summer months, the

Courtesy Montrose Memorial Library.

Bluff Park, Iowa.

railroad offered discounted tourist fares from Mount Pleasant to Bluff Park.

20 That is Summit Avenue – the prettiest residences in the country.

(p. 83, Letter 23)

Will is talking about a 4.5-mile-long boulevard from downtown St. Paul to the Mississippi River. The avenue was lined with gilded-age mansions. James J. Hill, the man behind the Great Northern Railroad, built a 36,000 s.f. home at 240 Summitt Avenue. Completed in 1891, the final cost totaled $931,275.01, which included construction, furnishings, and landscaping for the three-acre estate.

Summit Avenue was named one of America's "Great Streets" in 2008. The area where the oldest homes are located still has the look

Courtesy Minnesota Historical Society.

Back of James J. Hill mansion in St. Paul.

of a grand Victorian boulevard. James J. Hill's house was acquired by the Minnesota Historical Society in 1978 and today is a museum.

21 Dr. Heacock (p. 84, Letter 24)

Dr. James H. Heacock was the brother of Howard P. Heacock, owner of Heacock's Mill. The 1890 Sanborn Fire Insurance map shows Heacock's Mill which was accessed at 8th Street and Harris Avenue. It was built on piles over the water and was one of the very early sawmills on the Fairhaven waterfront. Howard Heacock was well known for his 1888 patent that improved lumber mill production. The home of James and Howard Heacock can be found at the northeast corner of 15th Street and Mill Avenue.

22 The restaurant where I board, and which is the only one in town where anything fit to eat can be had, (p. 84, Letter 24)

This dining emporium known as the Fairhaven Restaurant was located on the north side of Harris between 9th and 10th streets. Will had a different opinion of the restaurant than the review that appeared in the *Fairhaven Herald* on December 29, 1890:

> "One fact in connection with the restaurant that contributes largely to its popularity is the surprising promptness with which all orders are attended to. The attendants are courteous, polite and accommodating while the cooks are the very best that can be obtained. Messrs. Farley & Oesterlea understand their business thoroughly and are restaurant men of long experience."

23 Gasworks are now being built which will supply all three towns.

(p. 86, Letter 24)

Just the month before Will mentioned it, the Bellingham Bay Gas Company had been incorporated with capital of $200,000, much of it provided by the Fairhaven Land Company. It was built at the northern border of the now-expanded Fairhaven to service all of the towns around the bay. It made gas from coal that was brought from the Fairhaven Mine at Sedro-Woolley on the newly constructed Fairhaven & Southern Railway. The gas plant began operations in December 1890 and continued until 1956, when natural gas pipelines reached Bellingham. The small red brick building at upper Boulevard Park along State Street is one of the original gas works buildings.

Remaining building from the gasworks, is located on State Street.

24 Methodist Church (p. 88, Letter 24)

The Methodist Episcopal at 16th Street and Mill Avenue was constructed on land donated by Fairhaven Land Company. Will may have been guessing about types of wood used in the Northwest, but the ceiling was made of redwood which was imported from Northern California. While the building has undergone extensive restoration and is now a residence, the redwood ceiling has remained intact since 1890.

Pat Wickline Collection.

Untouched ceiling.

25   I had heard of the accident on Lake Pepin during the storm (p. 89, Letter 24)
Headlines from Bismarck, North Dakota newspapers.

> July 15, 1890. "DROWNED – THE STEAMER CAPSIZED IN LAKE PEPIN WITH TERRIBLE LOSS OF LIFE – IT IS ESTIMATED THAT 130 PEOPLE FOUND A WATERY GRAVE."

> July 16, 1890, "RED WING PRESENTS A HEART RENDING SCENE OF MOURNING, WEEPING AND ANGUISH – THE CAPTAIN OF THE BOAT WAS JAILED FOR HIS SAFETY"

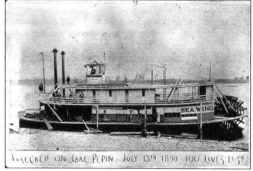

Known as the "Sea Wing" disaster after the name of the steamer, the final death count was 98 persons. Many were from the most prominent families of Red Wing, Minnesota.

Courtesy Minnesota Historical Society.

26   The leading drug store in the city is in this building (p. 93, Letter 26)
Will is talking about the Higginson & Hardy Pharmacy located in the Mason Block at the prime southeast corner spot of 12th Street and Harris Avenue. The Fairhaven Pharmacy moved to this location in 1895. (Fairhaven Pharmacy would later move into Fairhaven's historic Terminal and Monahan buildings before settling down in 1929 in the newly constructed one-story building at the northwest corner of 12th and Harris – diagonal from the Mason Block, where it continues to operate to this day.)

Whatcom Museum
The Fairhaven Pharmacy in the corner of the Mason Block. George Finnegan in the center and at the left is proprietor Fred Offerman. Photo by Rembrandt Studio in 1905 for an album of 280 storefronts, "Business Houses of Bellingham," used to promote Bellingham at the Lewis & Clark Centennial Exposition in Portland, Oregon.

27 Millionaire for a Landlord. (p. 97, Letter 27)

Will refers here to Allen C. Mason of Tacoma. Mason was a real estate developer who made a fortune selling real estate in Tacoma. He started with nothing in 1883, amassed a fortune in just a few years, built a huge mansion, bought a newspaper, built a gas works in Olympia and invested in irrigation projects in Eastern Washington and a streetcar line in Tacoma in association with Nelson Bennett, a major developer of early Fairhaven. He built the Mason Block in Fairhaven where Will Gray opened his first office and which still stands at Harris and 12th in the Fairhaven district of Bellingham. Mason unfortunately lost his fortune in the economic crash of 1893, but is still remembered as a man who did more to build Tacoma than any other. On December 6, 2008, a statue of Mason was dedicated as part of the Allen C. Mason Plaza in the Proctor District of Tacoma.

Courtesy Gary Knudson & Associates

Early character sketch used in design of Mason Plaza, Tacoma, WA.

28 By the way are you giving "Normal" the go by this year? (p. 99, Letter 28)

The Iowa Wesleyan University catalog offered "Normal Training," which in the jargon of the day meant teacher training for elementary teachers. The term is a translation of the French term, *Ecole Normale*, a name which was given to the first experimental school in France for educating teachers. The concept of such training was new and the term spread to the United States. "Normal Schools" sprang up at the college level across the country. Bellingham's college was initially dedicated to the teaching of teachers. It was called "The Western Normal School" for many years until finally in the 1940s as its curriculum broadened, it became Western Washington State College and finally Western Washington University.

29 Orcas Island, one of the fruit islands of the Sound (p. 116, Letter 34)

The San Juan Islands, with their superior climate and fertile sunny valleys, quickly proved to be prime farming country. In the early days before roads, boat transportation further favored the agricultural development of the islands. While San Juan Island led in the production of grains and field crops, Orcas Island proved perfect for growing fruits and berries and became famed for its orchards of apples, pears, peaches and plums. Hugh Templin must have become enamored of its opportunities, for he was soon to move to its commercial center, the village of Eastsound. In 1897 he built a long dock with a warehouse at its end and on the shore, a general store in the family tradition. Templin's store was a fixture in Eastsound until it closed in 1992. It is the present location of Island Market.

30   I ran across two or three little things today in the September "Century" that just struck me as very beautiful. (p. 125, Letter 36)
Will was an avid reader of magazines such as *Harper's, Schribner's* and *Century*. The article "Friend Olivia" that he mentions in the September *Century* can be accessed online through the Cornell University Library's Making of America Collection (MOA). This digital library of primary sources in American history was a collaborative effort between Cornell University and the University of Michigan and comprises the digitized pages of books and journals of the 19th century.

31   The Washington Press Association meets here for three days (p. 126, Letter 36)
To celebrate the event, a spectacular triangular arch bridged Harris Avenue at 11th Street. The arch was decorated with bunting and cedar boughs, emblazoned with "Washington Press Association Welcome."

The members of the Press Association arrived by steamer, which docked at the foot of Harris Avenue. As they made their way up Harris, with their 14 carriage procession led by a brass band, the view up Harris Avenue was not just of the magnificently decorated arch, but also the architectural glories of Fairhaven: the onion-domed Blonden block at 11th (now vacant and the site of a double-decker bus), and farther up on 12th the massive Mason Block where Will had his office and the soaring tower of The Fairhaven. The Hotel Fairhaven, had opened just in time for the event.

32   Tomorrow night a grand ball will be given at the Hotel Fairhaven
(p. 126, Letter 36)
The grand ball was held for the Washington Press Association. Invitations were issued by the Committee of the Invitation: F.J. Hamilton, Z.W. Christopher, I.S. Richards, A. Sherman and C.D. Francis.

Dr. Gray was treating Mr. Hamilton's son and was occasionally invited to dinner with Mr. and Mrs. Hamilton. Sherman was Clint Howard's partner.

The "Official" Formal Gala Opening did not happen until September 15, 1890. We are missing the newspaper accounts of that grand evening as the September 16, 1890 edition of the *Fairhaven Herald* has not yet been located.

33   Have another case of typhoid on my hands now. There is a regular epidemic of that here now. (p. 126, Letter 36)
Typhoid fever is a deadly disease caused by poor sanitation and lack of hygiene. It was a common cause of death in the 19th century, taking even such notables as Queen Victoria's consort Prince Albert. It is caused by the bacteria Salmonella Typhi. Fairhaven did not have sewers in 1890. Poor sanitation was endemic and in the warm months typhoid fever was commonplace. In the summer and fall of 1890, Fairhaven experienced an epidemic of the fever that took 135 lives and sickened many others. The effort to install sewers began immediately culminating in 1891 with a $250,000 bond issue. The sewers led directly to Bellingham Bay.

Willowbank School 1909.

Photo by Alex DeLuna.
Willowbank School 2009.

34 **The little Willowbank tyrants will soon be holding high revel.** (p. 126, Letter 36)
Anna taught at Willowbank School, about 10 blocks from her home. The school was built in 1870.

35 **You are right in believing that you cannot forget with the hospital so near you** (p. 135, Letter 39)

The Iowa State Hospital for the Insane at Mount Pleasant was completed in 1861. The 400-bed facility, situated on 178 acres with an imposing gated entrance, was at Asylum and East Washington Streets, just eight blocks from Anna's home. Her father, James Kurtz, was committed to the hospital shortly after Anna's birth in 1863 and died there in 1864. The hospital was a major employer in Mount Pleasant and attracted physicians, psychologists and academics to the area.

Courtesy Mount Pleasant, Iowa, Public Library.
The gates to the hospital faced East Washington Street, the street that Anna Kurtz lived on.

36 **The Sisters of the Sacred Heart are going to build a hospital** (p. 143, Letter 42)
In 1890, three Catholic nuns of the order of Saint Joseph of Peace were sent to Fairhaven with orders to start a hospital. They arrived on August 19 and immediately met with Father J.B. Boulet, a missionary priest, and J.J. Donovan, a leading Catholic citizen working for Nelson Bennett and the Fairhaven Land Company. They devised a plan to raise money in the community. Donovan was able to get a donation of a full block of land high on the hill on 17th Street just north of Adams Avenue, and by January 9, 1891, a hospital had been constructed and opened. It was dedicated St. Joseph Hospital.

37 **Certain rumors that have been set afloat by members of the Fairhaven Land Company.** (p. 150, Letter 45)
The Fairhaven Land Company was formed by Nelson Bennett and Charles X. Larrabee in 1888. It bought Fairhaven from Dan Harris, bought Bellingham, merged it with Fairhaven, attracted investors, and spun off companies which built the railroad, the hotel, the water company, and the gas company. It advertised and promoted their fledgling town internationally and was the driving force behind the growth and booming of Fairhaven. The company was led by Bennett and Larrabee and their capable lieutenants E.L. Cowgill, E.M. Wilson, J.J. Donovan, A. McKenzie and others.

38 I could imagine myself back in Stratford-on-Avon (p. 153, Letter 47)

Will is referring to Stratford, Ontario, Canada, less than 100 miles from Port Huron, Michigan. Stratford was first settled in 1832. The town and river were named after England's Stratford-upon-Avon, of Shakespearean fame. In 1859 Stratford was incorporated as a town and divided into five wards: Avon, Falstaff, Hamlet, Romeo and Shakespeare. In 1864, two years after Will was born, the town held Shakespeare tercentenary celebrations.

Will's affinity for Shakespeare might well have started very early in life. He would have visited Stratford on the route from his home in Port Huron, Michigan, to his father's parents in Belleville, Ontario.

39 There is a large natural park that has been beautified until it is very fine, (p. 154, Letter 47)

The park that Will refers to is Beacon Hill Park, located just one block from downtown Victoria, and described as an oasis of both natural and landscaped beauty. In 1882 land was set aside for a municipal park on a hill that was formerly a burial site for the First Nations Coast Salish people. The stone bridge had been constructed a year earlier in 1889. The oak trees are known as Garry oaks. Some of the trees seen in the park today were almost 200 years old in 1890.

40 There is a theatre and a Joss House (p. 157, Letter 48)

Joss House is the general term used by Europeans in this time period on the West Coast referring to a Chinese place of worship. Larger cities such as San Francisco or Victoria had diverse Chinese populations, and they needed places of worship – Joss Houses. Chinese religions are by nature non-exclusive, espousing a framework for life rather than a deistic dogma, so these places of popular worship could include elements of Daoism, Confucianism, Buddhism and particular local pagan beliefs.

41 I had heard rumors that the engagement between Anna Crane and Leigh Woolson was off (p. 158, Letter 48)

Leigh met and fell in love with another woman and broke his long engagement with Will's dear friend Anna Crane.

The *Iowa Wesleyan* reported:

> "AND LEIGH, HE DID A WOOING GO.
> They may have 'met by chance,' but in certainly a very unusual way, for he came from Mt. Pleasant and she from Missouri Valley, and they met in Boston. We suppose that it was wisely arranged centuries ago that all this should come to pass, — only one of those devious, circuitous routes we creatures are sometimes called upon to take to find the gold at the end of the rainbow. Perhaps the name first attracted him, Lillian Esther Mandeville, poetic and elegant; then the blue eyes and black hair, the onyx and the amethyst… . The class of 1887 can scarcely imagine the mischievous Leigh a sedate married man, but such is the case."

42 Allow me to state that I think you did just right in regard to Clara Cole.

(p. 159, Letter 48)

Courtesy Mount Pleasant, Iowa Public Library

Cole House from *Victorian Period Home Architecture*.

Clara Cole was the daughter of one of the wealthiest families in Mount Pleasant. Their home was located on 13 acres with a pond. Clara was an enthusiastic member of P.E.O. and would hold fundraisers at their home. Anna, belonged to Pi Beta Phi (formerly I.C. Sorosis). There was an intense rivalry between the two friendship societies, which might explain Anna's exclusion from a social gathering.

The Cole House looks very much the same today and has been owned for many years by Fred Crane, grandnephew of Hervey Crane. Six of the 13 acres has been turned over to the Mount Pleasant park system. Today the pond is known as Cole's or Crane's pond.

43 It is in the Mason Block. (p. 164, Letter 50)

Described in the December 29, 1890 Holiday Edition of the *Fairhaven Herald:*

> "This handsome brick block was commenced early in the spring of the present year, and was built by Allen C. Mason, of Tacoma. It is 100 x 100 feet and was completed in July last and every room engaged and occupied by the first of August. The building is three stories in height, the lower floor containing five stores, the second floor being occupied as offices, and the third floor by the Cascade Club. The building cost about $50,000."

44 The Fairhaven railroad company is having some fun at the expense of that suburb just at present. (p. 165, Letter 50)

When the moguls of the Fairhaven Land Company completed the Fairhaven & Northern line to Blaine they had built a long curving trestle across Bellingham Bay, intersecting the Colony Wharf, which extended out over the tide flats from the Colony Mill at the falls on Whatcom Creek. The Fairhaven Land Company had recently purchased the mill and wharf, giving them a toehold in rival Whatcom. In what had to be a show of hubris and an intentional poke at the pride of their rival, C.X. Larrabee built a small building at the intersection and had painted on the roof facing Whatcom, "FAIRHAVEN NORTH." The citizens of Whatcom were outraged.

45 Will stop now and peruse some *Materia Medica* – did you ever hear of that before? (p. 166, Letter 50)

Will is referring to the homeopathist's primary manual, a listing of diseases and their symptoms and the remedies and doses for each. *Materia Medica* was the foundation stone of homeopathic practice written by its founder, Dr. Hahnemann, and was studied as a distinct branch of study at the homeopathic medical department at the State University of Iowa. Will received 100% on his final examination on the subject. The various remedies were dispensed in tiny doses as illustrated in the accompanying photo. There were 793 pellets of heart medicine in the small bottle. The Humphrey's Company still exists.

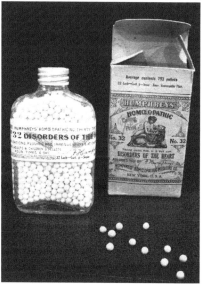

Gordon Tweit Collection.

46 Westward the Souf Mountains (p. 174, Letter 54)

We believe that Will was mistaken in his naming of the Souf Mountains. He probably meant to write Sooke Mountain, which is the southern peak of the Seymour Mountain Range on Vancouver Island. (The mountains of the Seymour Range are visible from Bellingham on a clear winter day, especially when they glisten with a new snowfall. Sooke Mountain rises just north of Sooke Inlet. To our knowledge there is no Souf Mountain.)

47 About Clint and Ed Robinson … they do run a lodging house. I don't think they want it known so keep mum about it. (p. 175, Letter 54)

Clint Howard and Ed Robinson owned Lawrence House on the north side of McKenzie Avenue, between 10th and 11th Street. The house was managed by their friend, Dave Kenworthy from Mount Pleasant.

Will did not mention that McKenzie Avenue was notorious for its "Sporting Houses" and that a "Lady" never ventured below 11th Street. It is unlikely that Lawrence House was used strictly for lodging. Its location, with rooms located just above several saloons, is highly suggestive, as is "female boarding" located directly behind the house (depicted on the Sanborn map).

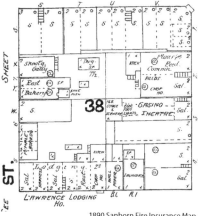

1890 Sanborn Fire Insurance Map.

The buildings to the right of the Lodging House were collectively known as "Devil's Row" and included the Tontine Saloon and Casino Theatre. The establishments are described in *Brothels of Bellingham* by Curtis Smith as "leading places of amusement and sport," or "dens of iniquity and a blight on the community," take your pick. It is no wonder that Clint and Ed wanted to keep their ownership of this hotel quiet.

48   Fairhaven had her good name for orderliness somewhat rudely damaged by a murder (p. 184, Letter 59)

On November 8, 1890, the *Weekly World* newspaper reported of the death of a young laborer named Armstrong by a "hobo" in The Royal Bodega Saloon. The next week an editorial followed decrying the lawlessness in town and reporting another shooting "affray" that week wherein one gambler shot another in a tavern. While the wound was not fatal, the shooter was set free under a mere $500 bond, "which it is always easy for such men to obtain from the saloon keepers in whose places they ply their calling." The editorial goes on to say, "In all probability a fine for carrying a concealed weapon will be the limit of the man's punishment. If such is deemed an adequate vindication of the majesty of the law, whose chief province it is to protect the persons and property of the people, then God help the people and the body politic."

Polk Directory, 1890. Washington State Archives: Northwest Region

49   To think that I should ever envy the festive Kopp! (p. 204, Letter 70)

Will is talking about William Frederick Kopp a student at Iowa Wesleyan. The "festive Kopp" graduated I.W.U. in 1892, went to law school and became a lawyer, prosecuting attorney for Henry County and postmaster for Mount Pleasant. In 1920 he was elected to the U.S. House of Representatives, serving six-terms as a Republican Congressman from Iowa's 1st congressional district between 1921 and 1932.

50   Monday morning work will be commenced on our $100,000 opera house.

(p. 216, Excerpt Letter 79)

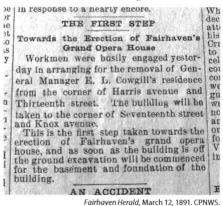

A first class opera house was championed by E. L. Cowgill, one of the original stockholders and general manager of the Fairhaven Land Company. As reported by the *Fairhaven Herald* in December 1890, "Mr. Cowgill is at present, making arrangements for the building of a grand opera house in Fairhaven which will involve the use of real estate worth more than $30,000 and the expenditure of more than $80,000 in cash."

Fairhaven Herald, March 12, 1891. CPNWS.

Cowgill was serious about the opera house, and had his home removed from the property at the northeast corner of 13th Street and Harris Aveniue to make way for the new building. The home's relocation up a very steep hill on Knox Avenue to 17th Street would have been a major accomplishment. Due to the economic downturn, Cowgill halted construction of the opera house after the foundation was excavated. The large hole at 13th and Harris was about 15 feet deep and remained until

Whatcom Museum.

Cowgill's house at 13th Street and Harris Avenue, before he moved up the hill.

1971. That year the area was filled in with the debris from downtown Bellingham's Sunset Building, which had burned. The location of the proposed opera house is now a parking lot.

51   Ed Robinson and myself were out taking a walk and went out on a high point that runs into the bay. (p. 218, Excerpt Letter 82)

Will had to have been referring to the large finger of glacial till which formed Deadman's Point. The point was a narrow hill protruding from the highlands behind it toward the northwest. It rose to about 70 feet tall and was situated approximately where Shipyard Point is now. It was first penetrated when the Great Northern Railroad line was built in 1890. Its further destruction occurred in 1917, when its gravel was used to fill wetlands and extend the shoreline for Pacific American Fisheries' shipyard. It was called Deadman's Point because it was used as a graveyard in the very early days. In 1890 the graves were moved to Bellingham's municipal graveyard, Bayview Cemetery.

52   Sign that directed to Dr. Teel's door (p. 220, Excerpt Letter 86)

Dr. Charles Seneca Teel came to Fairhaven from South Dakota in 1890 to practice general medicine and surgery. When the Fairhaven boom ended he moved his office to Whatcom (present day downtown Bellingham). He remained in Bellingham for the rest of his life, passing away in 1930. His son Charles E. Teel also became a physician and practiced medicine in Bellingham for his entire career. He died in 1965. They are both interred in Bellingham's Bayview cemetery. Grandson Charles Teel lives in the Fairhaven district of Bellingham to this day.

53   We had planned a trip to Esquimalt where the navy yard is and where John Bull keeps his big gunboats (Excerpt Letter 88)

The Royal Navy established their base in Esquimalt Harbour in 1865 as its Pacific headquarters. Esquimalt Harbour, just north of Victoria Harbour, replaced the Navy's earlier facility in Valpariso, Chile. "John Bull" was the popular nick-name for England, just as "Uncle Sam" is for the United States.

54 Yesterday was a great day in Fairhaven. (p. 225, Excerpt Letter 80)

In 1889, having completed the line from Fairhaven to Sedro-Woolley, C.X. Larrabee and his partners looked to the north with the desire to connect their railroad with the Canadian Pacific transcontinental line at New Westminster. The goal was to build a new line to be called the Fairhaven & Northern to Blaine, where the C.P. had agreed to connect. The last spike was driven on February 14, 1891. By that time Larrabee had sold his railroad to the Great Northern.

55 Dr. Van Winter and I are going to office together. (p. 226, Excerpt Letter 90)

Will Gray is referring to the new offices he shared with a dentist, Dr. Van Winter, on the second floor of the Thistle Block. The Thistles owned a retail store on Harris Avenue selling notions, general merchandise, stationery, pens and pencils. They apparently were successful, in 1891 they constructed a large frame building at the northwest corner of 11th Street and Mill Avenue and called it the Thistle Block. Their retail store occupied the street level, upstairs were offices and a 500 seat theater.

The theater was called the Thistle Opera House and in addition to opera, there were minstrel shows, dramatic productions of all kinds, as well as dance lessons and community meetings.

It is just possible that the youthful photograph of Will Gray was taken in the Thistle Opera House. Notice the theatrical backdrop.

LOUISVILLE, KY.   NEW YORK, N.Y.

Thistle's New Opera House

W. H. MOHR, Manager.

SATURDAY

MARCH 14th

Engagement Extraordinary

The C. D. Hess Grand Opera Company

Headed by the American Representative Prima Donna

Francesca Guthrie

Will give one performance of

La Traviata

Sale of seats opens Thursday. Prices $1 $1.50 and $2

Weekly World, March 13, 1891. CPNWS.

Biery Family Collection.

Will Gray

56 Ed Robinson and I went to Whatcom to attend the Episcopal services there.
(p. 230, Excerpt Letter 97)

Will is referring to St. Paul's Episcopal Church. A much grander structure was built in 1927. The original church is located across the street and today is used as a parish hall.

By December, 1891, there were 50 parishioners. Clint Howard and his wife Beth McCord Howard would become important members. When the new structure was constructed in 1927, Clint and Beth Howard donated one of the stained glass windows in memory of Clint's parents. Clint's father, DeWitt Clinton Howard, was an Episcopal minister in Mount Pleasant.

57 All we gained was a ride in the New Whatcom street cars which commenced running on that day. (p. 230, Excerpt Letter 97)

Bellingham Bay Electric Street Railway, commenced on March 29, 1891. Fairhaven distinctly saw it as a "New Whatcom" company, a rival, and did not allow it to go to Fairhaven. Fairhaven built its own trolley system in October, 1891 but it didn't connect with the Bellingham Bay railway, which ended at the top of State Street Hill.

Passengers going to Fairhaven exited the Bellingham Bay trolley and had to walk down an unpaved street to get to the Fairhaven Street Railway, and of course walk up an unpaved road on the return route. This situation existed from October to the following February, when the companies finally merged. Both towns wanted their name first so they decided to flip a coin – J.J. Donovan was deemed trustworthy by both sides. Fairhaven won the coin toss which resulted in the "Fairhaven and New Whatcom Electric Street Railway." New Whatcom disputed the results and continued to call it the New Whatcom Railway.

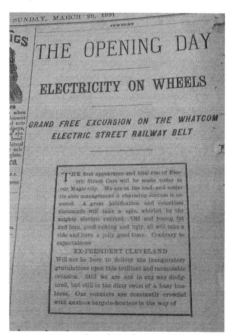

Center for Pacific Northwest Studies, WWU.
Fairhaven Herald, March 29, 1891.

58 We have recently put on another metropolitan air – we have a professional baseball team (p. 231, Excerpt Letter 98)

The Bellingham Bay baseball team was part of the Puget Sound League. For the team's "away" games, the Turf Saloon in Fairhaven became the 1891 version of a sports bar. The score was most likely wired to the Fairhaven telegraph office just around the corner on Harris, with runners going back and forth between innings, updating the bar's bulletin board.

The Turf Saloon was located in the Monahan Building, one of 17 historic buildings that still exist in the Fairhaven Historic District today. Owner Thomas E. Monahan had particular interest in the team as his son, Hugh, played right field.

Whatcom Museum.

Hugh Monahan at 10 o'clock position on the team photo.

Bellingham Bay had a rocky start that first month, but by May 12, 1891, "the boys have quit fooling and begun to play ball; Sunday's game was a beauty." At least that was the opinion of the *Bellingham Bay Bee* newspaper. Bellingham Bay beat Port Townsend.

59   Have also joined the Fairhaven Lawn Tennis Club (p. 235, Excerpt Letter 103)
May 23, 1891, was Opening Day at the Fairhaven Lawn Tennis Club, which was started by Roland Gamwell, President, and Charles Darling, Secretary. The courts were located at the top of Knox Avenue near 19th Street. The club was short-lived. In the 1950s, that corner would become Lord Nelson's mansion and later O'Cain's Nursing Home. Today that large area of property contains the building and grounds of SPIE.

60   He had a letter yesterday from Mrs. Babb (p. 240, Excerpt Letter 107)
Grace Woolson was the niece of P.E.O. founder Alice Bird Babb. Although the nature of her illness is unknown, an article in the *Iowa Wesleyan* reported that John Woolson and Mira Bird Woolson were sitting vigil for their daughter. Fortunately Grace recovered.

✿❀✿

Side Stories

RESEARCHERS FACE DIFFICULT DECISIONS. We learn so much about our subject, dozens and dozens of names and dates, stories about tragedies, incidents, deaths and births, we uncover wonderful photographs, we interview fascinating people. The process is one of collecting innumerable bits of intelligence. The historian finds each and every one of those bits fascinating.

The temptation to share these little discoveries is simply irresistible, and the thought of filing away one's discoveries into the bowels of an archive where they might not be seen for years is too painful to bear.

The writer of history has a different challenge. Writers must winnow through all of those archival facts, selecting the bits and pieces that will bring the story to life. We must share those "aha" moments that we have thrilled to and at the same time tell a fluid and understandable story.

Therein lies the dilemma. As writers of history we wanted very much to tell a straight-forward story of the Gray legacy, its beginnings in Iowa and its coming to fruition in the schools of Bellingham. We had learned so much about the Grays and their acquaintances, about Mount Pleasant and its cultural history, about old Fairhaven and the legacy that the Grays left to Bellingham; but we could not include it all into our narrative without running the risk of weighing down the story to the point that the readers would lose their way.

What were we to do with those orphan facts, these important side stories that could not find a home? We decided to include them at the end of the book and call them just what they are: Side Stories that we loved too much to cast into the street.

~ the Authors

- The Stone House on the Corner
- Anna's Desk
- The Gray Residences
- The Doctor's Offices
- The Templins of Orcas Island
- The Abraham Lincoln Connection
- Iowa Wesleyan College
- P.E.O.

The Stone House on the Corner

"Two years ago tonight I marched my way to 'the stone house on the corner' with fear and trembling and some hope in my heart and there heard the sweetest word that a man ever hears in his life."

Will Gray letter, August 21, 1890

Photo taken January 9, 1892.

401 E. Washington. The Crane family demolished this house in January 1892, to make way for construction of a new home.

"We were much surprised to find the plan of the new house, advertised in this months Harper's, Scribner's and Century. Uncle Hervey has books from several places but liked those of Barber's from Knoxville, Tennessee, but see if you don't think it's cute, Cottage Souvenir No. 2. It's not much like Mount Pleasant houses, is it? We call it the House of Seven Gables. It did seem a little queer that it happened to be the one advertised. Uncle Hervey says he knew enough to pick out a popular plan. The old house is down clear to the foundation now."

Anna Kurtz letter to Will in Le Mars, February 10, 1892

WHEN THE DECISION WAS MADE TO REPLACE the old stone house, Uncle Hervey and Aunt May took an interesting course; they chose a standardized "mail order" plan.

In 1891, architect George F. Barber of Knoxville, Tennessee, published Cottage Souvenir No. 2, which included plans for 58 variations of an elaborate Victorian house. Cost of the plans ranged from $8.50 to $45.00 and included a full set of working drawings, consisting of plans for each floor and the basement, specification sheets and even a sheet of color choices to be used on the exterior. Barber confidently assured customers that the plans contained everything that the builder needed. Changes to

Courtesy Mount Pleasant, Iowa, Public Library.

Photo by Alex DeLuna.

401 E. Washington, 1909.   401 E. Washington, 2009.

the home could be made for an additional fee, or made with the builder. While Barber was not the first to publish house plans, he was certainly one of the most popular. When Barber's firm stopped selling plans in 1908 he had produced over 20,000 sets of plans, both mail order and custom.

Pre-nuptial letters from Anna (in Mount Pleasant) to Will (on the western border of the state in Le Mars) tell of her decision to marry in the uncompleted new house because it sat on "home" ground. Those letters evidence the warm relationship that Anna seemed to enjoy with her Uncle Hervey.

Thousands of Barber mail-order designed homes were built in the United States. Hundreds of them have been identified and still exist today. One of those homes was built in Bellingham in the same year that the Cranes built in Mount Pleasant. In 1892 R.I. Morse, the pioneer founder of Morse Hardware Co., selected a Barber design and built his home at 1014 Garden Street in what was then the town of Sehome. The house, slightly modified, still stands. It has long been considered by many to be a Victorian original, unaware that there were scores of nearly identical houses built across the country.

Whatcom Museum.

1892 R.I. Morse house, Bellingham, Washington.

Courtesy Mount Pleasant, Iowa, Public Library.

Anna's room, January 1892.

Anna's Desk

THE VOYAGE OF DISCOVERY THAT THE HISTORIAN SAILS is not unlike the experiences of a sea voyage. There are days of boring calm when nothing seems to happen, no excitement, perhaps a tickle of interest as another small fact or piece of information is gleaned from this archive or that book, or the occasional interview – all this tucked away into the research file. And then, Whamo! The storm hits, Eureka! Batten down the hatches! The piece of a puzzle that you did not even know you were working on drops into place. The bells ring, the lights flash and your heart pounds as you come to a new reality. All of those boring little bits come together and become an exciting new realization. These are the moments that the historian lives for and that justify all of that slow poking around in musty archives. The story of Anna's desk was like that. Let us tell you how it happened.

We suppose it really began when Neelie first made contact with two women in Mount Pleasant – Martha Hayes, Chair of the Mount Pleasant Historic Preservation Committee and a Life Member of the Board of Trustees of Iowa Wesleyan College, and Pat White of the Mount Pleasant Historic Preservation Committee and Secretary Treasurer of the Henry County Heritage Trust. These two women had been immensely helpful sending us photos and newspaper clippings and information about the folks and families that people "My Darling Anna." They sent photos of the Cranes' old stone house that Anna grew up in.

A few days later, Joyce Morse, 94 (daughter-in-law of Morse Hardware founder, R.I. Morse), mentioned that her husband David's niece Margaret Morse Watts had been a close friend and confidant of Miss Gray and might be important for us to talk to. Brian then visited the 92-year-old Mrs. Watts and filmed an oral history interview. Present at the interview was her son Bill Watts. He mentioned after the filming that Margaret Gray had given two pieces of furniture to his mother. Would Brian like to see them? Of course the answer was yes. He was shown the furniture and he casually photographed them, a salon table with spool legs and a delicate small Victorian desk, gifts to Margaret Morse Watts from Margaret Gray in the last years of her life. Then Bill, for no particular reason pulled out the central drawer of the desk and looking under it found written on the bottom, "Dr. W.R. GRAY, Le Mars, Iowa." Those photos also went into the computer archive awaiting a later decision as to inclusion in the book.

More than a month later another email arrived from Mount Pleasant with two attached images. The first was an interesting 1890-era photo of the interior of the Cranes' stone house. The second image showed the back of the photo. Written on the back are the words, "Southeast corner of Anna's room in the old house." Whoa! Now we were riveted on the photo. This was the actual bedroom of our heroine. How incredible! Now this picture was very important to our story. Griffin took a hard look at the photo dated to 1892. A glimmer of recognition jumped from the old photo. Is it possible? Does that Victorian desk in the photo look like the desk that he had just photographed at the Watts home? A quick comparison of the computer photos and it was confirmed.

Voila! There it was. Without a doubt, Anna's desk in the photo of her 1892 room was the very same desk that her daughter Margaret Gray had given to good friend Margaret Morse Watts, and the very desk that Brian had photographed. One hundred and seventeen years had passed since the little desk had been photographed in Anna's room in Mount Pleasant. This was the very desk that Anna had sat at as she read Will's letters and penned her loving replies. This was the very desk on which Will Gray had written his name under the drawer so that ownership could be proved if it were lost in trans-continental shipping. The proof was indisputable. This was Anna's girlhood desk.

This was the kind of moment that keeps historians coming back for more.

The Gray Residences

WILL GRAY NEVER ACHIEVED HIS OFT MENTIONED DESIRE of owning his own home. During his first stay in the Fairhaven of 1890 and 1891, he was of course a lonely, engaged and underfunded bachelor urgently trying to establish his medical practice. We know that he slept in his office in the newly finished Mason Block, taking his meals in restaurants about town. As his financial condition slowly improved, the letters indicate that he engaged in a permanent boarding arrangement with the Fairhaven Restaurant, an eating establishment with a distinctive horseshoe-curved dining counter. The Fairhaven Restaurant occupied the entire ground floor of the building at 905 Harris Avenue on the north side of Harris between 9th and 10th.

When Will returned to Iowa in 1891, still a single man, he moved into Gray Club, managed by his mother. He opened offices above the Henry Savings Bank in Mount Pleasant but only occupied them for a few months.

An opportunity in Le Mars, near the western border of Iowa, found Will once again living in his office. He rented an office in the Le Mars Opera House Block and to save money slept in it, just as he had in the Mason Block in Fairhaven. We believe that he brought his bride to that office ten months later and that they lived there during the entire time they were in Le Mars. Their daughter Margaret was born in that office in the Opera Block, a fitting beginning for her theater career. In 1889 Will sold his Le Mars practice and moved back to Mount Pleasant. We do not know where he practiced medicine during this interlude, but we do know that he, Anna and their daughter lived with the H.E. Snider family, sharing a house on North Main Street.

From *Mount Pleasant Beautiful*, 1909. Courtesy Mount Pleasant, Iowa, Public Library.

The Snider House on North Main street.

Whatcom Museum.

1617 McKenzie Avenue circa 1901. (Could that possibly be Anna at the top of the stairway?)
The steeple of the Scandinavian Methodist Church is seen near the N.W. corner of 18th & Donovan.
The lovely home at right, with smoke coming from the chimney, is located at 1608 McKenzie and
is still there today.

Fairhaven Residences

House #1. 1617 McKenzie Avenue. Upon the Gray's return to Fairhaven in 1901, Will
and Anna rented lodgings on the gentle slope rising behind the Fairhaven business
district near the corner of 17th Street and McKenzie Avenue. A look at the 1904 Sanborn map revealed that the Grays had rented at least part of what appeared to be a
commercial building. The Sanborn shows a long rectangular structure with a two-
story front portion and a long platform in the rear raised ten feet off the ground. It is
probable that it was some sort of a retail store, with living quarters on the second story above the store, as was common in that day.

A visit to Jeff Jewell, photo historian at the Whatcom Museum, revealed the photo shown above. Here you will see the rear of the false-fronted building that the Grays
lived in and the platform raised ten feet off of the ground.

The large building beside it is Germana Hall, which Gordon Tweit remembers
as the place where the German population met, and which they let their Norwegian
neighbors use while Our Saviors Lutheran Church was being built.

The Grays lived at 1617 McKenzie Avenue for two years before moving on sometime in 1903.

Whatcom Museum

House #2. 1121 15th Street. The next home for the Gray family was on the steep 15th Street hill just below Wardner's Castle. The one-and-one-half story frame house was typical for its time with a simple peaked roof and a woodshed out back. They lived here for three years, from 1903 to 1907.

House #3. 1103 15th Street. In 1907 the Grays made a small move up the street, but a huge shift in terms of living space and social standing. They moved just one house up the street into the massive mansion built by James Wardner at the height of the Fairhaven Boom. The house was so large and occupied such a commanding position over the town that it had been dubbed "Wardner's Castle," a name that it enjoys to this day.

Whatcom Museum.

John Earles and family standing in front of their home, Wardner's Castle, in 1906.

Wardner had long since moved on to greener pastures and had sold the house to John Earles, one of the owners of the large Earles-Cleary saw mill in the center of the Fairhaven waterfront. Earles had to move out of town quickly and unexpectedly for health reasons. He left the furnished mansion in 1907 and the Grays immediately moved in. It seems highly unlikely that a young and not very well-to-do physician could afford to pay the rent for Fairhaven's largest 17-room mansion. We think that Earles needed a trustworthy occupant to tend the big house in his absence and the Grays were willing. It must have been quite a lark to suddenly be occupying a house of such distinction and grandeur.

Whatever the reason, whatever the arrangement, it did not last for long. Margaret Gray would later say that while the mansion had the first central heating system in town, it was not adequate for the job. They had to rely on the fireplaces to keep the house warm. The costs and difficulty of getting horse-drawn wagons of wood up the hill proved more than they could manage. The Grays spent just one winter there but they did take advantage of the size and celebrity of the "Castle" by hosting a big Christmas party that winter of 1907.

House #4. 1027 16th Street. In the spring of 1908, the Grays made one more move up the hill. This time to a more modest home owned by lawyer Thomas Newman and his wife Rita. Thomas Newman was a well connected lawyer. He was soon to become a partner with Mount Pleasant immigrant Clint Howard in the law firm of Newman and Howard. The firm counted among their clients the Fairhaven Land Company, the Bellingham Bay Improvement Company, and other major players on the Bellingham Bay scene. They were perhaps the leading law firm in the county.

Whatcom Museum.

Newman House.

Newman's father-in-law, Z.W. Christopher, had built his home in 1890. Newman, later lived there with Rita and daughter Elizabeth until 1908. By that time the Newmans were prospering and their social aspirations led them to abandon their modest house on 16th Street. They moved to the northwest corner of Knox Avenue and 19th Street into the substantial mansion of "Lord" Newton.

Henry Newton was a glib Englishman who had built a salmon cannery in Chuckanut Bay in 1898. He also built an imposing home at 1829 Knox Avenue at the very top of the street. "Lord" Newton, so named because of his English accent and imperious manner, was unable to continue his Knox Avenue lifestyle and his mansion became available. The Newmans, enjoying the heady pleasures of financial success, moved in.

The Grays rented the Newmans' cast-off house on 16th Street and lived there for five years until financial reverses forced the Newmans to return. Illustrating the connectedness of history in a small town, the Newmans' daughter Elizabeth lived in the inherited house with her husband Frank Klassen until her death in 1971. She was well into her eighties, and that very year author Brian Griffin and his wife Marya bought the Newman home, which abutted the back end of their home at 1607 Knox Avenue.

The Griffins demolished the dilapidated old house. In the attic rafters they found eleven of the 1891 Fairhaven Birdseye maps protected in a large cardboard storage tube. Those precious Birdseyes comprised eleven of the fifteen known originals of this classic historic stone lithograph. The Griffins gifted one of them to Village Books in Fairhaven on the condition that it would be forever hung in public view. It can now be seen on the wall beside the staircase on the lower floor of Village Books.

House #5. 1130 14th Street. The Grays' next home may have been a residence for the Grays, but it began life in 1890 as a boom-period hotel.

The Davey House, named after its owners, sported the typical tall false front on the streetside, hiding the peaked gables of its shingled roof when looked at from 14th Street. A bold sign was raised at the rear of the building trumpeting that name to the town below; perhaps even the passengers on arriving steamers in the Bay could have seen it. Further signage on the roof and sides proclaimed HOTEL and FURNISHED.

The Gray family moved into the upstairs rooms of the former hotel as renters in the summer of 1913 and they were to remain there for the next thirty-five years. The walls of the old hotel were still papered in the very luxurious but gaudy wallpaper of a previous remodel; most of that top floor was still broken up into hotel-like small rooms. The heat was supplied by one or more space-heating oil stoves. It was far from the luxury that they had briefly known in "Wardner's Castle," or even the middle class respectability of the Newman house on 16th Street. It could only have been a bit depressing, but nevertheless the Grays settled in for their thirty-five year stay.

Their landlord, Jules E. Sorbin, apparently lost interest in his investment by the 1920s. County tax records show that Mr. Sorbin failed to pay the real estate taxes. In 1924 the county sued him for back taxes and accrued interest. The court found him to be in arrears $3.18 in taxes, plus $2.02 in interest for a grand total of $5.20. The County advertised the delinquency as the law

Whatcom Museum.

The Davey House, 1890, near the corner of Mill Avenue and 14th Street.

required, but Mr. Sorbin still did not pay his debt. The county would not be denied and after a judicious amount of time had passed, a large sale of delinquent properties was advertised. There were a great many of these properties throughout the county to be sold, many of them in Fairhaven.

The county sheriff conducted an auction on the courthouse steps and the general public was invited to bid on whichever properties interested them. The sale was held just before Christmas in 1930. The interest and charges on the Davey House had by that time climbed to $5.80.

The widowed Anna attended the auction that chilly December 23rd. The County records show that Anna Kurtz Gray had bid on and won lot 14, block 16, of the Fairhaven Land Company's 1st Addition to Fairhaven, with a bid of $23.84.

Finally she owned her own home.

Gordon Tweit Collection.

The Davey House, circa 1913. Edith Chichester, daughter of G. Bernard Chichester standing in front.

Anna and daughter Margaret lived on in Davey House until 1948 when Margaret bought a house at 1000 15th Street, just across Douglas Avenue from Lowell School.

By age 88, Anna's condition had deteriorated to the point that her daughter could no longer look after her. She was moved into a nursing home. Margaret chose O'Cain's Nursing Home at the top of Knox Avenue. The large old mansion, built by Henry "Lord" Newton and lived in by the Newmans, had been converted to a care center and was to be the home where Anna Kurtz Gray would breathe her last breath on February 16, 1954. She was 90 years old.

Gordon Tweit Collection.

Henry Newton's mansion, later O'Cain's Nursing Home.

The Doctor's Offices

DR. WILL GRAY HAD MEDICAL OFFICES in many different places in his career. His seemingly endless search for the perfect location may say something about the challenges he faced in establishing a successful practice. In several instances his choice of an office gives us a glimpse at his interests in life.

The Mason Block, Fairhaven, 1890. The fledgling doctor began his medical practice in rooms 30 and 31 of the Mason Block on July 29, 1890. In August he changed to

rooms 34 and 35. He was the first tenant of the large brick building at the corner of Harris Avenue and 12th Street. His choice of offices was an excellent one, as the Mason Block was directly across Harris Avenue from the Fairhaven Hotel, still under construction when he moved in. The huge hotel was the central feature of the growing town.

Will was in a prestigious location but his financial limitations required that he choose the

Today the Mason block is known as Sycamore Square.

less expensive offices without a view of the street. Rooms 34 and 35 were down a back hallway toward the rear of the building. Mason Block housed four other doctors and Fairhaven's best pharmacy. The young doctor slept in his offices.

The Thistle Opera House, Fairhaven, 1891. Financial necessity, Will's interest in theater, and the intrigue of a new location led to new offices in a brand new building containing a theater. Will shared a three-room suite with a dentist, Dr. Van Winter. The two young professionals would each save $5.00 per month in the new building and Will had the added incentive of being near the theatrical world that he loved. The Thistle Block occupied the corner of Mill Avenue and 11th Street just north of the present day Village Books.

Whatcom Museum
1890s view of the Opera House, looking east from the waterfront.

The Henry Savings Bank, Mount Pleasant, 1891.
A new bank was built in 1891, just before Will's
return to Mount Pleasant. The handsome corner
building with its jaunty awning stood at the
corner of Main and Monroe on the town square.
Will rented offices on the second floor above the
bank for the short time that he stayed in Mount
Pleasant. The Henry Savings Bank building still
stands, designated as a historical landmark.

The Opera Block, Le Mars, Iowa, 1891 to 1898. It
was probably not a surprise to Will's friends and
family that his new offices in Le Mars should be in
the Opera Block. It was typical in the 1890s that
theaters were frequently constructed in buildings
which had commercial spaces on the street level

Photo from *Mount Pleasant Beautiful*, 1909.
Henry Savings Bank.

and offices on the upper floor co-existing with the theater space. Will's passion for the
performing arts no doubt led him to office in theater-commercial combination buildings. We don't know how spacious his offices were, but we believe he lived in them until the marriage and probably afterward. Daughter Margaret was born in the offices.
The Le Mars Opera Block no longer exists.

Mount Pleasant, 1898 to 1901. Will Gray sold his Le Mars practice in 1898 and returned to Mount Pleasant. He practiced there for three years until returning to
Fairhaven. We do not know the location of his office during this period.

Courtesy of Lemarscomm.net

Le Mars Opera Block, tall building on the left.

Nelson Block, Fairhaven, 1901 to 1903. Upon his return to Fairhaven, Will Gray rented offices on the second floor of the newly constructed Nelson Block over the bank which occupied the busy corner of 11th Street and Harris Avenue. We don't know which office he had but we hope it was the corner suite with a commanding view over the intersection. The Nelson Block still dominates that corner just across Harris Avenue from the Terminal Building.

Gordon Tweit Collection.

The Nelson Block in the 1920s.

Knights of Pythias Building, Fairhaven, 1903 to 1906. Will moved just a bit up 11th Street into the older Knights of Pythias building. The building was the home to both the Knights of Pythias and the Masonic Order, which had their meeting halls on the third floor. The large brick building still stands on 11th Street. It has been home to a hardware store, Village Books, the Colophon Cafe, and numerous other businesses over

Gordon Tweit Collection.

Knights of Pythias building in the 1970s.

Knights of Pythias stairway, photographed in 2009.

the years, but its upstairs rooms remain essentially unchanged from the day that Will Gray rented them. Photo shows the staircase that Will Gray's patients climbed to pay a visit to his office.

Nelson Block, 1906 to 1910. In 1906 Dr. Gray moved his offices back to the second floor of the bank building at the corner of 11th and Harris in the Fairhaven district of the now consolidated City of Bellingham.

The Exchange Building, 1911 to 1913. The economic center of Bellingham was now clearly centered on Holly Street in what had been the town of Whatcom. In recognition of that reality Dr. Gray moved his office from Fairhaven to the large brick building at the corner of Holly and State Street that now houses the Y.M.C.A.

Bellingham National Bank Building, 1913 to 1922. Will Gray's final office move occurred in 1913 when he moved to the recently completed bank building at the very center of town at Cornwall Avenue and Holly Street. The Bellingham National Bank Building was then the most prestigious address in Bellingham and housed most of its doctors and lawyers.

The Templins of Orcas Island

SINCE 1897 THE TEMPLIN FAMILY HAS BEEN A MAJOR INFLUENCE ON ORCAS ISLAND. They are frequently mentioned in Will Gray's letters and provide an interesting example of how entire families contributed to the great American migration and the settlement of the West.

In the 1880s the Templin brothers, Isaac and Hugh, were owners of a dry goods store with their brother-in-law John Woods. The store, called Templin & Woods, was located on the prominent town square in Mount Pleasant, Iowa. In 1889 brother Isaac, intrigued by the money-making potential in the Pacific Northwest, left the dry goods business and moved to the booming town of Fairhaven to try his hand at the real estate business. He and a partner named Henderson bought dozens of building lots from the Fairhaven Land Company and set up shop at 1105 Harris Avenue just one door uphill from the Terminal Building. They called their business Henderson & Templin. Hugh and Mary (Mrs. Templin), arrived in Fairhaven by 1889.

Meanwhile, back in Mount Pleasant, John Woods must have been restive. Daughter Lulu and her husband had become "boomers" in Tacoma by June of 1890. By November, Will reports that John Wood's son Charlie, with a surveying party, had come up the Skagit Valley and briefly stopped in Fairhaven. The Templins' optimistic views of the opportunities in booming Fairhaven influenced the partners to pull up stakes and move their store to Fairhaven. John and Sarah Woods arrived on Bellingham Bay in 1891 with two of their younger children. They moved in with the Templin family of seven. They all lived in a large house, near the southeast corner of 16th Street and Douglas Avenue – one big family of cousins and in-laws united by blood and a business adventure that was doomed to failure as the Fairhaven Boom began to fade.

Courtesy Mount Pleasant, Iowa, Public Library.

Will Gray commented in a July 1, 1891, letter to Anna, "It was a great piece of folly in Templin & Woods to move their stock of goods out here at this time. They don't know what they are going to do with them yet." John Woods and his family gave up three months later and returned to Mount Pleasant to re-establish the dry goods business in their original location.

Orcas Island Historical Museum.

Templin's Store, Eastsound. Karl Templin, in white meat jacket, standing center.

Hugh Templin and his family did not return to Iowa. Hugh operated a shingle mill on the Fairhaven waterfront. Hugh was intrigued with Orcas Island. Will Gray's letters contain several mentions of Hugh's trips to Orcas, "the fruit island in the Sound." He must have been fascinated with its beauties and opportunities. In 1897, Fairhaven's boom sagged into a deep depression. Hugh and his family moved to the tiny village of Eastsound, the largest village on Orcas Island. Hugh was 57 years old, Mary Eliza was 55. They brought the family with them: Jessie Carleton 34, Edgar Francis 31, Alfred Harold (Harry) 26, Karl 16, and Ralph Carter 11. Isaac Templin remained in Fairhaven until his death in 1901 during a visit to Iowa.

They also brought with them the aged patriarch of the family, Ephraim Killpatrick. Ephraim and his wife, Sarah, had moved from Mount Pleasant to Fairhaven to be with their daughter Mary Templin. Sarah Killpatrick died there in 1895. Ephraim lived on in Eastsound until 1900 when he passed away at the age of 92. The Killpatricks are buried at Bayview Cemetery in Bellingham, Washington.

The move to Orcas Island must have been a beneficial one for the Templin family, for the general store that they established there in 1897 achieved legendary status for generations of islanders and the thousands of visitors that flock to Orcas in the summertime. Templin's store occupied several successive buildings and anchored the center of Eastsound until the old store was demolished in 1992 and a new shopping complex called Templin Center was constructed. A Templin descendant operates that store to this day.

Hugh and Mary Eliza lived out their lives on Orcas Island as did five of their children. There are many Templins and Templin relatives living on the "Fruit Island in the Sound."

Orcas Island Historical Museum.

Orcas Island Historical Museum.
Templin's second store in 1949.

Leith TemplinCollection.
Younger Hugh Templin.

Leith Templin Collection.
Mary Eliza Templin.

Leith Templin Collection.
Hugh Templin in his later years.

The Abraham Lincoln Connection

TEMPLIN FAMILY LORE includes half-remembered stories of Templin children playing with the grandchildren of Abraham Lincoln. These family oral traditions are known to be accurate and are rooted in the Mount Pleasant relationship of family patriarch Judge Ephriam Killpatrick and U.S. Senator James Harlan.

Ephraim Killpatrick, the father of Sarah Woods and Mary Templin, was a formidable man. He was born in South Carolina in 1808 and went with his parents to Kentucky when it was still a wilderness, and then settled with them in southern Illinois in 1819, passing the years of his youth among the pioneers of that rich section of what was then the "far west." There he taught school and studied law, and there he served in the same regiment as Abraham Lincoln in the Black Hawk War.

Killpatrick moved to Mount Pleasant about 1838 and practiced law. He was both clerk and a judge of the district court for a number of years, and then during the Civil War he accepted an appointment to government service as private secretary to Senator Harlan. As a Senator in Washington, D.C., Harlan's friendship with President Lincoln became close. He was selected to escort Mrs. Lincoln to the President's second inaugural ball, and the President's son, Robert, escorted Harlan's daughter, Mary. In 1865, Harlan was appointed by Lincoln to serve as his Secretary of the Interior. With the assassination of Lincoln in April 1865, Harlan would serve under Andrew Johnson's administration instead. Harlan's close relationship with President Lincoln was recognized when he became the President of the Lincoln Monument Association.

Mary Harlan and Robert Todd Lincoln married. That marriage resulted in three Lincoln grandchildren who spent their summers with their maternal grandparents, the Harlans, at their Mount Pleasant home. Mary Harlan Lincoln also spent summers with the children at her parents' home, and Robert took the train from Chicago to join them on some weekends. The Harlans, Killpatricks, and Templins were all neighbors and friends. Hugh Templin's mother, Mary Worster Templin, was proprietor of the Harlan House, a hotel located near the town square owned by the Harlans.

Harlan-Lincoln House, postcard circa 1909, then home of the President of Iowa Wesleyan.

The Lincoln grandchildren spent many summers in Mount Pleasant with the Harlans and family oral history relates that Jessie Templin, Hugh's eldest daughter, was a playmate of Mary and Jessie Lincoln.

In 1895 Harlan's home was deeded to Mary Harlan Lincoln. In 1907, Mary donated the home to Iowa Wesleyan as a tribute to her father. A charming discovery was made many years ago during an early renovation. A door panel was found with the heights of the three Lincoln and Harlan grandchildren marked by Senator Harlan in 1883. That door can still be seen in the Harlan-Lincoln House, which is now a museum and part of the Iowa Wesleyan campus.

Iowa Wesleyan College

THERE IS A STRONG PRESENCE of Iowa Wesleyan College throughout *My Darling Anna*. (In Will Gray's day, the school was known as Iowa Wesleyan University, the name it was given in 1855. It did not become Iowa Wesleyan College until 1912.) The location of the Mount Pleasant home of Will Gray, known as Gray Club, is now part of the Iowa Wesleyan campus. The large house that Anna Crane shared with her eight siblings has been the residence of the College President since 1924.

At its beginning in 1842, the school was named the Mt. Pleasant Literary Institute; later renamed the Mt. Pleasant Collegiate Institute. Classes were held in Pioneer Hall which was constructed in 1844-1845 and remains on the campus today. When James Harlan was named president in 1853, he raised funds to construct a second building known as "Old Main" and expanded the curriculum to grant the baccalaureate degree. At his urging the Collegiate Institute was renamed Iowa

Courtesy Iowa Wesleyan College Archives.

The Chapel was constructed in 1893.

Wesleyan University to emphasize its sponsorship by the Iowa Conference of the Methodist Episcopal Church. Harlan would go on to become a Senator in Washington, D.C., and advisor to Abraham Lincoln, but returned briefly as president of the university again in 1869 before serving more time in the U.S. Senate.

In 1854 few institutions of higher education admitted women. That year the first catalog of Iowa Wesleyan advertised that students of both sexes were admitted on equal terms and to the same advantages. In addition to Liberal Arts it established departments of Theology, English, German, Law, Pharmacy and Anatomy. In 1912 the University became Iowa Wesleyan College and changed the focus to teaching Liberal Arts instead of professional training.

Mount Pleasant's preoccupation with education started with its early settlers. Samuel Howe started a school in 1841 above the jail in an old log cabin, and would go on to form Howe's Acadamy. He is credited with inspiring many students who would become influential citizens of Mount Pleasant and carry on the tradition of valuing education. James Harlan had been principal of Iowa City College and was elected Iowa's first Superintendent of Public Education. Both Howe and Harlan are credited with helping Mount Pleasant achieve the reputation as the "Athens of Iowa" for its exceptional educational institutions. They did not do it alone. Many prominent members of Mount Pleasant including Wellington Bird, W.R. Cole, Washington Irving Babb, Belle Babb Mansfield, and Alice Bird Babb, contributed to the reputation as professors, trustees and supporters of Iowa Wesleyan.

View of Iowa Wesleyan from Gray Club on North Main. Chapel with it's original spire, on left.

It is impossible to mention Iowa Wesleyan without mentioning the seven women undergraduates who joined together on January 21, 1869, to form the P.E.O. Sisterhood, which continues today as an important educational philanthropic organization. More information on this organization can be found on the following pages. Two rooms have been set aside in the Old Main building on the campus of Iowa Wesleyan College where visitors can view the actual room where the first meeting was held and look at other early memorabilia of the organization. A few notable nineteenth century graduates of Iowa Wesleyan include:

1859   Lucy Killpatrick (Byrkit), the first woman graduate with a B.A. degree at an institute of higher learning in the United States;

1866   Belle Babb (Mansfield), the first woman admitted to the Bar in the United States, in 1869;

1885   Susan Mosely (Grandison), the first female black graduate of Iowa Wesleyan, and perhaps the first in the nation.

A statue of Belle Babb Mansfield stands on the Iowa Wesleyan campus, representative of not only personal accomplishment of a graduate of the institution, but also of the welcoming and progressive climate of the Mount Pleasant community.

Statue of Belle Babb Mansfied with Old Main in the background.

P.E.O.

THESE THREE LETTERS MEAN TO THE KNOWING a North American women's Philanthropic Educational Organization which has had a long and distinguished record of promoting educational opportunities for women in the United States and Canada. The organization funds scholarships, provides loans, awards, and grants and owns and operates a women's college. We have included them in this book because the history of P.E.O. is deeply entwined with our story, with Mount Pleasant, with Iowa Wesleyan College and with many of the characters that people this book.

Postcard circa 1900-1902, listing seven founders: Alice Bird Babb, Mary Allen Stafford, Hattie Briggs Bousquet, Franc Roads Elliott, Alice Virginia Coffin, Ella Stewart and Suela Pearson Penfield. Alice is in the cameo photo. Old Main appears on the right with Pioneer Hall in the background.

The roots of fraternal-type organizations go back in time to the 1850s when Greek letter fraternal orders were being conceived on college campuses and there was a national interest in the formation of secret friendship societies. At the nation's colleges, men were the first to organize fraternal bands of "brothers," with secret hand shake grips, slogans and regalia, Their rituals were marked by lofty idealistic goals proclaimed during secret initiations midst oaths of loyalty and allegiance to bonds of fealty. In that growing age of fraternal orders, women also felt the pull to form societies of their own.

In the spring of 1867, at Monmouth College, in Monmouth, Illinois, twelve young women founded a sorority which they named I.C. Sorosis. The next year, one of its founders, Libbie Brook, volunteered to spread the organization and convinced her parents that she would be able to concentrate more on her studies if she were to attend Iowa Wesleyan University in Mount Pleasant, fifty-five miles across the Mississippi River in Iowa. Her parents fell for the scheme and by December 21, 1868, she had succeeded in organizing the second chapter of I.C. Sorosis at Iowa Wesleyan, thereby creating the first national fraternity for women. I.C. Sorosis changed its name to Pi Beta Phi in 1888.

This event was not shared with the general campus population until New Year's Eve of 1868, when the Iowa Wesleyan Beta Theta Pi fraternity held a bum (casual gathering) at a local restaurant in Mount Pleasant. Several girls walked in wearing gleaming I.C. Sorosis arrows, making it clear that Libbie Brook had achieved what she set out to do.

When some, but not all, of a close-knit circle of seven friends were invited to be a part of Libbie's group, they decided to stay together and form a society of their own. On Thursday, January 21, 1869, during a "vacant bell" (not a class hour) the girls rattled some doors in the Old Main building and found the music room unlocked. They scurried upstairs to the chapel room and brought down the Bible, and in the music room the seven women took the oath written by Alice Bird. Thus was organized the first chapter of the P.E.O.

The girls approached Anna Kurtz's uncle, Hervey Crane, who owned a jewelry store, and asked him for samples of a pin for the girls to look at. They decided to use the star for their emblem. Hervey placed the order and the seven women agreed to keep quiet until they got their pins. It is unknown when the delivery was made, but pins in hand, the seven new P.E.O. members decided to outdo the I.C. Sorosis girls who had planned to "come out" during a required Chapel gathering. With the help of Franc Roads' mother, the girls quickly whipped up identical aprons – the left side of the bib higher than the right to prominently showcase their new P.E.O. Star pin. Just as the I.C. Sorosis girls were about to enter the Chapel (with identical blue calico dresses for dramatic effect), the seven P.E.O. members quickly emerged to make their grand entrance. It was a girlhood rivalry, plain and simple, and would continue for many years.

Hervey Crane supplied those meaningful stars to P.E.O. initiates for years. The original pin was flat and larger than the smaller, concave pin used today.

The connection of P.E.O. and *My Darling Anna* continues, as the property that was once the home of Elizabeth and Will Gray was sold to Iowa Wesleyan College. In 1927 the P.E.O. Memorial Library was constructed on that site as a joint venture; the College provided the land, P.E.O. built the building. The name of the building honored the original seven founders. It became executive and administrative offices for P.E.O. and the library for the College. Currently, the executive offices of P.E.O. are in Des Moines, Iowa, and the building is used for administrative offices for Iowa Wesleyan.

Courtesy Iowa Wesleyan College Archives.

P.E.O. Memorial Library, south view, circa 1927.

Today the organization is known as P.E.O. International with almost 250,000 members throughout the United States and Canada. The P.E.O. Memory Room, located in that original Music Room in Old Main, has a large collection of items from the founders and early P.E.O. members. That so many items dating back to the organization's foundation were saved showed great foresight and an enduring faith in the future.

Anna Kurtz was an early member of P.E.O. rival I.C. Sorosis. Her daughter, Margaret Gray, was a longtime member of P.E.O. The wife of Anna's cousin Frank, Mae Crane, was an original member of the first P.E.O. Chapter F, which was organized in Bellingham in 1904.

Margaret Elizabeth Gray
"Miss Gray"

Introduction to
Margaret Elizabeth Gray
Special Section

"Miss Gray"

THE ULTIMATE TRIUMPH OF THE CULTURAL TRANSFER from Mount Pleasant to Fairhaven and the legacy of Will and Anna Gray are found in the life and career of their only child, Margaret Elizabeth Gray. This special section of *My Darling Anna* (and the hour-long digital recording that accompanies it) is our tribute to this beloved teacher.

In a very personal way this is also author Brian Griffin's gift to Margaret's memory and to all of those readers who share his memories of her. Those who did not know her will gain insight into her career and character and the particular influence that she had on so many young lives during her long teaching career.

It is also appropriate in this special edition to acknowledge Gordon Tweit, who was a longtime friend of Miss Gray. Gordon's extensive knowledge of Fairhaven and the Gray family, along with the archival collection in his personal museum have been of immense value and assistance in the writing of *My Darling Anna*. The authors are forever in his debt.

Another member of the Tweit family, Gordon's sister Eloise Tweit Rall, has made an important contribution to this special section with the loan of the celluloid 78 RPM records of her and Norris Brannstrom singing duets from the 1945 and 1946 operettas in which they played the leads. The transcription of the duets was made possible by the unique technical skills of the American Museum of Radio and Electricity, a world-class museum located in Bellingham's downtown cultural district.

The 1971 interviews with Miss Gray by Galen Biery and Haines Fay were found in the Biery Collection of the Center for Pacific Northwest Studies at Western Washington University and their inclusion on the CD make a large contribution to the historical record of the Bellingham community.

This special supplement to *My Darling Anna* is offered in recognition of the contributions which Margaret Elizabeth Gray made to the cultural life of her community in her long career as an educator.

Photo of Margaret Gray on page 311 from FHS *Aurora*, 1921. Gordon Tweit Collection.

BHS *Shuksan*, 1958.

The Final Curtain Call, Part I

MARGARET GRAY STOOD IN THE WINGS as the company took its final curtain call to wildly enthusiastic applause. This operetta, *Kismet,* had been a grand success, like most of the operettas in all of the years back to 1938. That was the opening year of a striking new and modern Bellingham High School. The operettas had begun that first year with Victor Herbert's, *The Red Mill,* which began a long and unbroken succession of operettas performed on the stage of Bellingham High's 1,735-seat auditorium. Margaret was fond of telling her budding thespians that their house was "larger than most of the theaters on New York's Broadway."

Margaret Gray was a matronly woman wearing an old-fashioned gown which hung to the floor and draped her ample frame. Her gray hair was tastefully tied back in her customary bun and she presented her usual mien of inner peace, dignity and almost motherly interest in her students.

She had been a teacher in Bellingham schools for 45 years; the last 20 years at Bellingham High School.

This 1958 production, *Kismet,* was to be her last, as she would retire at the end of the school year. She would be 65 on the upcoming April 16th. Margaret Elizabeth Gray had become an icon: "Miss Gray," the drama teacher, the beloved and respected counselor to all who aspired to the stage, who respected the language, and who loved the theater. Each year Miss Gray gathered the talented and interested young people in the high school who dreamed of dramatic glory or simply responded to the beauty of language and theater or who were beginning to find in themselves a talent for singing or speech or performance. She was beloved for nurturing their budding talents with her skill, wisdom and grace.

For a moment as she watched her young wards taking their bows, her thoughts drifted back to her father, long gone these 36 years. Her father, Dr. Will Gray, who had always loved theater. She knew that he would have been proud of the legacy she had created, and for passing his love of drama on to those hundreds, no thousands, of young students she had taught. She thought of her mother, Anna, whose career as a teacher had nurtured her own passion for the profession.

As the waves of applause flooded the stage, the realization that this would be her last curtain call overcame her. She grasped the heavy folds of curtain beside her and closed her eyes. The passing of time and years and lives and the story of her family replaced the happy sounds around her.

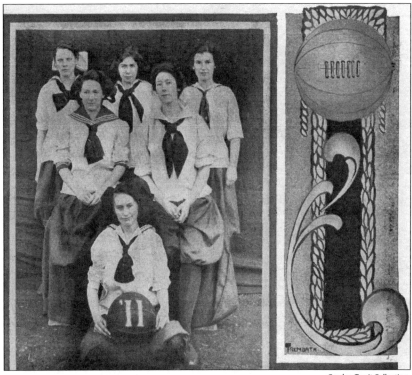

Gordon Tweit Collection.

Margaret was on the girl's basketball team (2nd row right), FHS *Aurora,* 1911.

Gordon Tweit Collection.

Margaret Gray, faculty member, FHS *Aurora,* 1919.

Gordon Tweit Collection.

Valedictorian Margaret Gray, FHS *Aurora,* 1911.

Dedication

To Miss Margaret Gray

In appreciation of her unfailing help, not only to the Senior Class, but to the entire school, the Class of 1921 affectionately dedicates this book

Gordon Tweit Collection.

Yearbook dedicated to Margaret Gray, FHS *Aurora,* 1921.

MARGARET GRAY WAS TO TEACHING BORN. Margaret was a brilliant student and the valedictorian of her high school class. She got her beginning teaching certificate at the Normal School, the forerunner of the present Western Washington University. She was soon teaching at Glendale, a rural school near Lynden north of her Bellingham home. The next year, 1915, she

Gordon Tweit Collection.
Margaret Gray, faculty member, FHS *Aurora,* 1923.

taught at Lowell Grade School near her 14th Street home in Fairhaven. After two years at Lowell, summers at the University of Washington to get an advanced degree, and a year of being a roving arts teacher throughout the district, she landed the job she wanted. She was assigned to Fairhaven School where she taught in the grades and later the high school. She taught English and history and was soon assigned as an assistant in drama to G. Bernard Chichester.

Now she was in her element; she was teaching what her father had been teaching her all of her life – English literature, history, drama, and theater. In the beginning the Fairhaven productions were modest and the stage in the gymnasium was adequate at best. Miss Gray explained that two great pillars on either side of the stage impeded the movement on the tiny stage, but they "made do."

Margaret Gray began teaching drama at Fairhaven High School assisting the regular drama teacher G. Bernard Chichester and the school's musical director Miss Dorothy Griggs in the production of *The Polished Pebble,* an operetta *The Bosun's Bride,* and *Captain Crossbones.* In 1926 she co-directed an operetta *The Gypsy Rover* with Miss Doris Johnson. Miss Johnson had sung with the choir of St. Olaf's College and contributed her musical knowledge while Miss Gray was responsible for the acting and set design. The next year the school did *Mr. Bob,* a two-act comedy which she directed. Margaret became deeply involved in all aspects of Fairhaven High theater in addition to her other teaching responsibilities.

Gordon Tweit Collection.
G. Bernard Chichester, FHS *Aurora,* 1926.

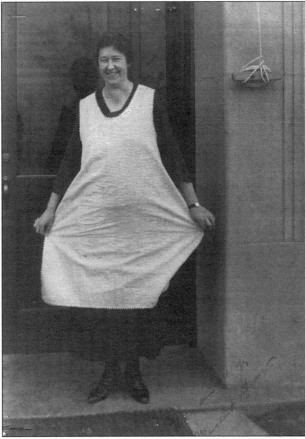

Gordon Tweit Collection.

Margaret Gray, FHS *Aurora,* 1925.

Bellingham's south-siders experienced tragedy on December 31, 1935, as their beloved Fairhaven High School burned in a raging fire. Only the gymnasium survived. While the fire certainly was a disaster, it did result in the beneficial decision to build a new consolidated high school that would serve all of the students of Bellingham, both from the north-side and the south-side. It would reduce and finally eliminate the bitterness of the cross-community rivalry that still lingered after the 1903 consolidation of the several cities around the Bay.

Construction of Bellingham High School was begun promptly after the fire. During its two-year construction, Bellingham's high schoolers and teachers operated on a shift basis at the surviving north-side high school in the building that became Whatcom Middle School. The teachers and students from one of the schools would attend the first shift, then the other school would do their shift.

Miss Gray described those years as a terribly difficult time. The building was badly over-crowded despite the shift system. Teachers on the first shift were asked to leave the grounds when their shift was over because they were

Looking Backward

In which the Aurora staff says farewell to Fairhaven

By SALOME GOODMAN

"No more pencils, no more books, no more teachers"—that was back in the grades, when we could say that every summer, for we knew we would be coming back to everything in the fall. But now—nothing to come back to, except four gaunt, charred walls, that once looked over a beautiful campus to give us a welcome.

As the passing of a friend, as the sinking of the sun into the horizon, as the passing of the night—Fairhaven is gone. No one better knows what this means than one who attended Fairhaven in the days when it was a grade school, later was graduated from what had become a high school, then came back to teach. That is a record not possessed by any other person.

Speaking of records, any one who has seven All-American *Auroras* to her credit is not to be forgotten. One might also mention all the successful plays, carnivals, and *Auroras* she has produced. Besides, she has been one of the best loved of teachers. And now to doff our hats to her — Miss Margaret Gray.

It is with a heavy, aching heart that she must turn away forever from what has been almost a home — a place where she has met, been friends with, and learned to love, and now must leave, so many dear friends. She goes, never to enter the friendly halls of Fairhaven that hold for her the sweetest memories of never-to-be-forgotten days.

Gordon Tweit Collection.

From the FHS *Aurora*, 1936.

getting in the way of those teaching the second shift. Students were confused and education probably suffered. The disruption and chaos however all seemed to be worth it when the 1938 school year opened in the all new perfectly modern Bellingham High School.

The facilities for drama and theater in the new school were stunning, with a huge professional-quality stage and an auditorium that seated 1,735 on the

main floor and balcony. Although the theater was changed and reduced in size by the recent 2000 remodel, it is still the envy of most high schools in the state.

The original auditorium was a drama teacher's dream and Margaret Gray was

Gordon Tweit Collection.

Bellingham High School auditorium, BHS *Shuksan*, 1938.

perfectly positioned. Mr. Chichester, the head of the high school drama department, retired in 1938 and Miss Gray took over the job.

John Roy Williams, the district music director, wanted to do an ambitious operetta in their brand new Bellingham High School theatre. They decided to put on *The Red Mill* by Victor Herbert. Warren Frank and Barney Stewart starred in the comedic roles. *The Red Mill* was a huge success and established the collaboration of Williams and Gray in the first of a long and continuous run of operettas that began a legend and a tradition at Bellingham High School that continues to this day. *The Red Mill* in '39 was followed by *Rio Rita* in '40, then *Naughty Marietta, Desert Song,* and *The Chocolate Soldier.*

Gordon Tweit Collection.
John Roy Williams, BHS *Shuksan,* 1945.

1944 ushered in an era of special talent when tenor Norris Brannstrom starred in *Blossom Time,* and was joined the next year by soprano Eloise Tweit. These two outstanding young talents sang the leads in *The Merry Widow* in 1945 and, the following year, in *New Moon.* Tweit and Brannstrom both went on to further musical education on the East Coast and Brannstrom to a professional career. Their participation in Bellingham High School operettas represented a high water mark in this long-standing tradition.

Despite the great artistic success of *New Moon,* the year 1946 was to be a bitter one for the high school program. Music Director John Roy Williams collapsed of a heart attack and died while mowing his lawn one warm summer weekend. The longtime musician and music director for the Bellingham School District was deeply respected and gravely mourned.

Gordon Tweit Collection.
New Moon featured Eloise Tweit and Norris Brannstrom as leads. BHS *Shuksan,* 1946.

In the old theater tradition of "the show must go on," John Roy Williams was replaced that summer of 1946 by a new Music Director, John Monroe, and that fall the new team of Gray and Monroe continued the tradition with Eloise Tweit and Jim Phalmer singing the leads in *Katinka*.

Margaret Gray's private life took a turn for the better in May of 1948 when she was finally able to get her mother to move from the dilapidated old hotel building that they had lived in for so long. Margaret had purchased a small house at 1000 15th Street, just across Douglas Avenue from Lowell School. While the house was nearly as old as their former lodgings, it was small, convenient and very well constructed.

1000 15th Street in 2009.

Margaret loved it. She could look across the street at the school where she had once taught – the school which her father had enjoyed a role in building when he was on the Board of Education. The house was described by friends as filled with old Victorian furniture and the accumulations of several generations. Margaret herself described the decor as "late attic or early basement."

Margaret's life was clearly centered on Bellingham High School, her students and their theatrical endeavors, however she also enjoyed an active social life. She was a member of P.E.O., the organization so connected to her roots back in Mount Pleasant.

She had many friends and adoring former students to socialize with. One of her good friends was Margaret Morse Watts. Margaret Morse was a young teacher hired by School Superintendent C. Paine Shangle in the early 1940s. Shangle, known for his close watch on School District expenditures, was in the habit of hiring new teachers at the "temporary substitute" wage classification and then keeping them in that pay level as long as possible. Margaret Morse, daughter of Morse Hardware Co. President Cecil Morse, was paid as a "temporary substitute" even though she was a permanent teacher. Margaret Gray earned Morse's lasting gratitude when she attended a School Board meeting and convinced the Board that Superintendent Shangle's practice of hiring "permanent temporary substitutes" was unfair and unethical. Margaret Gray won the day! Margaret Morse got a raise and became a lifelong friend and confidant.

Morse Watts recalls Miss Gray with great fondness, saying that while she was a warm and engaging friend, she was also a rather private person, not sharing with friends much of her inner feelings and personal life.

Miss Gray's professional responsibilities went well beyond the annual Operetta for which she shared responsibility with the music director. She was entirely in charge of the annual *What a Show,* a fall variety show which frequently turned up useful talent for other school productions. She was also in charge of all student dramatic events, most prominent of which was the Senior Play. To round out her duties, she taught several drama classes which were heavy on elocution, and occasionally English and history classes. Many children of loggers, mill workers and fishermen were given their first taste of classical literature in Miss Gray's room 203.

BHS *Shuksan,* 1942.

Miss Gray was also in charge of the Stage Crew, a mostly male group who built the stage sets, worked the curtains, changed the scenery and managed the lights for all school productions and events. Service on the Stage Crew took on a special aura under her tutelage. Ian Monsen, class of 1944, led the Stage Crew in his senior year while also serving as Student Body President. Monsen never knew how its members were selected, but he is proud to this day of having belonged.

Each year Miss Gray assembled a stalwart group of boys who could build sets, work lights and handle the heavy curtains. They were frequently chosen from the school's athletic teams. They all shared several required attributes: They were capable, proud of their roles and they were reliable. They were also Miss Gray's boys. She seemed to have a special affinity for her male students.

Each year Margaret developed another small group of students who gave her great loyalty and affection. This group was formed of boys who sang or acted in her productions and showed a particular interest in theater. She did not seem to develop similar close relationships with girls. Even though more than 50 years had passed, every person, male or female, who we interviewed about Miss Gray volunteered the observation that she seemed to favor the boys. Author Griffin experienced her almost maternal warmth of favor himself, being on the periphery of a group of her favorites for the 1950 year. The clear favorite in that group was Richard Wahl. He was also the most passionate about drama and theater, and he went on to a career as an ABC radio correspondent.

We wonder if her special relationship with male students was somehow psychologically connected to her strong relationship with her father and a difficult relationship with her mother Anna. Margaret resembled her father in many ways. She shared his height and his facial features and we believe his personality and interests. He was a sensitive, intuitive and cultured man and was deeply revered by his daughter.

Certainly the traits, interests and characteristics exhibited by Margaret during her life were reflections of his strong influence. Margaret would undoubtedly credit her love of theater and her love of language to the Shakespearian scholar who was her father. Even the fact that she never married might be a measure of her devotion to him. It is possible that there was never room in her life for another man. His premature death must have been a crushing blow to this sensitive woman.

BHS Shuksan, 1942.

Miss Gray and Ernie Dawe.

Whatever the motivation, Margaret Gray took a great interest in large numbers of students of her era and imparted to them a lifelong sense of worth, and an appreciation for the theater arts of speech and presentation and communication that would serve them well for their lifetimes.

Margaret Gray was to complete twenty storied years at Bellingham High School before retiring in 1958. What she had accomplished was to be her legacy and also that of her parents.

"Miss Gray"

BHS *Shuksan*, 1958.

The Final Curtain Call, Part II

SHE FELT A TUG AT HER SLEEVE and her reveries were broken. The applause had finally subsided and an expectant hush had fallen over the auditorium. "Come Miss Gray," the young male lead whispered, "it is time for your curtain call." He took her by the hand and led her in front of the drawn curtain into an avalanche of rising sound; the audience leapt to its feet as one and with hands clapping over their heads, greeted this beloved teacher with calls of "bravo" and "thank you."

By the time she had reached center stage the applause was deafening and her eyes gleamed with new-started tears. Again her thoughts flashed back in time to her parents and their love for her and for each other; she thought of the letters that her father had written so long ago and that she had kept all these years, reading them from time to time to bring him back to her. Those letters chronicled the young couple's struggles and presaged the legacy which had triumphed this night.

Lonnie Morgan, who had sung the leading role of Hajj in *Kismet* that last night, gently held her hand at center stage as she gracefully bowed acknowledging the thunderous applause.

Waves of emotion flooded the auditorium and were flowing across the footlights. After the stage crew electrician rigged the microphone, Lonnie asked for quiet and with a voice trembling with emotion reminded Miss Gray and the audience that the twenty roses that she was about to receive were for each operetta that she had produced.

Then twenty of her former students who had played in those productions, one at a time, came onto the stage to present her with a red rose. There were few dry eyes in the auditorium.

⊹⇒⊙⇐⊹

Christmas Greetings

Dear…

1958 – a never-to-be-forgotten year, with happy memories of the past, dreams that came true, and plans for the future.

In January, I announced that the time for my retirement had arrived, after forty-six years of teaching, with forty-five in Bellingham. They have been rich and rewarding years, and my work with young people has brought joy and happiness to me.

In March, the Musical, "Kismet," marked the end of my dramatic productions, with a total of one hundred twenty different shows. The last performance had a surprise ending, (for me) with memories of the 1938-1958 operettas. Members from the casts presented me with a red rose for each production, and, so, my final curtain was rung down.

June 5th was my last day in school; the stage had been put in order, my cupboards emptied, my desk cleared out, and I closed the door on room 203. That chapter of my life was finished, and I was about to start a new one.

July and August saw my plans completed for a trip to Europe. I chose an independent tour of the places which I especially wanted to see. My transportation, hotels, and an interpreter to meet me in each city were included in the tour.

September came, and, after busy days of final preparations, packing, dinners, and farewells, I left home on September 9th. I departed from Seattle by Pan American Polar Flight, direct to London, with seventeen and one half hours of flying time.

After five wonderful days in London, I went by motor coach to Oxford, Stratford-Upon-Avon, Coventry, York, and north to Edinburgh. From Glasgow, I flew to Copenhagen, then by train to Amsterdam, Brussels, Cologne, Heidelberg, Zurich, Munich, Vienna and Venice.

Motor coach tours took me from Venice to Florence, and then to Rome. I was in Rome in the interim between the death of the pope, and the election of a new pope. I resumed my trip by train to Pisa, Milan, Cannes, Paris, and back to London.

There were eight weeks filled with sight-seeing, plays, new impressions, a variety of transportation, hotels, food, fascinating experiences, and every-where I found kind and helpful people. I had time to stroll down avenues, browse on side streets, tour museums, enjoy the parks and do some shopping.

The time was all too short, but I was grateful that I could take such a trip, and relieved that my feet, my back, and my money held out.

In the fall of her retirement year she took a long anticipated trip to Europe and she reported on her adventures with this Christmas letter to her friends.

Miss Gray lived on in her home on 15th Street for many years, enjoying the adulation and respect of the community, friends and former students. Her treasured memories of those great years at Bellingham High School were so precious that she never wanted to dilute them by returning there. Gordon Tweit tells a poignant story of the day he was to be given a Bellingham School District Golden Acorn award at the high school for services to the District. He received a phone call from Miss Gray saying, "Gordon, I am very sorry but I cannot attend your award ceremony, I simply cannot bear to return to the scene of so many happy memories."

Margaret was asked in her 1971 interview with Haines Fay, "Is there anything that stands out in your mind over all the years you were a professional teacher, … something particularly worthwhile or gratifying to you personally?"

Margaret replied:

> "I would say that the biggest thrill that I had, was watching somebody develop from somebody shy, inexperienced and lacking security, and to see that person come along and become successful … with a feeling of 'I can accomplish something.' I believe that is the most important."

The legendary and beloved Margaret Gray passed to her reward at the age of 80, on May 14, 1973. She was buried beside her parents in Bayview Cemetery.

If the beginning of the Gray story began at a train station in Mount Pleasant Iowa in 1890, it ends in 1958 with the retirement of Margaret Gray from her position as drama teacher at Bellingham High School. No! That cannot be correct! The truth is the story has not ended yet, it just goes on and on carried by the legacy of Will and Anna and Margaret to new generations. The passion which began in the theaters of Chicago as a young Will Gray thrilled to the plays of Shakespeare is still to be found in the tradition of fine musicals produced in the Bellingham School District. Perhaps none was better than the 2008 production of *Les Misérables* produced at Bellingham High School featuring talent from each of the three Bellingham high schools. The legacy is to be found among the scores of Margaret Gray's former students who credit her with an inspiration, the spark of an aspiration, the sudden recognition of the beauty of language and an appreciation of words well spoken.

Bellingham High School
Operettas in the Margaret Gray Era

1939: *The Red Mill* 1906 operetta by Victor Herbert

1940 : *Rio Rita* 1927 musical by Tierney and McCarthy

1941: *Naughty Marietta* 1930 operetta by Victor Herbert

1942: *Desert Song* 1926 operetta by Sigmund Romberg

1943: *The Chocolate Soldier* 1908 operetta by Oscar Straus

1944: *Blossom Time* 1921 operetta by Sigmund Romberg

1945: *The Merry Widow* 1906 operetta by Franz Lehar

1946: *The New Moon* 1928 operetta by Sigmund Romberg

1947: *Katinka* 1915 operetta by Oscar Harbach

1948: *The Firefly* 1912 operetta by Rudolf Friml

1949: *The Red Mill* 1906 operetta by Victor Herbert

1950: *A Waltz Dream* 1908 operetta by Oscar Strauss

1951: *Sweethearts* 1924 operetta by Victor Herbert

1952: *A Connecticut Yankee* 1949 musical comedy
from a book by Mark Twain

1953: *Brigadoon* 1947 musical by Lerner and Loewe

1954: *The Vagabond King* 1925 operetta by Rudolf Friml

1955: *Rose Marie* 1924 operetta by Rudolf Friml

1956: *Carousel* 1945 musical by Rodgers & Hammerstein

1957: *Oklahoma!* 1943 musical by Rodgers & Hammerstein

1958: *Kismet* 1953 musical by Wright & Forrest

Acknowledgments

Our gratitude for assistance in researching *My Darling Anna* must begin by thanking Susan Fahey for introducing us to the Gray letters in the first place. Susan is the Assistant Regional Archivist at the Northwest Regional Archives in Bellingham. We must also thank James Copher, Reference Archivist, for his usual stellar assistance in our research efforts. The Center for Pacific Northwest Studies at Western Washington University is another invaluable source of information used in our book. The Center's Archivist, Ruth Steele, also earns our thanks for her help and cooperation.

We are indebted to Jeff Jewell, Photo Historian of the Whatcom Museum, for many of the photos in *My Darling Anna*. Jeff oversees an extensive collection of more than 200,000 images in the Whatcom Museum Photo Archives. His encyclopedic knowledge of Bellingham history and his always friendly assistance have become legendary to all those involved in local history research.

Co-author, Neelie Nelson, spent a week in Mount Pleasant, Iowa, researching for the book. There she discovered and befriended two historians who have been of immeasurable help, Pat White and Martha Hayes. Lynn Ellsworth, the Archivist at Iowa Wesleyan College, quickly found the lovely cover image of Anna and could always be relied upon for additional assistance and photographs. Some information came from people that we only met via the Internet, Betty Winterringer from Le Mars, Iowa, and Jeannette Bauman, from Ontario, Canada, whose husband, Bruce, is the great grandson of Will Taylor.

We are grateful to Alex DeLuna, our summer intern, who slogged through miles of microfilm, various directories, and copies of deeds and wills. Alex, a history major at Roanoke College, learned about the mundane, as well as the exciting aspects of historical research.

"It takes a village" most certainly applies to this book. Support, advice and memories have come from so many: Gayle Helgoe, Bev Johanson, Margot Larrabee, Joyce Morse, Janet Oakley, Eloise Tweit Rall, Chuck Robinson, Margaret Morse Watts and Emily Weiner.

Kate Weisel has our gratitude for her design and final preparation for the production of this book. Her professional expertise and dedication of time were of immense value.

And finally, we must thank Fairhaven pharmacist, Gordon Tweit, who shared his personal museum, his extensive knowledge of the people and places chronicled in this book, and opened his heart to assist us in this book about a family that he remembers and for whom he had great affection. The treasures that he dug up from his collection and from his keen memory continually thrilled and astonished us. Much credit for this book goes to Gordy.

Gordon Tweit, 1945.

Producing a book is a major enterprise and it takes the talents and efforts of many people. We are grateful to each and every one of you.
~ Brian & Neelie

Information Sources

Bibliography

Bellingham Bay Directory 1890. R. L. Polk & Co.

Edson, Lelah Jackson. *The Fourth Corner, Highlights from the Early Northwest.* Bellingham, WA: Whatcom Museum of History and Art, 1968.

Fairhaven Directory 1890-91. E. M. Day Publisher.

Griffin, Brian L. *Boulevard Park & Taylor Avenue Dock on the Old Bellingham Waterfront.* Bellingham, WA: Knox Cellars Publishing Co., 2007.

The History of Henry County Iowa. Chicago: Western Historical Company, 1879.

Koert, Dorothy and Galen Biery. *Looking Back: The Collectors' Edition: Memories of Whatcom County/Bellingham.* Bellingham, WA: Grandpa's Attic, 2003.

Minaker, Dennis. *The Gorge of Summers Gone, a History of Victoria's Inland Waterway.* Victoria, B.C., 1998.

Mt. Pleasant Beautiful 1909. Republished by Mt. Pleasant Beautiful Committee: University Press. Mount Pleasant, IA, 1988.

Portrait and Biographical Album of Henry County, Iowa. Chicago: Acme Publishing Company, 1888.

Reeves, Winona E. *The Blue Book of Iowa Women: a History of Contemporary Women.* Mexico, MO: Missouri Printing and Publishing Company, 1914.

Radke, August C. and Barbara S. Radke. *Pacific American Fisheries, Inc.: History of a Washington State Salmon Packing Company, 1890-1966.* Jefferson, NC: McFarland & Co., 2002.

Roth, Lottie Roeder. *The History of Whatcom County Vol. I & Vol II.* Chicago: Pioneer Historical Publishing Company, 1926.

Smith, Curtis F. *The Brothels of Bellingham, a Short History of Prostitution in Bellingham, WA.* Bellingham, WA: Whatcom County Historical Society, 2004.

The Iowa Wesleyan, Vol. 1, January 1886 – Vol. 5, December 1890. Published by the students of the Iowa Wesleyan Universty, Mount Pleasant, IA.

Turbeville , Daniel E. *An Illustrated Inventory of Historic Bellingham Buildings 1852 – 1915.* Bellingham, WA: Bellingham Municipal Arts Commission, 1977.

Van Miert, E. Rosamonde Ellis. *The Fairhaven Hotel Journal, 1889-1956.* Bellingham, WA: E.R.E. Van Miert, 1993.

Widmer, Melba Rae. *Victorian Period Home Architecture: Mt. Pleasant.* Mount Pleasant, IA: Chamber of Commerce, 1989.

Internet Resources

Ancestry.com

City of Bellingham "Fairhaven Historic District"

Cornell University's "Making of America"

Harper's Magazine

Henry County, Iowa, USGENWEB Project

The Library of Congress

Newspaperarchive.com

P.E.O. International

ViHistory

Whatcom GenWeb, submissions by Susan Nahas

Institutions

Bellingham Public Library: Bellingham Washington
 Fairhaven Herald, Bellingham Herald microfiche newspaper collection

Center for Pacific Northwest Studies at Western Washington University:
 Bellingham, Washington
 Howard Buswell Collection, Galen Biery Collection,
 Weekly World and *Fairhaven Herald* Newspaper Collection

Chicago Title Company: Bellingham, Washington

City of Victoria Archives: Victoria, British Columbia

Iowa Wesleyan College Archives: Mount Pleasant, Iowa

Mount Pleasant, Iowa, Public Library: Mount Pleasant, Iowa

Royal B.C. Museum, B.C. Archives: Victoria, British Columbia

State Historical Society of Iowa: Iowa City, Iowa

University of Iowa Archives: Iowa City, Iowa

Washington State Archives, Northwest Region: Bellingham, Washington

Whatcom Museum: Bellingham, Washington

Personal Interviews

Fran Becque, Ph.D., Historian, Pi Beta Phi

Elizabeth E. Garrels, President, P.E.O. International Chapter

Carolyn Hallett, Fairhaven Homeopath

Martha Hayes, Chair, Mount Pleasant Historic Preservation Commission

Jeff Jewell, Photo Historian, Whatcom Museum, Bellingham, WA

Gary Knudson, Architect for Allen C. Mason Plaza, Tacoma, WA

Ruth Crane Looker, Mount Pleasant, IA

Dennis Minaker, Author, Victoria, B.C.

Joyce Morse, Bellingham, WA

Ian and Ruth Munson, Bellingham, WA

Eloise Tweit Rall, Bellingham, WA

Arthur Tylor Richards, Victoria, B.C.

Gordon Tweit, Bellingham, WA

Margaret Morse Watts, Bellingham, WA

Pat Ryan White, Board Member, Henry County Heritage Trust

Other Sources

Atlas Henry County Iowa 1895. Compiled by Brooks & Whiting, Mount Pleasant, IA

Biery, Galen, *1971 Interview with Margaret Gray.* Bellingham, WA: Center for Pacific Northwest Studies

Fay, Haines, *1971 Interview with Margaret Gray.* Bellingham, WA: Center for Pacific Northwest Studies

Fire Insurance Plans of Victoria 1891

Sanborn Fire Insurance Maps, Fairhaven, WA: 1890, 1891, 1897

Sanborn Fire Insurance Maps, Bellingham, WA: 1904, 1913

Neelie Nelson and Brian Griffin with Gordon Tweit's collection.

About The Authors

BRIAN GRIFFIN comes by his interest in Bellingham history naturally. He was born there more years ago than he cares to tell. His interest in Fairhaven and in the Gray family are also understandable. He has mostly lived within the bounds of old Fairhaven and does so to this day, but more importantly, he was a student of Margaret Gray and insists that he is a beneficiary of the Gray Legacy. He recalls the intimidation and then the exhilaration of reading Shakespeare out loud in her drama class and credits her with his ability to speak in public and to enunciate.

Griffin has written a previous local history book, *Boulevard Park,* as well as two books about native bees. *The Orchard Mason Bee* and *Humblebee Bumblebee.* He lives with his wife Marya on the south hill above Fairhaven and is currently working on the complete history of Fairhaven to be entitled simply *Fairhaven.*

NEELIE NELSON comes by her love and fascination with Fairhaven history through immigration. She and her husband Steve moved to Bellingham from California just over two years ago, but they have bonded and immersed themselves into the community with great passion and success. It was Neelie who learned of the Gray Letters from Susan Fahey and insisted that they should be published. Neelie considers genealogy research a "gateway" into the love of history. Her years of genealogical research experience were put to use in the book.

Neelie's mother, Mrs. Barnes, would like it to be known that the name she gave her daughter Eileen in 1954, is a perfectly good name and she doesn't understand why Neelie insists on spelling it backwards.